Communities and
Networks

Communities and Networks

Using Social Network Analysis to Rethink Urban and Community Studies

KATHERINE GIUFFRE

polity

First published in 2013 by Polity Press

Polity Press
65 Bridge Street
Cambridge CB2 1UR, UK

Polity Press
350 Main Street
Malden, MA 02148, USA

ISBN-13: 978-0-7456-5419-5
ISBN-13: 978-0-7456-5420-1(pb)

A catalogue record for this book is available from the British Library.

Typeset in 11 on 13 pt Scala
by Servis Filmsetting Ltd, Stockport, Cheshire
Printed and bound in Great Britain by MPG Books Group

For further information on Polity, visit our website: www.politybooks.com

Contents

Acknowledgments

I would like to thank, first of all, Jonathan Skerrett at Polity, for his enthusiasm for this project and his kindness, helpfulness, support, and insight in seeing this book through from the very beginning all the way to the finish.

I would like to thank the following for permission to use copyrighted material: Social Forces for permission to use table 2.9 and figure 2.3 from Ronald Breiger's "The duality of persons and groups," University of Chicago Press for permission to use table 3.1 from Barry Wellman and Scot Wortley's "Different strokes from different folks," Nancy Howell for permission to use figure 3.5 from *The Search for an Abortionist*, Steven Borgatti for permission to use table 3.5 and table 3.6 from the UCINET data files, Harvard University Press for permission to use figure 5.1 from Paul Boyer and Stephen Nissenbaum's *Salem Possessed*, the American Sociological Association for permission to use figure 6.1 from Roger Gould's "Multiple networks and mobilization in the Paris Commune, 1871," and the Annual Review of Sociology for permission to use figure 8.1 and figure 8.2 from Duncan Watts's "The 'new' science of social networks." In addition, Stephanie Denton of the US Bureau of Labor Statistics expeditiously provided the data used for the correspondence analysis in chapter 7. Three anonymous reviewers provided extremely helpful critical feedback and thoughtful advice on the manuscript.

Finally, I would like to thank the members of my family for being so enormously supportive. Aiden Giuffre gave the manuscript a close reading and careful editorial attention, Tristan Giuffre gave very valuable hugs when the going got tough, and Jonathan Poritz gave both of those and everything else from mathematical expertise to homemade pumpkin pie. He proved once again that he is not only decorative, but also functional. This book is dedicated with love to him.

1   What is network analysis and how can it be useful?

Humans are inherently social beings. We have lived in communities as long as we have been human. We form communities and, in many ways, communities form us. Our lives in communities shape who we are and how we approach the world. Understanding how communities work is vital to understanding our lives, but communities are complex and analyzing them can be difficult. They are spaces both of cooperation and of conflict. They can give us both a sense of belonging and one of alienation. They can root us in a place and also allow us to transcend the confines of geography.

For example, in the 1690s the Puritan village of Salem, Massachusetts, erupted in a paroxysm of witch-hunting the likes of which had never before been seen in North America. In the 1930s, community after community of solid citizens in Germany turned on their neighbors and succumbed to Nazism. What was happening at the level of the community to make the citizens of these places behave in these ways?

In the early twentieth century, Jewish immigrants from Eastern Europe to Chicago gradually assimilated into the American culture. In the late twentieth century, however, Indochinese refugees to Boston were the victims of arson by their neighbors who wanted the Indochinese out of their community. How and why do different communities react differently to the presence of outsiders in their midst?

In the 1960s, the residents of the ghetto in Washington, DC, responded to the assassination of Rev. Martin Luther King, Jr., with days of riots and looting. In the 1980s, the residents of New York City responded to the AIDS crisis by building a broad network of organizations intended to respond to a wide-ranging population of people in need. How and why does crisis elicit such different responses from different communities?

1

Community members can provide social support for each other in a variety of ways and that support can play a part in, for example, the explosion of innovative thinking that characterized Silicon Valley at the end of the twentieth century. But community members can also exert enormous pressure on each other to conform to established traditions, customs, and ways of thinking or risk being ostracized from the group and all of the social goods that it provides. How do members of communities navigate this tension between support and suffocation? Are there new types of communities emerging in the twenty-first century that are better able to maintain the balance between having too much community support and having too little?

These examples illustrate some of the ways in which communities are complex, many-faceted phenomena. Analyzing communities and communal life, therefore, is fascinating, but can at times seem overwhelming. Social network analysis helps make sense of all of this. Using social network analysis to look at community structures can give us a new perspective, new insights, richer understanding, and surprising answers to questions like the ones above and many more. The rise of social network analysis in the past half century has opened up wide ranges for exploring the questions of how human life is organized on a variety of levels and in a variety of disciplines. This book will look at how incorporating network analysis into urban and community studies can help us to understand questions and issues in those fields and can lead us to think about problems in new and fruitful ways.

What is structure?

Network analysis is the study of structure. But what do network analysts mean when they use the term "structure"? Berkowitz writes that "[t]he idea that social systems may be *structured* in various ways is not new. In fact, all of the established social sciences have evolved some notion of *structure*. But, until recently, no field had taken the idea of a *regular, persistent pattern in the behavior of the elementary parts of a social system* and used it as a central or focal concept for understanding social life" (1982: 1, emphasis in original). Wasserman and Faust add, "Regularities or patterns in interactions give rise to structures" (1994: 6–7).

What this means in the context of network analysis is that the persistent patterns of *relations* among the participants in a system become the core of the analysis. It is the relationships between the members of the system rather than the individual *attributes* of those members that are the key component of understanding the system. For example, network analysts would focus on the web of relations among various artists and galleries (rather than, say, the talent of individual artists) in order to understand why some artists find success in the art world and others do not (Giuffre 1999). The logic behind this thinking is part of our everyday understanding of how the world operates when we say things like, "It's not what you know; it's who you know." Network analysts do not stop at merely "who you know," however, but investigate much more deeply into the persistent patterns of those relationships. These patterns of relationships are what we call "structure" (Wasserman & Faust 1994: 3).

Much social science research in a variety of fields focuses exclusively on individual attributes (like talent, in the example above) and ignores important information about the patterns of relations among the members of the system (Wasserman & Faust 1994: 6–7). Network analysts, however, argue that "structural relations are often more important for understanding observed behaviors than are such attributes as age, gender, values, and ideology" (Knoke & Yang 2008: 4).

Social network analysis, then, concentrates on relations among the members of a system rather than on the individual attributes of those members. This is because patterns of relations have consequences. Again, this is the kind of everyday thinking we employ when we say that people looking for jobs should "activate their networks," or that the "environment" in Silicon Valley is conducive to producing innovative thinking, or that the American economy suffered as the country lost its "position of dominance" in the system of global trade, or even that a friend going through a difficult time needs others to rally around with emotional support. In fact, one of the earliest examples of the type of work that we now think of as network analysis was Moreno's 1934 study of how the "social configurations" surrounding individuals affected their psychological well-being (Moreno 1934). More generally, "[t]he central objectives of network analysis are to measure and represent these structural relations accurately, and to explain both why they occur and what are their consequences" (Knoke & Yang 2008: 4).

Because the relations among the members of a system can have profound consequences, it is important to understand how those relations fit together – how they are structured. Network analysts, therefore, gather data on the *relations* among the actors as their primary source of information. This relational data, Scott writes, is "the contacts, ties and connections, the group attachments and meetings, which relate one agent to another and so cannot be reduced to the properties of the individual agents themselves. Relations are not the property of agents; these relations connect pairs of agents into larger relational systems" (2000: 3).

Relational data is not about the individual members of a system (who have relations), but about relations (which occur among members of a system.) This difference may seem trivial (or even non-existent), but it is really a change in worldview, bringing the importance of the structure of relations to the fore in our understanding of how the world works. Focusing on the structure of the relations rather than on the attributes of the parties in those relations is the key to understanding network analysis. Wasserman and Faust note that "[o]f critical importance for the development of methods for social network analysis is the fact that the unit of analysis in network analysis is not the individual, but an entity consisting of a collection of individuals and the linkages among them" (1994: 4–5).

Networks as metaphors

Although the methods by which we can analyze relational data are relatively new, relational thinking has a long history in the social sciences. As far back as 1845, for example, Marx wrote in the *Theses on Feuerbach*: "VI: Feuerbach resolves the religious essence into the human essence. But the human essence is no abstraction inherent in each single individual. In its reality it is the ensemble of social relations" (Marx 1978 [1845]: 145). That is, Marx argues that it is our relations with others – our real, lived relations – that make us who we are.

In the early twentieth century, the work of Georg Simmel pushed the relational thinking behind network analysis to new heights. Simmel, one of the founders of the field of sociology, wrote prolifically on the relationship between individuality and social forms, especially during the transition to modern urban life. Simmel's idea of the development of individuality (discussed in more detail in chapter 2) is based on a notion of the dynamic between social circles and individuals with each forming and being formed by the other. Simmel's study of these social forms – which he referred to as the "geometry" of social relations – was the basis of "formal sociology." The "forms of sociation" are made by individuals who are tied together in relations. Simmel particularly concentrates on *exchange* as the form of interaction through which society is formed; religion, economy, and politics, he argues, are all based on exchange. "Exchange," he writes, "is the purest and most concentrated form of all human interactions in which serious interests are at stake" (Simmel 1971: 43). Social circles are themselves formed by these interactions – we are linked together through exchanges. We can see here the basis of the idea that networks are formed by relations between actors and that these networks have consequences. For Simmel, the creation of society itself is the result of these exchanges.

Simmel argues that exchange "lifts the individual thing and its significance for the individual man out of their singularity, not into the sphere of the abstract but into the liveliness of interaction" (1971: 69). This relational thinking, especially the primacy given to the role of exchanges between individuals, played a key role in the later development of network analysis. The "geometric" mindset brought relational thinking more clearly into focus.

But at first, Berkowitz notes, networks "were employed as little more than metaphors for the things social scientists were really trying to deal with: a friendship group was *like* a 'star' with one central point; a work group was *like* a small 'pyramid'; or the spread of a rumor was *like* a 'chain'" (1982: 2). While these metaphors helped social scientists conceptualize more clearly about the phenomena that they were studying, to truly be able to analyze in detail the spread of actual information through actual networks, social scientists needed more than just compelling metaphors; they needed method.

The relational thinking exemplified by Simmel was part of many disciplines in the social sciences, but it was an anthropologist, John A. Barnes, who is usually credited with first using the term "social network" in 1954 (Wasserman & Faust 1994, Knoke & Yang 2008) in his study of a Norwegian island parish. Barnes drew on Moreno's work on "social configurations" and emotional well-being (mentioned above) and, specifically, on Moreno's ground-breaking tool for analyzing these configurations: the sociogram (Moreno 1934). It was the advent of the sociogram that allowed network thinking to move from metaphor to method.

Metaphor into method

A **sociogram**[1] is a picture of a **network** of relations, where the members of the network are represented by points and the relations between them are represented by lines connecting the points. The map in the back of an airline's in-flight magazine showing the airports connected by the airline's flights is an example of a sociogram, for instance. So is the organizational chart of a company showing the chain of command in decision making or a family tree showing kinship connections. Sociograms are familiar to us now – so familiar, in fact, that it is difficult for us to conceive of the revolutionary impact that Moreno's work had in the social sciences. "Before Moreno, people had spoken of 'webs' of connection, the 'social fabric' and, on occasion, of 'networks' of relations, but no one had attempted to systemize this metaphor into an analytical diagram" (Scott 2000: 9–10).

Once the analytical diagram had been developed, it was available for analysis along a number of different lines. The mathematics for the analysis came from graph theory. Graph theory is the mathematical study of graphs, which (not to be confused with bar graphs, pie charts, and other types of graphs that we think of colloquially) are simple structures consisting of a set of vertices (represented by points in a sociogram) some of which are connected by edges (the lines connecting the points in a sociogram.) Edges may have additional characteristics such as direction (going from one vertex to another and not simply connecting two vertices) or color or weight. Topological techniques in graph theory yield results about the coarse properties of graphs, such as when they are connected, have certain special paths (Eulerian or Hamiltonian, for example), or can be colored with a certain number of colors. Probabalistic, linear algebraic, discrete geometric, and other, purely numerical techniques can answer questions about **densities** of edges (that is, the proportion of actual ties which exist in the network) in certain graphs, the rate of propagation of some kind of signal through a graph, or of the solutions of differential equations defined on a graph, for example. Often a graph is used as a simplified version of a complex situation (such as in geometry or differential equations) where results about the graph

---

[1] Network terms that appear in **bold** when they are first discussed in the text are defined in the glossary.

will give approximate answers to the full, original problem. Graph theory has been extensively used in computer science to model communications networks, the connections on a single computer chip, the relationships between the components of a large software system, and so on. Graph theorists can analyze not only a sociogram, but also the translation of a sociogram into a *matrix* (see below). Graph theory provided the mathematical method to analyze social networks.

What is a social network?

A social network is a type of graph – a set of vertices and edges. Or, less abstractly, a social network is composed of a set of actors and the relations among them. What, then, is an "**actor**" and what constitutes a "**relation**" between actors?

"Actors" can be any social entity that is engaged in interaction with others of its type – individual persons can be actors in a network, and so can small groups like families, larger groups like civic organizations, bigger groups like corporations or even nation-states. Actors can be much more than people sharing friendships mediated through a "social networking" site like Facebook. Some examples would be workers in a tailoring shop in Zambia who attempt to organize a strike (Kapferer 1972), composers working in the Hollywood film industry (Faulkner 1987), monks forming cliques in a monastery (Sampson 1969, White et al. 1976), families vying for political dominance in Renaissance Florence (Padgett & Ansell 1993), corporations connected by shared board members (Useem 1978), public and private agencies engaged in interagency collaboration to improve school safety (Cross et al. 2009), political parties forming coalitions (Centeno 2002), or nations importing guest workers from other nations (Massey et al. 2002).

Actors are all members of the system being analyzed, but they do not necessarily all have relations with each other. Some composers working in the Hollywood film industry may work together on projects repeatedly; some may never have any contact with each other. Some countries may be active trading partners; some may have no relations of any kind. Moreover, although network analysts use the term "actors" for the members of the network, that does not necessarily mean that they "act" or that they have agency. Family members in a kinship network "act" merely by being born. Some artists are "actors" in the art world by failing to get gallery representation – by being ignored and unable to form **ties**. Actors are represented as points or **"nodes"** in a sociogram. The lines that connect the actors represent their "relations".

Actors are tied together by specific types of relations. These ties can be almost anything. When we think of social networking sites, we often think of individual people being tied together through friendship ties, but individuals could also be linked together by kinship, by belonging to an organization together (as in Useem's [1978] corporate interlocks), by attending events together (as Davis et al.'s [1941] club women did), by disliking each other (as some of the monks in Sampson's [Sampson 1969, White et al. 1976] monastery did), or by a whole host of other types of relations. On a larger scale, nations, for example, could be tied together by shared trade or diplomatic relations, by links of tourism, by sending and receiving guest workers and so on. Once we define what particular type of tie we are studying, we can then see which pairs of actors in the network are linked together by sharing a tie of that type (Wasserman & Faust 1994: 18–20). Two actors in a network that are tied together are called a **"dyad"** and the dyad is the most basic building block of a network.

Like the edges that graph theorists studied, ties can have properties such as direction and **strength**. A tie is directionless when it is mutual; I am related to my cousin in the same way that she is related to me, for example. But some ties have direction – they are sent from one node to another. An employer pays an employee and not the other way around. A boss directs an underling. Even ties such as those of friendship or affection may have direction – think, for example, of unrequited love. Ties can also have strength. I can be acquainted with someone, be friends with him, or be the very best of friends with him. Nations may engage in no trade with each other, engage in some trade with each other, or be primary trading partners.

It is important to remember that these properties are properties of the *tie*, not of the actor. It is only by looking at the flow of goods and money *between* two countries that we can tell if they are strong partners or not.

Further developments

Simmel's formal sociology and the relational thinking that underlay it had an enormous impact on the development of social science in the twentieth century. Further advances were made in the 1950s by a group of anthropologists at Manchester University, including John Barnes (who first used the term "social network," as mentioned above), Clyde Mitchell, and Elizabeth Bott (whose work will be discussed in much greater detail in chapter 3). These researchers concentrated on specific case studies and developed many network analytical concepts, tools, and terms to help them describe and explain the social structures that they uncovered. These empirical studies laid the groundwork for further methodological and theoretical developments that began to appear in the 1960s and 1970s – especially from Harrison White and his students at Harvard.

It is impossible to overstate the importance of White to the development of social network analysis. There were three especially important parts of White's work: the development of algebraic methods for dealing with structure, the development of multidimensional scaling, and the training of a generation of important network researchers (Scott 2000, Berkowitz 1982.)

Using algebraic methods, White and François Lorrain developed a technique for identifying **structurally equivalent** nodes. (We will discuss structural equivalence in depth in chapter 6.) Using structural equivalence to reduce networks to models allows researchers to compare structures and positions across different networks. "Lorrain and White's method was able to realize, for the first time, all of the power implicit in the social network concept. First, it operated simultaneously on both nodes and relations. . . . Second, it enabled researchers to deal with a given network at all levels of abstraction" (Berkowitz 1982: 5). The second technique, multidimensional scaling (which we will discuss in detail in chapter 8), is a method for mapping social distances onto geographic space. Like structural equivalence, multidimensional scaling allows researchers to build models based on the actual relations between actors in the network rather than having to impose a priori categories and understandings on the social world before beginning to analyze it. Network analysts now had methods by which they could compare positions across networks, compare network structures, build models to explain and understand action, and so on.

White was also responsible for training future generations of network researchers who produced some of the most important and ground-breaking network studies. For example, Granovetter's study of the strength of weak ties (discussed in chapter 4), Lee's study of women seeking illegal abortions (discussed in chapter 3), Wellman's studies of urban community networks (discussed in chapters 3 and 8), and Breiger's work on the duality of persons and groups (discussed in chapter 2) were all encouraged and informed by White. These are only a few of the brilliant researchers who began their work in network analysis with White.

This very brief overview is certainly not a full discussion of the development and usefulness of social network analysis, but has been restricted mostly to those aspects of it that are most important for this book. The shift in worldview that undergirds network analytical thinking – the shift from analyzing attributes to analyzing relations – has had an impact on every discipline in the social sciences, as well as in many fields in the natural sciences and the humanities. More complete discussions can be found in Berkowitz (1982), Collins (1988), Watts (1999a and 2003), Scott (2000), Barabási (2003), Freeman (2004), Azarian (2005), and Knoke and Yang (2008), just to name a few. The most in-depth and comprehensive book is Wasserman and Faust (1994).

Why use network analysis?

Network analysis provides an important and interesting lens with which to look at communities because it is concerned, most fundamentally, with the *relations* among the people and groups who make up those communities. It is these relations themselves which are at the heart of what it means to belong to a community – rather than to merely coexist in the same general geographic area as other individuals. The nature of the types of relations that we have with others affects how we behave, what we believe, how we understand the world around us and how we navigate through it, what constraints we labor under, and what avenues of opportunity are open to us.

The nature of our relations with others is fundamental to our lives. Network analysis allows us to examine those relations directly. By doing so, we can gain a clearer picture of human life in communities and a richer understanding of our world. We can also find surprising insights into questions that might otherwise seem intractable. The virulence of the Salem witch crisis, for example, seems mysterious and unexplainable – a bizarre aberration among the sober-minded Puritans. But when we look at the structure of the relations of the inhabitants of Salem Village during the end of the seventeenth century (as we will do in chapter 5), we will see how the underlying logic of the social networks at play made the tragedy of 1692 not only understandable, but almost inevitable.

In this book, we will see how using the perspective provided by social network analysis – focusing on the relations among people rather than on their individual characteristics – can give us new insights into the working of our communities. This deeper understanding may even help us be better able to have a positive impact on our own communities.

Plan of the book

This book examines the ways in which different types of community structures allow for different possibilities for individual and group actions – deviance and conformity, successful challenges to outside authority and failures, the emergence of innovation, etc. Chapter 2 will look at some of the fundamental building blocks of communities and examine the ways in which communities changed with the rise of modernity. Chapter 3 will address issues of communal support systems and the resources which communities provide to us. Chapter 4 focuses on the ways in which we are shaped by our communities and made to conform to communal expectations. Chapter 5 will turn to fractured communities and explore both why they break apart and what the consequences of that might be. Chapter 6, on the other hand, examines ways in which communities can come together and foster collective action among the members. Chapter 7 examines how different types of community structures either do or do not generate creativity and innovation. Finally, chapter 8 turns to the rise of computer-mediated communication and "virtual" communities to see if and in what ways they differ from more traditional communities.

This book uses network analysis to delve into the issues of community structure, formation, and dissolution. We will see how network thinking can be used to explore issues about communities in fruitful and interesting ways and discuss how applying a network analytical perspective to these questions allows new insights to emerge. At the end of each chapter, there is a section called "A Closer Look" that discusses in more depth one technical aspect of network analysis so that we can understand what the analysis is doing, as well as understanding why and in what circumstances this particular aspect of network analysis would be a useful tool.

Software

The development of network analytical tools was certainly facilitated by the increasing access to computers that researchers have had in the past half century, and there are many network analysis software packages that are commercially available, including UCINET, Pajek, NetMiner, STRUCTURE, MultiNet, and StOCNET (Knoke & Yang 2008: 2). In order to understand the "Closer Look" sections, though, it is not necessary to have access to any type of network analysis software. These sections are meant to explain how the various techniques work and in what situations a researcher would want to use them. However, most of the tools and techniques are complex enough to require computer power in order to actually use them for analysis. UCINET (Borgatti et al. 2002) is an excellent general purpose program that allows users access to all of the techniques covered in this book (and more). I will use UCINET to give examples of data analysis throughout the book.

A closer look: basic network terms and definitions

It is important to understand the basic terms and definitions used by network analysts to describe the world. First of all, a *network* is a set of relations between actors – and by actors we can mean individuals, groups, organizations, even entire nations. Friends in an informal friendship group can be actors in a network – so can nations in trade relationships. We call these actors *nodes* in the network. The important point is that the actors are in a situation or system where they may or may not have relations with each other.

These relations between nodes are called *ties*. Ties are the connections that actors have with each other. The content of the ties can be lots of things. You could have a tie of kinship with people, for example. These people are your relatives. Or you could have ties of affection or of enmity. You could have ties of the exchange of favors or loans of money. You could have ties of sharing memberships in clubs or organizations or of attending certain events together. Ties are the connections that the actors could have with each other. Not every member of a social network will be tied to every other member of that network by a particular type of tie – all that matters is that they *could* conceivably be tied together.

Ties can have *direction*. That is, you could have a tie of liking

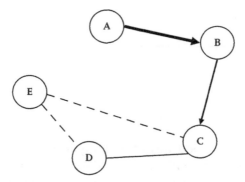

Figure 1.1 Sociogram: nodes and ties

someone who does not like you back. Lines of authority usually have direction. Other ties are directionless, such as ties of kinship or shared membership in organizations. Ties of "knowing" are often directionless.

Ties also have *strength*. There are a couple of different ways in which we can think about the strength of ties. One way is by the intensity of the relationship. You could love someone or you could like them or you could even just merely tolerate them without feeling too much about it. Or we could measure the strength of a tie by how many different types of content that the tie contains. For example, you might be roommates with someone and that is the full extent of your relationship. We would call that tie **uniplex**, meaning that it has only one dimension. Or you might be roommates with someone and also be that person's friend and take classes together and work at the same job and even be related to that person. This would be a **multiplex** relationship and might be stronger than the uniplex relationship.

Nodes and ties can be put together to show a map of relationships called a *sociogram*. Figure 1.1 is an example sociogram. The circles represent the nodes (each of which is given an identifying letter as its "name") and the lines represent the ties. Dark lines are strong ties, dashed lines are weak ties, and regular lines are ties of medium strength. Ties with an arrow on one end of them indicate a tie with direction, so that although A likes B in this example, B does not return the favor (if this is a sociogram of "liking.") Ties that do not have arrows on them are directionless ties, which could mean that they are reciprocated (C likes D and D likes C back) or that the type of tie (such as being cousins) does not lend itself to having a direction.

Table 1.1 Matrix of figure 1.1

	A	B	C	D	E
A	0	1	0	0	0
B	0	0	1	0	0
C	0	0	0	1	1
D	0	0	1	0	1
E	0	0	1	1	0

Sociograms are a good way of looking at the picture of the social structure, but they are not easy to analyze, especially when they get very large. Imagine a sociogram of the political networks in the US House of Representatives. It would be a tangled, unreadable mess. A better form to use for the analysis of the network data is a **matrix**.

A matrix is a grid of numbers arranged in rows and columns. Table 1.1 is the matrix translation of the sociogram in figure 1.1. The rows and columns are labeled with the names of the actors in the network. We will name this matrix "M."

To understand how to read the information presented in the matrix, we need to know a few more terms. First, the matrix is arranged in **rows** and **columns**. Rows are read from left to right and columns are read from top to bottom. The intersection of each row and column is called a **cell** and each cell has a **value**. The values in the example matrix here are either 1 or 0, depending on whether or not the two actors whose row and column intersect in that cell have a tie or not. If the actor in the row of the cell sends a tie to the actor in the column of the cell, the cell value is 1. Otherwise, it is 0.

If we wish, we can indicate the strength of the ties in the matrix. Instead of using 1s and 0s to merely indicate the presence or absence of a tie between two nodes, we can use the cell values as a measure of strength. If the ties are multiplex, the values in the cells could, for example, be the number of different types of relations that the nodes share. Or suppose we were measuring trade relations among nations; the cell values could be the annual amount of exports between pairs of nodes expressed as dollar amounts. Or we could use a simpler metric merely indicating "strong," "medium," or "weak" ties. In table 1.2, we can see the matrix translation of figure 1.1, but now the cell value is 3 if the tie is strong, 2 if the tie is medium strength, or 1 if the tie is weak. Nodes which have no tie between them are still coded 0.

Along with having a value, each cell also has an address. It is important to remember that the matrix is always read in the order of

Table 1.2 Matrix of figure 1.1 with tie strength

	A	B	C	D	E
A	0	3	0	0	0
B	0	0	2	0	0
C	0	0	0	2	1
D	0	0	2	0	1
E	0	0	1	1	0

row and then *column*. The cell addresses follow this pattern as well. The cell whose address is $M_{2,3}$ is the cell that is in the matrix that we have named M and is the intersection of row 2 and column 3. The cell whose address is $M_{3,2}$ is the cell in the matrix that we have named M and is the intersection of row 3 and column 2. You can see that in the example of table 1.1, those cells have different values. This is because this example matrix is not **symmetric**; some nodes send ties to others in the matrix and those ties are not reciprocated. B, for example, sends a tie to C, but C does not send a tie to B. When noting ties that have direction in a matrix, the actors who are listed as the headings in the rows are always considered the "senders" of the ties and the actors who are listed as the headings in the columns are always considered the "receivers." So we can read across the B row and see that there is a 1 in the C column, indicating that B has sent a tie to C. But when we read across the C row, we see that there is a 0 in the B column indicating that C has not chosen to send a tie to B.

The main diagonal of the matrix is the cells where the sending and the receiving node are the same. That is, $M_{1,1}$, $M_{2,2}$, $M_{3,3}$, $M_{4,4}$ and $M_{5,5}$ in table 1.1 are the cells of the main diagonal. As you can see, the values of each of these cells is 0. That is because we did not allow nodes to have ties to themselves in this example. You could imagine, however, situations in which nodes would be tied to themselves. Suppose, for example, the nodes were the attendees at a cocktail party. We could imagine the host circulating among them with a tray of hors d'oeuvres, handing out some to his guests but also eating some himself. The tie would be receiving an hors d'oeuvre; some ties would be from the host to his guests and some would be from the host to himself. When nodes have ties to themselves, those ties are usually indicated in the sociogram by an arrow curving back to the node. In the matrix, the value of the main diagonal cell for that node would no longer be zero. Figure 1.2 and table 1.3 are the sociogram and matrix examples of this. As you can see, both B and D are now

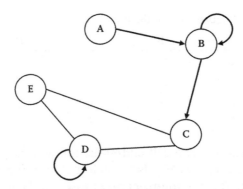

Figure 1.2 Sociogram: nodes and ties, including ties to self

tied to themselves and the value of their cells in the main diagonal is
1.

You may also notice that symmetric matrices have the same values
in corresponding cells above and below the main diagonal, while
asymmetric matrices, such as the one in figures 1.1 and 1.2, do not.

These are some of the basic terms with which we will be working in
the following chapters. More terms will appear as we move through
the concepts, but these are enough to get us started.

Entering and displaying matrices in UCINET6

It is quite simple to enter network data into a matrix in UCINET6
(Borgatti et al. 2002.) Once you are in the program, click on the
"Matrix Spreadsheet Editor" icon at the top of the screen. (You can
also access this editor by using the dropdown menu under "Data" and
then "Data editors.") This will open a spreadsheet into which you can
enter your data just as it would be in a matrix like the ones we have
been using in this chapter. Notice that you have the option of entering
data in either "Normal" or "Symmetric" mode. If you are entering a
square, symmetric matrix (where there are no directional ties), you can

Table 1.3 Matrix of figure 1.2

	A	B	C	D	E
A	0	1	0	0	0
B	0	1	1	0	0
C	0	0	0	1	1
D	0	0	1	1	1
E	0	0	1	1	0

save time by choosing Symmetric mode and then you will only have to enter the data for each pair of relations into one cell. For example, in Normal mode, if A and B are tied together, you would need to enter a "1" in the A,B cell and also into the B,A cell. But in Symmetric mode, the UCINET program will automatically enter a "1" into the B,A cell for you once you have entered it into A,B. If you are not entering data into a square, symmetric matrix, use the Normal mode.

The blue boxes at the top and side of the spreadsheet are for row and column labels. In a network of individuals, these would be their names or ID numbers. In most matrices, the labels are the names or IDs of the nodes, but in some matrices there may be other labels. For example, if you were analyzing a network made up of women attending social events together (as in Davis et al. 1941), the rows would be the names of the women and the columns would be labels for the events. This would not be a square matrix (unless by chance there happened to be the same number of women in the group as there were events held). The cell entries would be a "1" if the woman in the row had attended the event in the column and a "0" otherwise. We will discuss how to analyze these types of matrices in chapter 2.

When entering the data, you can save time and can perhaps work more accurately by entering only the 1s into your matrix. It is often much easier to note only the ties that exist. But you cannot properly analyze matrices that have empty cells. Use the "Fill" button at the top of the Spreadsheet Editor to fill all empty cells with 0s once you have finished entering your data. Trim the matrix to the appropriate dimensions by entering the number of rows and the number of columns in the boxes on the right-hand side of the Spreadsheet Editor, then click on an empty cell in your matrix. Then click on the "Fill" button at the top of the screen. This will automatically fill all empty cells with 0s.

Save your matrix by clicking on "File" at the top of the screen and choosing "Save as" from the dropdown menu. Give your dataset a name in the "File name" window and then click "Save." Your dataset is now saved and you can close the Spreadsheet Editor. You can add more data to your matrix or make changes in it by opening it in the Spreadsheet Editor at any time in the future. Open the "Matrix Spreadsheet Editor" just as before, click on the "open file" icon and click on your data file to open it.

To see the matrix on which you want to work, instead of "Matrix Spreadsheet Editor," choose the "display" icon and click on your data file. (Again, this function can also be accessed by using the drop-down menu under "Data.") Note also that UCINET comes preloaded with data files that we can use as examples. These are stored in the "datafiles" file folder. (If you have accessed the Display function by using the dropdown menu under "Data," just click on the ". . ." button next to the "Data Set Filename" window in order to get access to the list of datasets.) Double click on "datafiles" and scroll down to "sampson," for instance, and double click on it. What you should see are a series of matrices showing the relations between the monks whom Sampson studied (1969). Matrix #1 shows the ties of "liking" between the monks at Time 1. Notice that this is a square matrix (with the names of the monks in the same order down the row labels and across the column labels), but that it is not symmetric. Some monks said they liked others who did not choose them back. The cell values also indicate the strength of the tie.

If you close the Sampson dataset and open "davis," you will see a different kind of matrix. The rows are 18 women from Davis et al.'s study *Deep South* (1941) and the columns are 14 social events that the women could have attended. A "1" in a cell means that the woman in the row attended the event in the column; a "0" means that they did not. We will analyze this matrix in chapter 2.

When you are finished with your work and have saved it, you can exit UCINET by choosing the "Exit" icon from the top of the screen or by choosing "Exit" from the dropdown menu under "File."

2 What is a community? Where does it come from?

In his *Life of Johnson* (1791), James Boswell recorded Samuel Johnson's famous quip that "the prospect of hanging concentrates the mind wonderfully." What is true for individuals and hanging could arguably also be true of societies and revolutions. The eighteenth and nineteenth centuries were an age of revolutions in Western Europe and North America. Political revolutions swept through this part of the world with alarming frequency, permanently changing the way in which those societies organized themselves. At the same time, the Industrial Revolution upended the day-to-day lives of thousands of workers who left the land and their agricultural lives and moved into factories in the cities as urbanization exploded. People from all different walks of life were gathered together in these newly expanding cites and came into contact with a wide variety of new and different ideas and ways of living. This revolutionary upheaval wonderfully concentrated the minds of some thinkers about society. Societies had been formerly held together by custom and tradition, but with the old ways being destroyed, social theorists concentrated on discovering how societies functioned and how they would now be held together. These theorists hoped that understanding how societies worked would mean that the end of the old ways would not be the end of human civilization. "What is a society?" they asked themselves. "How does it manage to function? And, most importantly, how will it manage to function in this new world where all the traditional ways of doing things have been swept away?"

Gemeinschaft und Gesellschaft

Ferdinand Tönnies (1855–1936) was one of the early writers on these issues. He published his most famous work, *Gemeinschaft und*

Gesellschaft, in 1887. "Gemeinschaft" is often translated as "community" and, for Tönnies, it is analytically distinct from "Gesellschaft," often translated as "society." Community is "a common and binding system of positive law, of enforceable norms regulating the inter-relation of wills. It has its roots in family life and is based on land ownership. Its forms are in the main determined by the code of the folkways and mores. Religion concentrates and glorifies these forms of the divine will, i.e., as interpreted by the will of wise and ruling men" (1957 [1887]: 64). Gemeinschaft was intimate, supportive, and traditional. "Community," in Tönnies's conception, had a moral basis that held it together.

Gemeinschaft, in his conception, is the mode of life that existed for most Western Europeans before the age of revolutions swept through their world. Gesellschaft, on the other hand, is the newer form of social organization that Tönnies saw springing up in the eighteenth and nineteenth centuries. Gesellschaft, he writes, "derives from the conventional order of trade and similar relations, but attains validity and binding force only through the sovereign will and power of the state. Thus, it becomes one of the most important instruments of policy; it sustains, impedes, or furthers social trends; it is defended or contested publicly by doctrines and opinions and thus is changed, becoming more strict or more lenient" (1957 [1887]: 64). Gesellschaft, based on contracts and relations among dissimilar individuals, is held together by the laws of the state.

Tönnies, not surprisingly given his historical context, saw communities *evolving* into societies – a development which he viewed as being rather negative. Writing of the dissolution of traditional communities, Tönnies says, "[t]he substance of the common spirit has become so weak or the link connecting [a person] with the others worn so thin that it has to be excluded from consideration. In contrast to the family and cooperative relationship, this is true of all relations among separate individuals where there is no common understanding and no time-honored custom or belief creates a common bond" (1957 [1887]: 65).

Without the bonds created by traditional mores and folkways, Tönnies saw a society ruled, ultimately, by the fear of punishment for transgression rather than by the positive desire for harmony that he argued pervaded Gemeinschaft. "In this connection, we see a community organization and social conditions in which the individuals remain in isolation and veiled hostility towards each other so that only fear of clever retaliation restrains them from attacking one another, and, therefore, even peaceful and neighborly relations are in reality based upon a warlike situation" (1957 [1887]: 65).

We can compare and contrast Tönnies's rather dour view of modern society with his contemporary Emile Durkheim's (1858–1917) ideas about mechanical and organic solidarity as laid out in *The Division of Labor in Society*.

Durkheim: mechanical and organic solidarity

Durkheim wrote *The Division of Labor in Society* as his doctoral dissertation at the École Normale Supérieure. First published in 1893, *The Division of Labor* explores the development of society, and of individuality, through its forms of organization – especially as they are unveiled through the formation of laws. Durkheim is concerned with the problem of how social order is to be maintained in a society of increasingly diverse individuals. He begins first by looking at the two different types of solidarity that he finds in society – mechanical and organic. Laws and legal systems are the indicators of these types of solidarity, so it is through the study of these legal systems that Durkheim undertakes the study of social solidarity. He chooses the study of laws because they are an integral part of the successful workings of society. Indeed, they are a concrete measure of those workings and, therefore, a useful tool for analyzing the state of development of any particular society – because Durkheim, like Tönnies, viewed society as evolving from one state to another as modernization proceeds. "The visible symbol is law. In effect, despite its immaterial character, wherever social solidarity exists, it resides not in a state of pure potentiality, but manifests its presence by sensible indices" (1933 [1893]: 64).

The first type of law that Durkheim investigates is "repressive" law. By this, he means that body of laws whose function it is to punish transgressions. Implicit in the idea of punishing transgressions, however, is the question: "transgressions of *what?*" Durkheim's answer is that repressive law has the function of punishing transgressions against the body of specific, common sentiments that are shared by all (or almost all) members of a community – the "totality of beliefs and sentiments common to average citizens of the same society forms a determinate system which has its own life; one may call it the *collective* or *common conscience*" (Durkheim 1933 [1893]:

79). By exploring the essence of repressive law, Durkheim is able to develop the idea of the "collective conscience."

There can only be this type of conscience "common to average citizens" in those communities where there is little differentiation among the members of the community. That is, Durkheim argues, in situations where there is little division of labor (where most people do the same things and, therefore, have the same day-to-day life experiences) people will also share the same values. The lack of differentiation among community members with regard to their experiences, responsibilities, needs, and habits means that the understandings of the world and how it should operate will also be shared by the members of that community. Because people are not differentiated in their activities, Durkheim argues, they will not be differentiated in their values – they will have a *collective* conscience. The community is an entity that is more than the sum of its parts. The moral force of the collective conscience acts on the members of the community to create the feeling of a shared identity.

It is the collective conscience which holds society together in what Durkheim calls "mechanical solidarity." The collective conscience is most strongly developed and all-encompassing in societies where the division of labor has yet to differentiate individuals. The commonality of beliefs and sentiments will produce a populace with great solidarity because of the absence of heterogeneity and, therefore, of strife. "The social molecules which can be coherent in this way," he wrote, "can act together only in the measure that they have no actions of their own, as the molecules of inorganic bodies. That is why we propose to call this type of solidarity mechanical" (1933 [1893]: 130).

The members of the community are impelled to act, therefore, even in the most minute instances, in conformity with the collective conscience because it is the only conscience that they possess. The community must maintain a firm line against attacks on its common values or risk falling apart into chaos. This is mechanical solidarity, which has its expression in repressive law – law that is meant to punish transgressions against the collective conscience. Repressive law is the expression of the members of society acting to protect and reinforce the collective conscience. Durkheim argued that punishment "consists, then, in essentially a passionate reaction of graduated intensity that society exercises through the medium of a body acting on those of its members who have violated certain rules of conduct" (1933 [1893]: 96). The rules of conduct are determined by the collective conscience. Because all members of the community believe in the same values and ideas – because they share a collective conscience – the members of that society view any act that violates that communal ethos as criminal.

This type of solidarity not only does not require individuality, but is in fact in opposition to its development. It can, Durkheim writes, "grow only in inverse ratio to personality" (1933 [1893]: 129). Repressive laws are the expression of the reaction of those undifferentiated members to an attack on the collective conscience. Crime in this instance is defined as being any attack on the collective conscience, and by punishing that crime, the members of the community reassert their commonality.

Durkheim has a less rosy view of life in tightly controlled communities without much differentiation among the individual members than Tönnies does. The requirement of commonality of sentiments represses the possibility of individuality. Punishment is meted out to those who do not fall in line with the strictures of the common sentiment – individual expression which is at odds with the collective conscience is, in fact, an attack on the very heart of community solidarity. "All the acts which offend them are not dangerous in themselves, or, at least, are not as dangerous as they are made out to be," Durkheim writes. "But, the reprobation of which these acts are the object still has reasons for existing, whatever the origin of the sentiments involved, once they are made part of a collective type, and especially if they are essential elements, everything which contributes to disturb them, at the same disturbs social cohesion and compromises society" (1933 [1893: 107]). Or, as Aron more succinctly notes, "[t]he purpose of punishment is to satisfy the common consciousness" (1970: 19). This is the dark side of Tönnies's Gemeinschaft. Harmony and unity are maintained only by the exclusion of individuality. "Community" here is a repressive entity that works to oppose individuality in favor of categorical ("us" vs. "them," for example) identity.

But there are different types of societies – societies where the division of labor is more advanced and where the possibility exists for the development of individuality.

> The collective conscience varies in extent and force from one society to another. In societies where mechanical solidarity predominates, the collective consciousness embraces the greater part of individual consciousness. The same idea may be expressed thus: in archaic societies,

> the fraction of individual existences governed by common sentiments
> is nearly coextensive with the total existence. In societies of which dif-
> ferentiation of individuals is a characteristic, everyone is free to believe,
> to desire, and to act according to his own preferences in a large number
> of circumstances. In societies with mechanical solidarity, on the other
> hand, the greater part of existence is governed by social imperatives and
> interdicts. (Aron 1970: 15)

As it advances, then, the division of labor produces a different
and supposedly more advanced type of social solidarity – organic
solidarity – which finds its expression in "restitutive" law.

Organic solidarity is so called because it is analogous to the functioning of the various organs within the body of an animal. As their
functions become more specific and specialized – that is, as the
division of labor progresses – the organs themselves become more
interdependent. Members of a society where the division of labor
has differentiated the functions and duties of those members have
greater individuality because they are not interchangeable; they are
not so easily replaced. Therefore, the development of individuality
is not only facilitated, it is necessary. The organs of the body cannot
continue to function unless each organ carries out a specific and individuated task. The more specific and individuated the task, the more
dependent upon each other the organs become. Thus, the division of
labor in society is connected with the evolution of human beings into
individuals.

The solidarity ensuing from this differentiation is more tenuous
than is mechanical solidarity, and it is the function of restitutive law
to maintain the balances between and interworkings of the various
organs. The point of restitutive law is not to punish transgressions
against the collective conscience – which has been weakened by the
division of labor to the point where it can no longer provide a source
of community cohesion – but to ensure the orderly functioning of the
various differentiated "organs" of the community. The goal of restitutive law is to restore the workings of the interdependent system when
one part of the system has been thrown into disarray. This is usually
the body of civil law. Under restitutive law, for example, if someone
hits my car because she is driving too fast, the community does not
step in to shame her or, perhaps, cut off her offending lead-foot. This
solution would do nothing to help me continue my commute to work
for which I need my car. Instead, the state requires that she (or her
automobile insurance company) pay to have my car restored to its

working state so that I can continue to drive it to work. The goal of restitutive law is to restore the interdependent working of society.

Law, the state, and ultimately civilization itself work to maintain the solidarity of a society whose cohesion rests on differentiation and individuality, which could produce either strife or interdependence. The negative solidarity which Durkheim sees manifest itself in laws which serve to separate the conflicting members of a society is not sufficient to insure the maintenance of social cohesion. Some positive solidarity – such as the contract – must also exist to unite those members. Thus, interdependence must be ensured.

Societies with organic solidarity have a weak collective conscience. Societies with mechanical solidarity have a strong collective conscience. It is that similarity of thought and feeling that holds the mechanical solidarity society together – that sameness is the social glue. It is difference – and the resulting interdependence – that holds organic solidarity societies together. We can see how there is some correspondence between the ideas of Gemeinschaft and mechanical solidarity and between Gesellschaft and organic solidarity. Look for example at Tönnies's characterization of the transition from Gemeinschaft to Gesellschaft: "The state frees itself more and more from the traditions and customs of the past and the belief in their importance. Thus, the forms of law change from a product of the folkways and mores and the law of custom into a purely legalistic law, a product of policy" (1957 [1887]: 66). He goes on to say that the "state is hardly directly concerned with morality. It has only to suppress and punish hostile actions which are detrimental to the common weal or seemingly dangerous for itself and society" (1957 [1887]: 69).

We can also see how, without naming it, Tönnies recognized a diminishing role for the collective conscience in Gesellschaft.

> Previously, all was centered around the belief in invisible beings, spirits and gods; now it is focalized on the insight into visible nature. Religion, which is rooted in folk life or at least closely related to it, must cede supremacy to science, which derives from and corresponds to consciousness. Such consciousness is a product of learning and culture and, therefore, remote from the people. (1957 [1887]: 67)

While Durkheim sees the emergence of organic solidarity as an adaptation to the greater press of humans on space – an adaptation that will prevent the human race from dissolving into a survival-of-the-fittest fight of each person against the rest – Tönnies sees the loss of traditional communities and the emergence of Gesellschaft in a much more negative light:

> City life and *Gesellschaft* drive the common people to decay and death; in vain they struggle to attain power through their own multitude, and it seems to them that they can use their power only for a revolution if they want to free themselves from their fate. . . . The entire culture has been transformed into a civilization of state and *Gesellschaft*, and this transformation means the doom of culture itself if none of its scattered seeds remain alive and again bring forth the essence and idea of *Gemeinschaft*, thus secretly fostering a new culture amidst the decaying one. (1957 [1887]: 70–1)

Community, for Tönnies, involves an underlying collective moral foundation, shared in common among the members who feel themselves to be part of – and responsible to – the larger civic body. Without that foundation, we may have relations with others, but we will not have community.

Almost certainly, the context in which Tönnies was writing had an enormous impact on his feelings about the transition from traditional to modern life. He was living and writing during the very worst period of the Industrial Revolution, when unrestrained capitalism swept through Europe and North America sowing misery in its wake. That notoriously noxious period of human history was inevitably tied to urbanization. Urban life might possibly have been blamed for social ills that might better have been laid at the door of capitalism. (For a thorough discussion of this, see Fischer 1984.) Nevertheless, this criticism of the transition from Gemeinschaft to Gesellschaft, or traditional to modern life, or small town to urban jungle, or even face-to-face interaction to computer-mediated communication, is a line of argument that survives well into the present day. We will certainly see it again.

Durkheim, on the other hand, argues that it is the differentiation which is part of the division of labor and leads to us all being individuals. This is what he means when he says that individuals are formed *after* the society develops. Durkheim sees this as a positive development. Differentiation, specialization, and interdependency are positive adaptations to the rising press of population growth and provide a mechanism other than the fight of "all against all" for us to survive together – it is opposed to the nasty, brutish and short lives that natural selection means for the beasts.

Despite their differences, Tönnies and Durkheim share the view of a fundamental change in societies such that the basis of social solidarity is no longer categorical affiliation, but instead becomes interdependent relations, especially of exchange. As White et al. argue: "Perhaps *the* major thrust of classical social theory was its recognition of the historical dissolution of categorical boundaries for social relations, whether the change was perceived as a transition from status to contract (Maine), from *Gemeinschaft* to *Gesellschaft* (Tönnies), from mechanical to organic solidarity (Durkheim), from traditional to means-rational orientation (Weber), or from ascribed to achieved status (Linton)" (1976: 732–3). The conception of community, that is, shifts from an entity with a moral pull of individuals to a system of interlocking relations among its members. This is the type of relational thinking that is at the heart of network analysis. It is also at the center of Georg Simmel's formal sociology.

Simmel: individuality and social groups

The individual, for Simmel, is inexorably tied to the social form that she or he has created. The two, individual and society, are constantly in the process of creating each other. Individuals are defined by the social circles of which they are members. A college student, for example, is a member of the college at which she matriculates. But that doesn't give her much individuality on the campus; every other student is similarly situated in the social world. But perhaps she is also a member of the student government; that makes her somewhat more individual. Perhaps she is also a staff member of the school newspaper. She is more individual still. She has a particular major, comes from a particular place, and lives in a particular dorm. With every additional group affiliation, she becomes increasingly individual so that the accumulation of affiliations will soon mean that she is the only person on campus who sits at this particular intersection of social circles. She is unique and individual.

Likewise, the social circles are defined by the individuals who compose them, contracting and expanding, becoming more or less differentiated from other groups as they either narrow their membership rolls or broaden them. This duality of individual and social group is the interplay that Simmel explored in his 1908 "Group expansion and the development of individuality." There is a tension between freedom and equality, Simmel writes, because freedom includes the idea that an individual is free to develop her or his own eccentricities, peculiarities and even deviancies. These fully developed individuals cannot, however, be equal because they are incommensurable. Equality, as such, rests in the undifferentiated character of the elements that compose an extremely narrow social circle (much like mechanical solidarity before the division of labor has differentiated individuals). It is only in the expansion of this social circle that Simmel sees the route to the full development of the individual's capacities. "Individuality in being and action," he writes, "generally increases to the degree that the social circle encompassing the individual expands" (1971: 252). The expansion of the social circle will lead to a less individual character for that circle, but to the greater development of individuality for the members of that circle.

> The narrower the circle to which we commit ourselves, the less freedom of individuality we possess; however, this narrower circle is itself something individual, and it cuts itself off sharply from all other circles precisely because it is small. Correspondingly, if the circle in which we are active and in which our interests hold sway enlarges, there is more room in it for the development of our individuality; but as *parts of this whole*, we have less uniqueness: the larger whole is less individual as a social group. (Simmel 1971: 257, emphasis in original)

A narrow circle, therefore, by definition will not allow great differentiation among its members, but will itself have a more distinctive and individual character. Simmel sees the expansion of the social circle to be the intersection by the individual of an expanding number of increasingly narrow – and therefore more "individual" – social circles. This idea, which echoes Durkheim's arguments about the development of individuality connected with increasing organic solidarity, is relational. The uniqueness of the individual is based on her or his position alone at this nexus of a unique set of circles. This defines the individual as such. As social circles become ever more narrow (as, for example, the division of labor proceeds), the social values that they encompass become increasingly more specific and constrained, increasingly at variance with outside circles.

In his 1903 "The metropolis and mental life," Simmel laid the basis for the narrow circle/wide circle dichotomy that he elaborated in "Group expansion." It is only in the metropolis with its breakdown of the strictures of tight communal life (or, in Tönnies's terms, the movement from Gemeinschaft to Gesellschaft), Simmel argues, that

the individual at once attains her or his most characteristic development and also *transcends* the intermediate forms of association – that
is, the middle-sized social circles which exist in small towns – in
order to become part of the wider humanity. As Simmel argues, "[t]he
sphere of life of the small town is, in the main, enclosed within itself.
For the metropolis it is decisive that its inner life is extended in a
wave-like motion over a broader national or international area" (1971:
335). It is in the metropolis, Simmel argues, with its rich diversity of
others with whom we can associate that we are able to be our most
individual selves.

This type of relational perspective takes a different approach
than traditional conceptions of community. Tönnies and Durkheim
imagine community as more than merely a network of particularly
dense ties. It is also a *feeling of belonging* to the group. The group
is something more than just the sum of its members – something
more than even the sum of the members and the concatenation of
the relations among them. It is conceived of as an entity itself. The
collective conscience, for example, that Durkheim sees as integral to
mechanical solidarity still exists even in contemporary post-industrial
societies. We can see it many places – such as in the fervor of
opponents to marriage equality for gays and lesbians or in virulent
anti-immigrant sentiments.

But the networks perspective challenges this notion by looking
at the ways things like beliefs are transmitted and even produced
in networks. For example, we will see in later chapters how active
racism against Indochinese immigrants in Boston arose as a result
of particular network structures, how the identity of "Parisian" was
created by changing networks among the inhabitants of that city
in the nineteenth century, and how innovative thinking is fostered
under certain network conditions. A network analytical perspective
argues that even the *feelings of community*, as well as the moral beliefs
and sentiments that community members share, are created through
relations in networks.

Looking at "community" from these different perspectives has
implications for our analyses. What, for example, are the differences
between Anderson's "imagined communities" (1983) or Webber's
"community without propinquity" (1963) and the dense networks of
rich personal ties that exist not only in small towns and villages, but
even (as we will see) in large urban centers and seemingly impersonal
suburbs? On the one hand we have "categorical identities" (Calhoun

1998) while on the other we have complex webs of interpersonal relations that are often multi-layered and multi-faceted.

> Community life can be understood as the life people live in dense, multi-
> plex, relatively autonomous networks of social relationships. Community,
> thus, is not a place or simply a small-scale population aggregate, but
> a mode of relating, variable in extent. Though communities may be
> larger than the immediate personal networks of individuals, they can
> in principle be understood by an extension of the same lifeworld terms.
> . . . Within a community, as within a kinship-based social organization,
> an unmet person need not be completely a stranger, for he or she can
> always be placed within an intuitive field, identified by a readily recogniz-
> able kind of relationship (a distant cousin, someone related by marriage
> to a friend, etc.). This is not equally true of people met from outside the
> communal field. While some direct relationships extend far afield, this
> happens usually with minimal density of network formation. Most under-
> standings of strangers will be based not on ideas of the nature of their
> relationship to one, but on categorical identities: they are Blacks, Whites,
> rich, poor, Baptists, Jews, etc. (Calhoun 1998: 391)

Members of our communities can be fit into our networks; those who
are not members of our community are merely categorical "Others."

So while traditional conceptions of communities emphasized the
shared identity and the ways in which relationships were formed on
the basis of the moral order of the community, a network perspective puts the structure of the relations first and argues that beliefs,
feelings, ideas, and sentiments emerge from them. By analyzing the
network structures directly, we hope to gain a greater understanding
of what exactly a particular community is, how it functions, what
constraints and opportunities its members face, and how identity is
created in interaction – or even in the lack of interaction.

"The duality of persons and groups"

In the 1970s, Ronald Breiger (1974) began working on ways to take
Simmel's insights about duality and translate them into techniques
which would allow us to analyze social networks from the perspective
of both the person and the group. Understanding Breiger's work will
allow us to calculate things like density and look at real groups inside
of larger, more diffuse webs. Breiger builds on Simmel's fundamental idea that groups are made up of people (which is not terrifically
surprising) *and* that people are also made up of groups (which can be

a rather new way of thinking about ourselves). What does it mean to say that people are made up of groups?

Breiger asks us to "[c]onsider a set of individuals and a set of groups such that the value of a *tie* between any two individuals is defined as the number of groups of which they are both members. The value of a tie between any two groups is defined conversely as the number of persons who belong to them both" (1974: 181–2, emphasis in original). We can see here an intuitive fit with some of the ideas about the strength of ties that were discussed in chapter 1. Groups are linked together by sharing members – the more members they share, the stronger the tie between them. Likewise, individuals are linked together when they share membership in groups – the more group memberships they share, the stronger the tie between them. Groups are connected by people; people are connected by groups.

Breiger shows us that this insight into social structure allows us to analyze the connections between people and groups so as to find things like clique structures in the system. As his example, Breiger analyzes Davis et al.'s (1941) data about southern club women attending social events together to uncover the clique structure among the women and among the events. Duality means that there are two sides to questions like, "What organizations do you belong to?" From knowing that alone, we can make network diagrams of people and of groups.

Breiger's method for analyzing this data was to use matrix multiplication on the matrix of women and the events they attended. The "Closer Look" section of this chapter explains how to do matrix multiplication and how to interpret the results that it gives you.

The links between individuals and groups form the basis of social solidarity – they are the building blocks of communities.

Cohesion

But what does "solidarity" mean? One way to think about it is in the sense that Durkheim uses "mechanical solidarity" – a community has solidarity when its members share a collective conscience, a common body of beliefs and sentiments that give individuals a feeling of belonging to the group.

Another way to think about solidarity, though, is to think about "cohesion" – that is, the degree to which members of a community are actually tied to each other, either directly through personal contact or indirectly through joint group membership, as Breiger shows us that Davis's club women were. Cohesive groups are those in which the members are tied to each other in relations that are mutual (that is, the ties go both ways), are frequent, are more frequent to others in the groups than they are to those who are outside of the group, and allow all of the members of the group to reach each other, if not immediately directly, then at least through relatively short chains of contacts (Wasserman & Faust 1994: 251–2). Using network analysis, we can empirically observe and measure these properties. We can see if a group's members, for example, have more frequent ties with each other than they do with outsiders.

This type of definition seems to be at odds with our more common conceptions of "community" involving a commonality of belief and sentiment. However, Collins points out that "[t]he more tightly that individuals are tied into a network, the more they are affected by group standards ... Isolated and tightly connected groups make up a clique; within such highly cohesive groups, individuals tend to have very homogenous beliefs" (Collins 1988: 416–17). That is, the variation in cohesiveness of groups is connected to the variation in communal feeling that the members of the groups may have. We will see the emergence of this collective conscience and identity in later chapters.

A closer look: matrix multiplication

Suppose you have a list of groups, organizations, or events where each group etc. provides a roster of its members or attendees. Or suppose you have a set of resumes on which people list their group memberships – or calendars where they list the events they attend. And suppose you want to know what the social structure of these people or groups looks like – that is, you want to know which people are tied together by shared group memberships, or which groups are tied together by shared members, or even the degree of segregation and clique-ishness that exists in this world. The hard way to do this would be to successively match up each pair of rosters/resumes and mark down the similarities. The task would be daunting. For a small group of only 25 people, the number of possible pairs to be examined would be 300. On a small college campus with 1,900 students, the number of pairs to be examined would be 1,804,050.

The easy way to do this is through matrix multiplication, which

Table 2.1 Person-by-group matrix, PXG

	Film	Glee	Hockey
Amy			
Betty			
Carrie			
Dana			

allows us to quickly find and analyze the indirect ties between people that are formed by shared group memberships or between groups by shared membership rosters.

Start by making a person-by-group matrix. This is a matrix where the rows (going across) are people and the columns (going up and down) are groups. We might, for example, have four people – Amy, Betty, Carrie, and Dana – and three groups – Film Society, Glee Club, and the Hockey Team. The person-by-group matrix that we would set up for this would look like the example in table 2.1. We will name this matrix PXG for "person by group." (Remember from chapter 1 that matrices are always read row first and then column.)

We also need to know either (1) each girl's list of group memberships (their *resumes*) *or* (2) each group's list of members (their *rosters*). Suppose we have the girls' resumes: Amy belongs to the Film Society and the Hockey Team, Betty belongs to the Glee Club, Carrie belongs to the Film Society and the Hockey Team, and Dana belongs to the Glee Club and the Hockey Team. Or we could instead have the club rosters: the members of the Film Society are Amy and Carrie, the members of the Glee Club are Betty and Dana, and the members of the Hockey Team are Amy, Carrie, and Dana. Either set of information would allow us to fill in the cells of the matrix, putting a 1 in a cell if the person in that row belongs to the group in that column. This is shown in table 2.2.

We fill in the rest of the cells in the matrix with 0s, which indicate that the person in that row does not belong to the group in that column. This is shown in table 2.3.

Table 2.2 PXG with cell entries

	Film	Glee	Hockey
Amy	1		1
Betty		1	
Carrie	1		1
Dana		1	1

Table 2.3 Completed PXG

	Film	Glee	Hockey
Amy	I	O	I
Betty	O	I	O
Carrie	I	O	I
Dana	O	I	I

Reading across the rows, we can see each girl's resume; reading down the columns, we can see each group's roster.

But what about the connections of the girls to each other through shared group memberships? What about the connections of the groups to each other through shared members? Although the connections are easy to see in this very small example, we could look at much larger systems in this same way: how are corporations linked together by sharing members of their boards of directors, for example?

To be able to see these indirect connections, we can use matrix multiplication to reveal the connections between people resulting from shared memberships in groups or the connections between groups resulting from shared members. First, let's see how we could multiply our example matrix to see how the girls are connected through shared group memberships. We begin by making a **transpose** of the original matrix – this just means that we flip the original matrix across the main diagonal so that the rows become columns and the columns become rows. This is shown in table 2.4, which will call GXP (for "group by person").

Note that the information contained in each of the matrices is exactly the same. We can still read the girls' resumes (by reading down the columns) and we can still read the groups' rosters (by reading across the rows). We are now ready to multiply the two matrices together.

Set up a blank matrix to receive the results of your multiplication. In this case, we are looking for the indirect relationships of the girls to each other through shared group memberships, so we will set up a

Table 2.4 Transposed matrix GXP

	Amy	Betty	Carrie	Dana
Film	I	O	I	O
Glee	O	I	O	I
Hockey	I	O	I	I

Table 2.5 Blank person-by-person matrix

	Amy	Betty	Carrie	Dana
Amy				
Betty				
Carrie				
Dana				

blank person-by-person matrix (we will call it "PXP"), with the girls as both the rows and the columns. This is shown in table 2.5.

To fill in the value for the $PXP_{1,1}$ cell (that is, the cell in row 1, column 1 or the cell that has Amy in the row and Amy also in the column) we multiply the values in the first row of the original matrix, PXG, each by the corresponding value in the first column of the transposed matrix, GXP. We then add the multiplied values all together.

The values of the first row of PXG are: 1, 0, 1. The values of the first column of GXP are 1, 0, 1. (Although these are the same values in this instance, that will not always be the case.) The first value of the first row (which in this case is 1) is multiplied by the first value of the first column (which in this case is also 1): $1 \times 1 = 1$. The second value of the first row (which is 0) is multiplied by the second value of the first column (which also happens to be 0 in this case): $0 \times 0 = 0$. The third value of the first row (which is 1) is multiplied by the third value of the first column (which is also 1): $1 \times 1 = 1$. We then add all the products together: $1 + 0 + 1 = 2$. The value for the cell in the first row, first column of the person-by-person matrix is 2. Table 2.6 shows this.

We continue on in this way. To find the value for the cell in the *first* row, *second* column of PXP, we multiply the values in the *first* row of PXG by the values in the *second* column of GXP, and so on. The *third* row, *second* column of PXP, for example, will be found by multiplying the *third* row of PXG by the *second* column of GXP. In general, any cell with row *i* and column *j* in the new matrix will be found by multiplying together the *i*th row of the original matrix with the *j*th row of

Table 2.6 Person-by-person matrix with one filled cell

	A	B	C	D
A	2			
B				
C				
D				

Table 2.7 Final person-by-person matrix

	Amy	Betty	Carrie	Dana
Amy	2	0	2	1
Betty	0	1	0	1
Carrie	2	0	2	1
Dana	1	1	1	2

the transposed matrix. So, if our original matrix is called M and our transposed matrix is called M^I (the superscript I is the usual way that a transposed matrix is distinguished from the original matrix) and we call our multiplied matrix P:

$$P_{I,I} = (M_{I,I} \times M^I_{I,I}) + (M_{I,2} \times M^I_{2,I}) + (M_{I,3} \times M^I_{3,I}) + (M_{I,4} \times M^I_{4,I})$$
$$P_{I,2} = (M_{I,I} \times M^I_{I,2}) + (M_{I,2} \times M^I_{2,2}) + (M_{I,3} \times M^I_{3,2}) + (M_{I,4} \times M^I_{4,2})$$
$$P_{I,3} = (M_{I,I} \times M^I_{I,3}) + (M_{I,2} \times M^I_{2,3}) + (M_{I,3} \times M^I_{3,3}) + (M_{I,4} \times M^I_{4,3})$$
$$P_{I,4} = (M_{I,I} \times M^I_{I,4}) + (M_{I,2} \times M^I_{2,4}) + (M_{I,3} \times M^I_{3,4}) + (M_{I,4} \times M^I_{4,4})$$
$$P_{2,I} = (M_{2,I} \times M^I_{I,I}) + (M_{2,2} \times M^I_{2,I}) + (M_{2,3} \times M^I_{3,I}) + (M_{2,4} \times M^I_{4,I})$$
$$P_{2,2} = (M_{2,I} \times M^I_{I,2}) + (M_{2,2} \times M^I_{2,2}) + (M_{2,3} \times M^I_{3,2}) + (M_{2,4} \times M^I_{4,2})$$

And so on.

In this example, PXP will be a four-by-four matrix – four people listed down the side and the same four people listed across the top. It will have 16 cells, called $PXP_{I,I}$; $PXP_{I,2}$; $PXP_{I,3}$; $PXP_{I,4}$; $PXP_{2,I}$; $PXP_{2,2}$; $PXP_{2,3}$; $PXP_{2,4}$; $PXP_{3,I}$; $PXP_{3,2}$; $PXP_{3,3}$; $PXP_{3,4}$; $PXP_{4,I}$; $PXP_{4,2}$; $PXP_{4,3}$; and $PXP_{4,4}$. (Remember that the subscripts for the cell addresses always list the row first and then the column. So $PXP_{I,4}$ is the cell in the person-by-person matrix that is in the first row and the fourth column.) For each of these cells, we look at the cell address and multiply the row of the original matrix and the column of the transposed matrix to find the value for that cell.

If you multiply the matrices in this example, you should get a person-by-person matrix that looks like the matrix in table 2.7.

That is for the person-by-person matrix. But suppose instead we wanted to look at the group-by-group matrix. We simply flip the order of the original and the transposed matrices. That is, we would consider the transposed matrix to be matrix M (which we will use for its rows) and the original matrix to be M^I (which we will use for its columns). The empty matrix that we set up to receive the values that we calculate will have the names of the groups as the labels on the rows and columns and will have the same number of rows and columns as we have groups. Following the same rules for multiplying

Table 2.8 Final group-by-group matrix

	Film	Glee	Hockey
Film	2	0	2
Glee	0	2	1
Hockey	2	1	3

the matrices together that we used in the example above, but switching the order in which the matrices are used (that is, using the rows of the matrix that had been the columns and the columns of the matrix that had been the rows), we should get a group-by-group matrix that looks like table 2.8. (Unlike in regular multiplication, the order in which you multiply matrices matters.)

But what do these matrices mean? How do we read them and what do they tell us? Let's look at the person-by-person matrix first. Notice that the matrix is *symmetric* on either side of the *main diagonal*. That is, the value in the B,D cell (where the row for Betty and the column for Dana intersect), for example, is the same as the value in the D,B cell (where the row for Dana and the column for Betty intersect). The value in the A,C cell (where the row for Amy and the column for Carrie intersect) is the same as the value in the C,A cell (where the row for Carrie and the column for Amy intersect). This makes sense because the values in these cells tell us the number of groups in which the two people share memberships. In this example, Dana and Betty share one group membership. Amy and Carrie share two group memberships. By looking back at the original matrix, we can confirm that this is true: Dana and Betty are both in the Glee Club and are in no other groups together. Amy and Carrie are both in the Film Society and are on the Hockey Team together. So by multiplying the original matrix by its transpose, we now have a matrix of indirect ties which shows us how the girls are tied to each other through shared group memberships. We can see by looking at the person-by-person matrix that Amy and Carrie have a dyad of shared membership and that Betty operates in a different social world. Dana, however, pulls them all together. The sociogram translation of the person-by-person matrix in table 2.7 is shown in figure 2.1. Heavier lines indicate stronger ties. The arrows curving back into the nodes from which they came represent the groups to which each girl belongs. Betty only belongs to one group, so her self-tie is lighter than the self-ties of the other girls, each of whom belongs to two groups.

We can do the same thing with the groups and see the pivotal role

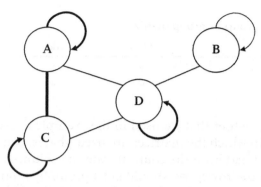

Figure 2.1 Person-by-person sociogram

played by the Hockey Team in holding the network of organizations together. Figure 2.2 is the sociogram translation of the group-by-group matrix in table 2.8. Again, heavier lines show stronger ties – that is, more members shared in common. Notice, for example, the very heavy line from H curving back in on itself. This is because H has three members, the largest of any group.

The main diagonal (the Amy,Amy cell, the Betty,Betty cell, the Carrie,Carrie cell, and the Dana,Dana cell in the person-by-person matrix or the Film,Film, Glee,Glee and Hockey,Hockey cells in the group-by-group matrix – in other words, the cells that have the same row and column or that show each person's or group's relationship to itself) tell us the total number of groups to which that person belongs in the person-by-person matrix and how many members each group has in the group-by-group matrix.

Breiger uses this technique on Davis et al.'s data to find the clique

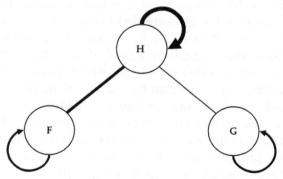

Figure 2.2 Group-by-group sociogram

Table 2.9 Person-by-event matrix of Davis et al.'s data (Breiger 1974: 186, used by permission)

	1	2	3	4	5	6	7	8	9	10	11	12	13	14
Eleanor	0	1	0	1	0	0	0	1	0	0	0	1	0	0
Brenda	0	1	0	1	0	0	1	1	0	1	0	1	1	0
Dorothy	0	0	0	0	0	1	0	0	0	0	0	1	0	0
Verne	0	0	0	1	1	1	0	0	0	0	0	1	0	0
Flora	1	0	0	0	0	1	0	0	0	0	0	0	0	0
Olivia	1	0	0	0	0	1	0	0	0	0	0	0	0	0
Laura	0	1	1	1	0	0	1	1	0	1	0	1	0	0
Evelyn	0	1	1	0	0	1	1	1	0	1	0	1	1	0
Pearl	0	0	0	0	0	1	0	1	0	0	0	1	0	0
Ruth	0	1	0	1	0	1	0	0	0	0	0	1	0	0
Sylvia	0	0	0	1	1	1	0	0	1	0	1	1	0	1
Katherine	0	0	0	0	1	1	0	0	1	0	1	1	0	1
Myrna	0	0	0	0	1	1	0	0	1	0	0	1	0	0
Theresa	0	1	1	1	0	1	1	1	0	0	0	1	1	0
Charlotte	0	1	0	1	0	0	1	0	0	0	0	0	1	0
Frances	0	1	0	0	0	0	1	1	0	0	0	1	0	0
Helen	1	0	0	1	1	0	0	0	1	0	0	1	0	0
Nora	1	0	0	1	1	1	0	1	1	0	1	0	0	1

structure among the women based on their attendance together at social events. The original matrix of women and the events they attended is presented in table 2.9, where the women's names are the row labels and the events are recorded in the columns. A 1 in a cell means that the woman attended the event; a 0 means that she did not.

Looking at the raw data in this way, it is impossible to see what kind of clique structure could be present here. But once Breiger has transposed the matrix and then multiplied it, he comes up with a person-by-person matrix which shows a clear divide between two cliques of women. Figure 2.3 shows Breiger's sociograms. (Note that not all of the women are included in the figure because a few of them were part of neither clique.)

By using matrix multiplication when we have person-by-group data (such as resumes, rosters, or calendars), we can begin to analyze the structure of the network. The discovery of the clique structure of the women in the Davis data appears evident when we look at the sociogram translations of the multiplied matrices. In future chapters, we will go further with the analysis, looking, for example, at the densities of the various parts of the network, the centrality of particular actors, and the structural equivalence of some actors.

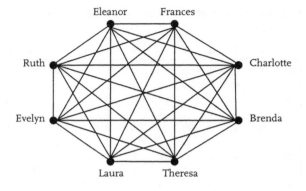

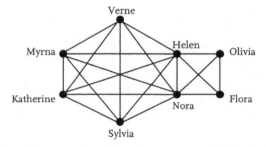

Figure 2.3 Sociogram of Davis et al.'s data (Breiger 1974: 188, used by permission)

Matrix multiplication in UCINET6

As you can imagine, doing the matrix multiplication of large data-sets by hand would be extremely cumbersome. Even multiplying small datasets can be rather tedious. To do matrix multiplication in UCINET, however, takes a matter of seconds. Start by taking a look at the matrix that you want to multiply by using the "Display" function. In this case, like Breiger, we will use the Davis et al. data. Click on the "display" icon at the top of the screen, double click on "datafiles," scroll down to "davis" and double click on it. Notice in the displayed matrix that the women are the rows and the events are the columns. This will be important later. Close the dataset once you have looked at it.

To transpose the matrix, click on the "Data" button at the top of the screen and choose "Transpose" from the dropdown menu. In the "Input dataset" window, you can either type in "davis" or click on the "..." button next to the window, click on "datafiles" and scroll over to

"davis" from the list. You can name your "Output dataset" (the transposed matrix) if you would like or UCINET will automatically give it
a name for you – in this case "davis-Transp." Click "OK." You should
now see the transposed dataset displayed with the events as the rows
and the women as the columns. Close the window.

Now we are ready to multiply the matrix by its transpose in order
to get either the person-by-person or the group-by-group matrix. Click
on the "matrix algebra" icon at the top of the screen (or choose "Matrix
Algebra" from the dropdown menu under "Tools"). You should see a
flashing cursor at the bottom of the screen in the window next to the
little arrow. The command for matrix multiplication is "prod" and the
syntax for the command is:

name of multiplied matrix = prod(name of first matrix,
name of second matrix)

(Be sure that there is no space between the command "prod" and the
parentheses.)

For this example, let's first look at the person-by-person matrix. We
will call it PXP, so our command will be:

PXP = prod(davis, davis-Transp)

If the program has executed our command successfully, the command
will appear in the log window at the top of the Matrix Algebra
Command Window. To see the PXP output file, use the "Display"
function and either scroll down to or type in the name PXP. You
should now see an 18 by 18 symmetric matrix with the names of the
women as both the rows and the columns. The main diagonal cell
values in this matrix tell us how many events each woman attended
(Evelyn went to eight events and Laura went to seven, for example)
and the other cell values tell us how many events the two women
went to together (Evelyn and Laura attended six events together;
Evelyn and Flora attended only one event together).

We can do the same thing for the events to look at the group-by-
group (or, in this case, event-by-event) matrix. We will call our output
matrix GXG and the command will be:

GXG = prod(davis-Transp, davis)

Notice that we have reversed the order in which we have input the
matrices to be multiplied. This time the transposed matrix is the
first matrix and the original matrix is the second matrix. This tells

the matrix algebra program in what order to multiply the matrices. An easy way to remember which matrix to put in first in order to get the output matrix that you want is that the first matrix should have as its rows the output that you want. That is, if you have people and groups and you want a group-by-group matrix, the first matrix should be whichever one (either the original or the transpose) has groups as its rows. If you want a person-by-person matrix as the output, the first matrix should be whichever one has people as the rows. (Remember that the order in which you multiply matrices matters.)

The output matrix is now our group-by-group matrix and we can use the Display function to see it. It is a 14 by 14 symmetric matrix with the events as both the rows and the columns. The main diagonal values tell us how many people attended each event (3 people at event #1, but 14 people at event #8, for example). The off-diagonal cell values tell us how many people attended both the events. Two people went to both event #1 and event #2, none of the people who went to event #14 also attended event #1, while all six people who attended event #3 also attended event #5, for example.

In the following chapters, we will see some of the ways we can organize this data to discover more about the structure of the network.

3 What do communities do for us?

In his classic treatise on Polynesian culture and history, *Vikings of the Sunrise,* Peter H. Buck wrote:

> The widely spaced islands between Fiji and South America remained unvisited by man until late in the world's history. They are included in a vast triangular area with its points at Hawai'i in the north, New Zealand in the south, and Easter Island in the east. . . . The scattered specks of land within the triangle are oceanic islands separated by abysmal depths. Never within the period of human migrations have they been joined together to offer an easy path to footmen. For untold centuries after the boundaries of the Pacific had been peopled by man, these islands remained isolated and unoccupied save by land shells, insects, reptiles, and birds. . . . The westerly winds and the constant trades blew over empty seas, for no primitive navigator had yet dared to raise a matting sail to waft him to waiting islands. . . . Beyond the eastern horizon, earth, sea, and sky awaited the coming of a breed of men who not only had an effective form of ocean transport but who had the courage to dare and both the will and the skill to conquer. The uncharted seas awaited the coming of the Polynesian navigators. (1938: 10–11)

Only relatively recently – probably within the last thousand years – did humans finally inhabit the far-flung islands of the Pacific. And only in the past 250 years did those societies come into contact with outsiders from Europe and North America – often with tragic results for the communities that had been built on those scattered islands. What can the social organization of such places tell us about life in the urban world?

Gift exchanges as social support and obligation

Marcel Mauss's 1925 study of the importance of "the gift" to the societies of the South Pacific is based on research in what he calls

"archaic" societies. The social functions of exchange in these societies, however, are similar in many ways to those in modern industrial
and post-industrial societies. The social relations – and obligations
– built by gift exchanges in the Pacific islands form a template for
understanding the relations of exchange in other social worlds. The
obligations of giving and receiving, the social ties created in these
exchanges, and the social support they engender are still vital aspects
of modern communal life.

In discussing gift giving, Mauss makes a key insight when he writes
that "it is groups, and not individuals, which carry on exchange, make
contracts, and are bound by obligations; the persons represented in
contracts are moral persons [i.e., legal entities] – clans, tribes, and
families; the groups, or the chiefs as intermediaries for the groups,
confront and oppose each other" (1967 [1925]: 3). Mauss argues that
gift exchanges are not merely transactions between two isolated
individuals – one who gives and one who receives – but rather bind
together the whole communities surrounding the exchangers. As
with Durkheim's organic solidarity or Tönnies's Gemeinschaft, social
solidarity is bound up in the ties created by exchange between differentiated others.

In looking at the literature regarding the Maori in the islands of
Polynesia, Mauss finds that important powers are attached to gifts.

> The *taonga* [a Maori word which means 'gifts', but also means 'burdens']
> are, at any rate with the Maori, closely attached to the individual, the clan
> and the land; they are the vehicle of their *mana* – magical, religious and
> spiritual power. In a proverb collected by Sir G. Grey and C.O. Davis,
> *taonga* are asked to destroy the person who receives them; and they have
> the power to do this if the law, or rather the obligation, about making a
> return gift is not observed. (1967 [1925]: 8)

It is apparent here that receiving a gift carries with it an obligation
on the part of the recipient – an obligation taken so seriously that
it carries the weight of life and death. The contract, then, to which
Mauss refers is one of extreme importance not only to the individual,
but also to the family, clan, and community of which that individual is
a part. Mauss recounts an explanation of the way that this obligation
worked given by a Maori informant:

> Suppose you have some particular object, *taonga*, and you give it to me;
> you give it to me without a price. We do not bargain over it. Now I give this
> thing to a third person who after a time decides to give me something in

repayment for it *(utu)*, and he makes me a present of something *(taonga)*. Now this *taonga* I received from him is the spirit *(hau)* of the *taonga* I received from you and which I passed on to him. The *taonga* which I receive on account of the *taonga* that came from you, I must return to you. It would not be right on my part to keep these *taonga* whether they were desirable or not. I must give them to you since they are the *hau* of the *taonga* which you gave to me. If I were to keep this second *taonga* for myself I might become ill or even die. (1967 [1925]: 8–9)

We can see in this discussion, laid out in perhaps more animate terms than we might be used to using, the *obligations* involved in generosity. Although we might not believe in a spirit that would sicken or kill us if we do not repay our social debts, anyone who has ever lived through a season of marriages (especially if it includes his or her own) will possibly recognize the social controls and tensions revolving around appropriate gift giving. In fact, there are three distinct types of obligations involved in gift exchanges: not only is there the obligation to repay gifts, there is also the obligation to give and the obligation to receive. "To refuse to give, or to fail to invite, is – like refusing to accept – the equivalent of a declaration of war; it is a refusal of friendship and intercourse" (Mauss 1967 [1925]: 11). Social support is not just a privilege or benefit; it is an obligation.

The socially imposed requirements of generosity help to bind the society together in mutual exchange. We can see the role in supporting social solidarity that gift giving plays. But it is established not only on the basis of friendship and harmonious intercourse, but also on the basis of forming a status hierarchy – that is, on the basis of social insecurity. With regard to the Native American tribes of the Pacific Northwest, for example, Mauss writes that "[n]o less important is the role which honor plays in the transactions of the Indians. Nowhere else is the prestige of an individual as closely bound up with expenditure, and with the duty of returning with interest gifts received in such a way that the creditor becomes the debtor" (1967 [1925]: 35).

Tied with the obligation to give, there is also the reciprocal obligation to receive, without which the system would break down. Again, this obligation is tied to honor and status as much as to friendship and the desirability of social intercourse. We begin to see why the word for "gift" and the word for "burden" are the same in the Maori language. In fact, Mauss tells us, "[o]ne does not have the right to refuse a gift or a potlatch. To do so would show fear of having to repay. . . . You accept the food and you do so because you mean to take up the challenge and prove that you are not unworthy. . . . Failure to give or receive, like failure to make return gifts, means a loss of dignity" (1967 [1925]: 39–40). Communities provide social support through obligations to give, to receive, and to repay. But support carries a burden of obligation.

The world the slaves made

The exchanges in these societies hold the societies together through mutual bonds of reciprocity that go on forever. Institutions like the Kula ring, an inter-island trading ritual, in Melanesia bind the different islands and kin groups together. Exchanges make relationships – network ties – that are long-lasting and could be vital to the continuation of the lives of the people involved. We can see the importance of these network ties when we look at the situation that Genovese (1974) writes about in *Roll, Jordan, Roll: The World the Slaves Made*. The antebellum slaves whose history Genovese tries to recover lived lives of extreme hardship under conditions of severe cruelty – not the least of which was the tearing apart of families. Yet Genovese argues that, even under such harsh conditions, the slaves made networks of connections and used those networks to help them survive (both physically and emotionally) the horrors they faced on a daily basis. How did people manage to build such a vital and sustaining community in the face of such overwhelming obstacles?

One of the most heartbreaking cruelties of slavery was the forced separation of family members – parents from children, spouses and siblings from each other, individuals ripped away from all loved ones. In the face of this, Genovese argues, slaves used names, especially surnames, as a mechanism by which to build and sustain contact with kinship structures.

We can see the importance of names when we consider that women who change their names when they marry often lose a significant portion of their personal social networks, especially their history. People who knew them before they were married may not be able to locate them now that they have a new name. Losing former friends and acquaintances can hamper women down the line. Indeed, Granovetter's research (1974) shows us that in the search for a job, these acquaintances from previous parts of one's life can play an important role in achieving success. Being able to claim a relationship with someone (and the obligations that may come with that relationship) is part of the exchange of gifts – and, in broader terms, of social support in general.

Genovese tells us that slaves were often very anxious to acquire surnames (1974: 445). The surnames were important because they were the marker of where a person belonged in the kinship structure. In many ways, a surname *establishes* kinship. Although it might seem strange to us, often slaves took the surname of their own master or of some other slaveholding family in the vicinity. This was even true in the aftermath of the Civil War which emancipated the slaves and finally allowed their separation from their masters.

Sharing names can be seen as a tie between nodes. By their choice of names, slaves were mapping out a pattern of social relationships which had been silenced, hidden, and neglected as unimportant to whites. But to the slaves themselves, claiming kin was a key act – especially in the hard times of the late nineteenth-century American south. To be able to rely on kin in times of need was a survival tactic. Genovese argues that the kinship ties among the slaves were strong and pervasive and that the web of family relations was of supreme importance to the slaves themselves. As evidence of this he notes that runaway slaves often went to see family members elsewhere, that the presence of children often tied enslaved parents to farms and plantations that they otherwise might have attempted to flee, and even that slave owners often kept families together on their plantations, not for any reason of sentiment or justice, but because of economic and safety concerns. Slaves would work harder and cause less trouble if they could be with their families. All of this, of course, was in the context of the omnipresent and heartbreaking separations that constantly occurred.

How did the community deal with these devastating continual losses? Genovese gives us a few answers, all of which can be seen in network terms. First, the slaves developed a system of establishing "fictive kin." "All except the most dehumanized slaveholders knew of the attachments that slaves had to their more extended families, to their friends, and to most of those who made up their little communities and called each other 'brother' and 'sister'" (Genovese 1974: 456). This practice builds strong ties of social support in local areas.

Second, slaves made a practice of visiting across to other farms and plantations whenever it was possible. Genovese tells us that Saturday nights, especially, were often occasions for parties to which slaves might come from many miles away to join in the festivities at one plantation. These occasions allowed networks of friendship to be built and to be maintained, and also made ties that reached outside the plantation to extend the web of relations further afield. In this context, slaves sometimes met others with whom they fell in love and married (even without the formal consent of the white establishment, who disregarded these marriages).

The marriages between slaves from different plantations were a double-edged sword for the slave owners.

> Marriages off the place meant considerable inconvenience to masters as well as to slaves. The masters of slave men had to forgo any claim to their children. Since slave marriages had no status at law and children followed the condition of the mother, the economic advantage fell to the masters of the slave women. But the masters of the men did not necessarily sacrifice their economic interests. They knew that a man who fell in love with a woman off the place would be a poor and sullen worker, and probably soon a runaway, if deprived of his choice. (Genovese 1974: 473)

The real threat to the slave owners, however, was not necessarily economic; it was rather the exchange of information through social ties that was facilitated by the movement of slaves around the area. Genovese notes that

> [t]he greatest complaint was that the slaves derived too much independence from their increased freedom of movement. The slaves began to think, wrote a hostile planter, that they have "an uncontrollable right to be frequently absent." They become indifferent to their master's interests and consider their wife's plantation their own home. Their presence disrupts the quarters, for *they bring news, habits, and attitudes from the outside*. (1974: 473, emphasis added)

We can see here that one structural outcome of this was the creation of a web of relations spreading out across the entire south – a web that could disseminate information and ideas among the slave population whom the masters desperately wanted to keep ignorant and isolated. Kin and friends could be found in many places – if you could reach them. This web of relations – as the masters realized in their opposition to interplantation marriages – had revolutionary potential. But it was a very tenuous web, dependent on memory and oral history, riddled with uncertainty. Were people still alive? Had they been moved again? Had they had children?

Certainly literacy among the slaves would have had an effect on the stability and viability of this network. A heavy reliance on oral communication has several implications for community building. One of the implications might be that the slaves would need places to come together where the spread of information could be more efficiently facilitated by the teller having simultaneous access to several listeners at once. Thus we see the importance of institutions such as churches where slaves could gather together without arousing the suspicions of the masters. Informal social gatherings – parties – were also key sites of network building and of the exchange of information.

Genovese notes that

> [t]he slaveholders brooded over the unreasonableness of their slaves, who preferred to party and court when they ought to have been resting up for the next day's labor. W.W. Gilmer of Virginia suggested that slaves had to be made to work hard or "they become restive, run about at night for want of exercise in the day, to pilfer, or visit, hear the news, etc. etc." He sputtered, "Adams and Co.'s Express can't beat them in the transmission of all sorts of reports; they travel from ten to thirty miles in a night, and many it seems do with less sleep than almost any other animal." (1974: 570)

The transmission of information through these connections was a serious threat to the slave owners' ability to control the culture of the plantations.

The role of the existence of such institutions as churches and social gatherings for community building continues to be relevant even today, when literacy (as Benedict Anderson [1983] reminds us) helps hold communities together. It is also important to note, moreover, that in actual fact, there were literate slaves everywhere. Genovese tells us that as a low estimate at least 5 percent of the slave population could read. Partly because of this, a literate black leadership was developing. Literacy creates a "locus of community" that transcends place and time.

The literacy of just a few slaves would change the structure of the flow of information. We can look at this in the form of a sociogram. Figure 3.1 shows a possible diagram of slave relations without literacy. Although there are connections among the slaves, including connections to slaves on neighboring plantations, the distance that information would have to travel between any two slaves in the network could conceivably be quite large. The shortest distance between A and B, for example, in figure 3.1 is seven steps. At such a distance, any information would probably be so degraded as to be worthless.

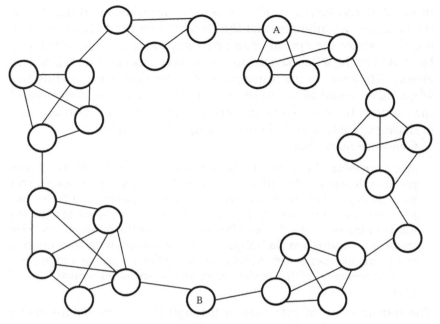

Figure 3.1 Sociogram of slave relations without literacy

Just adding one tie between two of the nodes in the sociogram (such as might happen if a letter were sent to a distant relative), however, dramatically decreases the distance between the two nodes. In figure 3.2, the shortest path between A and B is now only four steps, almost half as long as it had been.

If we add only one more literate slave to the network, as in figure 3.3, we can see how most of the slaves in the sociogram are now much closer to each other in terms of how many steps on average it would take for information to reach them. In chapters 4 and 8, we will discuss the work of Watts and Strogatz (1998) and we will see this network formation again. For now, we will just note that almost no node in figure 3.3 is more than three jumps away from the nearest literate source of information.

This structure – small supportive cliques of tightly knit strong ties connected to each other into a larger system – seems as though it would be perfect for organizing resistance to the institution of slavery. Yet the antebellum south saw little in the way of organized revolt by the slaves. Genovese argued (1974: 580) that the creation of a viable and supportive community by the slaves might have actually

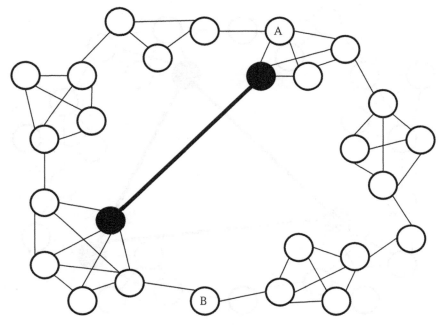

Figure 3.2 Sociogram of slave relations with two literate members

inhibited them from revolting. But a much more reasonable explanation can be found in the work of James Scott. In *Weapons of the
Weak* (1985), Scott argues that frontal assaults on the oppressors by
the disempowered and extremely vulnerable oppressed members of
the society are acts of extreme desperation, only engaged in when the
oppressed have absolutely no other options.

Scott argues the unceremonious cruelty with which the powerful
in society crush revolts by the powerless means that large-scale uprisings by the powerless are relatively rare and are usually only the last
resort of the desperate.

> It [seems] far more important to understand what we might call *everyday*
> forms of peasant resistance – the prosaic but constant struggle between
> the peasantry and those who seek to extract labor, food, taxes, rents, and
> interest from them. Most of the forms this struggle takes stop well short
> of collective outright defiance. Here I have in mind the ordinary weapons
> of relatively powerless groups: foot dragging, dissimulation, false compli-
> ance, pilfering, feigned ignorance, slander, arson, sabotage, and so forth.
> These Brechtian forms of class struggle have certain features in common.
> They require little or no coordination or planning; they often represent a

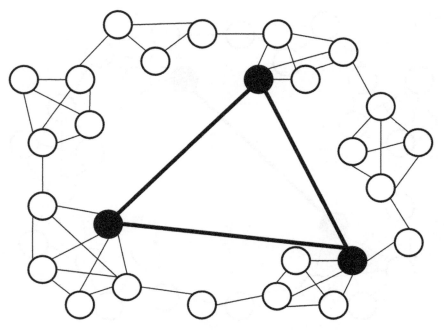

Figure 3.3 Sociogram of slave relations with three literate members

form of individual self-help; and they typically avoid any direct symbolic confrontation with authority or with elite norms. (1985: 29)

With particular regard to slavery, Scott writes that "[s]uch forms of stubborn resistance are especially well-documented in the vast literature on American slavery, where open defiance was normally foolhardy. The history of the resistance to slavery in the antebellum U.S. South is largely a history of foot-dragging, false compliance, flight, feigned ignorance, sabotage, theft, and, not least, cultural resistance" (1985: 33–4).

Given that frontal assaults are acts of extreme desperation, it is amazing that they happened at all. Genovese looks at some of the slave uprisings which did occur and analyzes the factors that they had in common. Many of these factors are related to social network structures and give us insights into what networks can provide for their members. Genovese tell us (1974: 590–1) that some of the key elements that distinguished situations where large-scale slave revolts actually did occur were when slave holdings were large and where the ratio of slaves to free blacks and whites was high. Another important

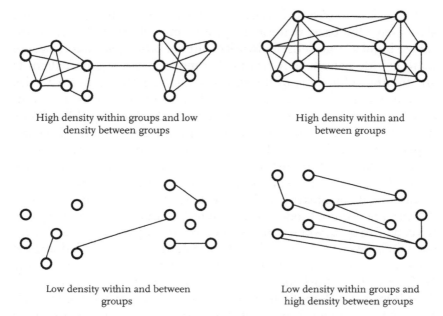

High density within groups and low
density between groups

High density within and
between groups

Low density within and between
groups

Low density within groups and
high density between groups

Figure 3.4 Variations in densities within and between groups

factor was that slave revolts were much more likely to happen in urban rather than in rural areas and where the relationship between masters and slaves was more businesslike and less paternalistic. And, finally, slave revolts were much more likely to occur when there was a division in the ruling class that split the powerful into different camps.

We can translate these factors into structural arguments. Specifically, many of these conditions are about the density of the various social groups. "Density" is the proportion of the number of ties that exists within or between groups to the number of ties that possibly could exist. There can be a more or less dense network of ties within a group. There can also be more or less dense networks of ties between groups. (See the "Closer Look" section of this chapter for a more detailed explanation of density.) Figure 3.4 shows some different situations.

For slave uprisings, the issue is having highly dense in-group ties and less dense out-group ties. First, the large holdings mean that slaves have the possibility of forming a critical mass with each other that is not diffused with ties to whites. This is also true in the cases of high slave-to-free and black-to-white ratios. In these situations, slaves have the basic material (an abundance of other slaves) necessary to build a large dense network of similar others. Situations where there is little paternalism also fit this model because paternalism is an attempt to fill some of the slaves' available network ties with ties to their white masters rather than with ties to other slaves. In a situation where direct action is risky and costly, McAdam (1988) tells us that people are more likely to engage in the action when they have the support of trusted others. We will examine this more in chapter 6.

One of the most interesting of the conditions for large-scale slave revolts is that there is a split in the white majority. The density of the ties among the whites is less than the density of ties among the slaves. We can see a more modern example of this in the Montgomery bus boycott of 1955–6, when white women broke with their husbands and used their own cars to provide transportation for their black domestic workers to and from work. The white women often had surprisingly (at least to their husbands) close ties to their black maids and saw their interests differently than their husbands imagined they would. Many white women found that they cared less about integration of public buses (which many of them – for class reasons – did not use anyway) than they did about the possibility of having to do their own cooking and cleaning. With a split along gender lines in the white opposition, the blacks in Montgomery had higher in-group density than their opponents did.

We can see that communities provide support of individuals in extremely harsh circumstances – support that could mean the difference between surviving or not in many cases. But what about in situations that are not so extreme – or so foreign to modern city life. What can communities, and the social networks that come with them, give to urban dwellers today?

Different types of support

Wellman and Wortley's (1990) work in East York, a suburb of Toronto, gives us some answers to the questions of what social support we can get from our communities and about who, precisely, provides that support and what types of support they provide.

Wellman and Wortley conducted surveys and extensive interviews with East York residents, gathering data about the respondents' social networks and about the types of social support that they received through their social ties. When we discuss "social support," we need to define just exactly what it is that we mean. As Wellman and Wortley point out, there are many different types of support. They looked for five specific types: emotional aid (such as giving advice or being a "shoulder to cry on"), small services (such as lending or giving household items or giving aid in dealing with organizations), large services (such as providing regular child care or helping with major household repairs), financial aid (small or large loans or gifts of money), and companionship (such as discussing ideas together or doing things together).

Wellman and Wortley then categorized the members of their respondents' networks by different role types (parent/child, sibling, extended kin, neighbor, friend, and organizational tie) to find out which types of ties provide which types of support. The authors also categorized the relationships along dimensions of strength, ease of access (proximity), employment similarity, age similarity, and whether or not the support happened in the context of couples or groups (rather than individually). In addition, Wellman and Wortley looked at the gender of the supportive other. There was not enough racial variation among the study population to analyze the role possibly played by race. Table 3.1 reports the *significant* variables that were found.

Wellman and Wortley found that the

> kinds of support provided are related more to characteristics of the relationship than to characteristics of the network members themselves. Strong ties provide emotional aid, small services, and companionship. Parents and adult children exchange financial aid, emotional aid, large services, and small services. Physically accessible ties provide services. Women provide emotional aid. Friends, neighbors, and siblings make up about half of all supportive relationships. (1990: 558)

That is, we get different types of support from different types of social ties.

One of the most interesting findings is that a very small number of strong ties provided most of the social support for the residents. This was true for all types of support. Each of us seems to rely on a handful of our closest friends and relatives to give us what we need. In terms of support, it seems, cities can look an awful lot like villages.

On the other hand, physical proximity is not the key to providing social support. Although physical proximity matters to things like

Table 3.1 Logistic regression on support dimensions (Wellman & Wortley 1990: 565, used by permission)

	Unstandardized coefficient	Standardized coefficient
Emotional aid:		
Strength	.62	.25
Gender	.95	.17
Parent/child	1.31	.10
Small services:		
Access	.18	.21
Strength	.52	.19
Parent/child	1.45	.10
Employment similarity	.63	.09
Age similarity	−.62	−.09
Couple	.80	.09
Organizational	−.87	−.08
Large services:		
Parent/child	1.90	.23
Access	.77	.18
Sibling	1.00	.13
Financial aid:		
Parent/child	2.16	.29
Employment similarity	.77	.10
Companionship:		
Strength	.88	.29
Sibling	−1.49	−.20
Extended kin	−1.76	−.17
Parent/child	−1.22	−.11
Group	.86	.11
Support breadth:		
Strength	.44	.37
Parent/child	.92	.20
Access	.05	.15
Extended kin	−.59	−.15
Employment similarity	.86	.11

Only variables significant at P < .05 are shown. N = 334.

providing small and large services – it is easier to borrow a cup of sugar from a neighbor than from a friend across town – other types of support are not dependent on proximity. Wellman and Wortley found that most other types of support could be provided by long distance – such as comforting chats on the telephone or helpful checks in the mail. This is important to keep in mind, especially when we ask about technology and the impact of things like the internet on people's lives. Virtual friends can't provide services, but they can provide other types of support. And this phenomenon has held for a long time – financial aid could be mailed from parents to children even hundreds of years ago, for example. Cities bring people into physical proximity so that they have access to many others, but immediate access is not necessary for all types of support.

It is also important to understand the role that families play in providing support, as urban life can sometimes remove individuals from family structures that pervade social life in more rural settings. Wellman and Wortley note that the "parent/child bond is the most supportive of all role types. It is also broadly supportive, usually providing all dimensions of support except companionship" (1990: 573). This is in contrast to more extended kin, who provide the least amount of support of any kind. So maybe urban life has stripped individuals of the extended family support that they might have had in a more rural setting, but not of the close and enduring bond between parents and their children.

Finally, it is interesting to take a look at the role of gender. Wellman and Wortley found that women provided much more emotional support to others than did men. Women turn to mothers/ daughters, sisters, and a rich variety of female friends for emotional support. Men, who have fewer female friends in their networks, rely on mothers, sisters, and wives for the emotional support that they do not get from their male friends and relatives. Some of the men in Wellman and Wortley's study even sought out female friends specifically for the emotional support that these women provide to them.

The main point that Wellman and Wortley make, however, is one about the role of networks in people's lives rather than about the characteristics of individuals in those networks. These authors argue that other than the importance of gender in giving emotional support, the personal attributes of the people involved are irrelevant to the support that they give. It is your *relations* with them – the type of tie that you have with others – that determines whether or not or to what extent they will be willing to help you out.

This is important because it tells us that the shapes of our networks matter. Although in terms of support it is important to have women and (especially) parents in your network, for many types of support, the individual characteristics of your supporters are not particularly relevant. It is important to have strong ties in your network – it does not matter to whom, specifically, you are strongly tied. It is important to have physical access (proximity) to others – it does not matter to whom, specifically, you are proximate.

This differs from our usual conceptions of how the world works. We think we are lucky that the people in our clubs are such a friendly bunch, that our strongest ties are such supportive and nice people, that our neighbor lets us borrow the lawnmower. But Wellman and Wortley argue that it is the networks that draw forth these attributes of friendliness and supportiveness from others rather than that the friendliness and supportiveness of the other leads us to form ties with them. This seems like a strong and counter-intuitive claim, but other studies of social networks – such as Bott's study of conjugal roles, discussed next – show similar findings.

Conjugal roles and social networks

Elizabeth Bott's study of family roles in England in the 1950s is one of the classic early empirical network studies. Bott argued that the characteristics (specifically the density) of the social networks external to a couple affect the internal domestic functions of that couple. Bott (1956, 1957) studied 20 London families in the 1950s and found that those families who had dense, tightly knit networks were more likely to have highly gender-segregated conjugal roles. How did this work?

Some of the families that Bott studied lived in neighborhoods where they had long-term relations with a number of others. The example Bott gives is of the working-class N family in the East End of London.

> The Ns felt that their neighbours were socially similar to themselves, meaning that they had the same sort of jobs, the same sort of background, the same sort of outlook on life. Because the Ns had grown up in the area, as had many of their relatives and neighbors, they knew a very considerable number of local people, and many of the people they knew were acquainted with one another. In other words, their social network was highly connected. In fact, there was considerable overlap of social roles; instead of there being people in three or four separate categories – friend, neighbour, relative, and colleague – the same person frequently filled two or three or even four of these roles simultaneously. (Bott 1956: 355)

That is, the ties were strong and multiplex.

The Ns had highly segregated conjugal roles, with each of them socializing separately with gender-segregated peer groups. They spent very little of their leisure time together. Inside the house, too, they had a clear-cut and very traditional division of labor into tasks that were considered "men's work" and tasks that were considered "women's work." However, Bott writes, "[o]ne man said in a group discussion: 'A lot of men wouldn't mind helping their wives if the curtains were drawn so people couldn't see'" (1956: 358–9). We can see in this comment the role that social pressure from the outside network played in the internal relations of the household.

But by far the most important and supportive relationships that women had were with their female kin. It was to their mothers, sisters, and other female relatives that these women turned for all types of support – emotional aid, large and small services, companionship, and so on. Bott noted that "a man living in the same local area as the Ns and having a similar sort of family life and kinship network summed up the situation by saying, 'Men have friends. Women have relatives'" (1956: 357).

One of the interesting insights that Bott's interviews turned up was the idea that husbands would be more likely to be egalitarian in the division of labor within their homes if only the neighbors – those friends whom they had known for years and years and who fulfilled multiple social roles in their lives – could not see them doing so. The pressure to conform to the expectations of the densely knit network in the neighborhood was felt not only in the external relationships that the couple engaged in, but even inside the house, where norms and mores were dictated by the prevailing attitudes of the network. It is interesting in Bott's study that the Ns repeatedly fail to even consider other ways of operating in the world. It doesn't occur to the Ns to question that he has his jobs around the house and that she has hers – or that other families might organize their lives differently. It doesn't occur to them that she might socialize with his friends or he might socialize with hers – or that these two groups might be brought together. These attitudes are part and parcel of the life of the whole network and are reinforced by the ordinariness of those attitudes among everyone with whom the Ns interact. Because "everyone does it" and because the Ns are so deeply embedded in this tight network of conformity, it does not occur to them to question the traditional gender roles which are so pervasive in their world. The dense network of shared assumptions that envelops the Ns makes the construction of the gender roles inside their home invisible to them.

Conversely, Bott found that families that had a "dispersed" (that is, less dense) network were more likely to have a joint, more egalitarian conjugal role-relationship. These families were no longer living in the original neighborhoods where they had grown up and were not, therefore, as closely tied to those around them. They were much less concerned with what the neighbors would think. The networks among their circles of friends were also less interconnected and less dense.

There are some interesting differences with the Ns. First, friends in these types of dispersed network families do not fill multiple roles (friend, co-worker, neighbor, and also kin) in the way that the friends of the Ns did. Second, this is a product of mobility. Because these families had moved around so much, Bott argues, their networks had become dispersed and the local neighborhood could not provide the all-encompassing community for them that the Ns' neighborhood did. As with Wellman and Wortley's Canadian study, the people in Bott's dispersed networks got their social support, for the most part, across distance. Bott tells us that in order to get the kinds of support (such as small services) for which Wellman and Wortley found that proximity was important, the people in the dispersed networks used cash – that is, they hired someone to do it. For example, Bott (1956: 361) notes that most of the dispersed network families either had or were looking to hire cleaning women and babysitters to live in the family, if possible, or at least live nearby. Where the Ns relied on neighbors and kin (who were often the same small set of people) to provide many of the types of social support that Wellman and Wortley discuss, the families in the more dispersed network relied on the market.

This type of network meant that out of necessity the couple had to rely more on one another than did the gender-segregated Ns and their friends. Thus, the conjugal relationship was of a vastly different character. Socializing was done as a couple and friends were joint friends of both the husband and the wife. There was also much more egalitarian division of labor inside the house, as well. Bott notes that the domestic duties were flexible and that both husband and wife participated. This was true in all areas of running the household, including child care (which the Ns saw as exclusively the responsibility of women) and managing the family finances (which the Ns saw as strictly the responsibility of men).

Moreover, with regard to the relationship between the husband and the wife, Bott found that "[i]t was felt that, in a good marriage, husband

and wife should achieve a high degree of compatibility, based on their particular combination of shared interests and complimentary differences. Their relationship with each other should be more important than any separate relationship with outsiders" (1956: 364–5).

That is, by throwing them on each other for support, Bott argues, the dispersed social network of these couples (which comes about as a result of moving from one place to another) leads the husband and wife to develop a more egalitarian and joint conjugal relationship. Without worrying about what the neighbors think, the husband and wife are more flexible in their division of labor and more inclined to value the other's opinions about everything from the desirability of certain people as friends to decision making in the home. When social support comes from one other person, that person has a lot of sway over one's thinking. The dispersed social networks of the movers make the spouse that most important other.

So we can see that different types of networks, specifically networks with different densities, can lead to different outcomes for the individuals who are members of those networks. But as Wellman and Wortley remind us, we can't just say that dense networks are supportive and dispersed networks are not. Rather, we have to ask what types of networks structures provide what types of support or resources to their members.

Agency in networks

Two important examples remind us that not every network contact provides support – or even wants to. Depending on the types of networks you have, your position in them, and the way in which they are constructed, you may be led to different types of outcomes. Hannerz's discussion of mau-mauing and flak-catching and Lee's study of the search for an abortionist demonstrate how the use of personal networks to get social goods like support may be even more complicated than just having or not having network ties. Not only does the existence of external network affect individual lives, but agency also plays a role in those networks. The members of networks are self-aware agents who make decisions about whether or not to use ties and how to go about using them.

An excellent example of agency in networks is Hannerz's discussion of Tom Wolfe's 1970 essay "Mau-mauing the Flak Catchers," in which Wolfe gives a devastatingly satirical portrait of mau-mauing:

This is a satire of the late 1960s poverty program in San Francisco. The bureaucracy was expected to support community organization, but did not know the community (and, one may suspect, had not given much thought to in what sense there was one). It was supposed to work with the grassroots leadership, but did not know where to find it. So, in Wolfe's interpretation, there was a wide open field for entrepreneurship: "Going downtown to mau-mau the bureaucrats got to be the routine practice in San Francisco. The poverty program *encouraged* you to go in for mau-mauing. They wouldn't have known what to do without it. The bureaucrats at City Hall and in the Office of Economic Opportunity talked 'ghetto' all the time, but they didn't know any more about what was going on in the Western Addition, Hunters Point, Potrero Hill, the Mission, Chinatown, or south of Market Street than they did about Zanzibar. They didn't know where to look. They didn't even know who to ask. So what could they do? Well . . . they used the Ethnic Catering Service . . . right . . . They sat back and waited for you to come rolling in with your certified angry militants, your guaranteed frustrated ghetto youth, looking like a bunch of wild men. Then you had your test confrontation. If you were outrageous enough, . . . [t]hey knew you were the right studs to give the poverty grants and community organizing jobs to. Otherwise they wouldn't know." (Wolfe 1970: 97–8) Mau-mauing, then, is an art of network manipulation. When people in one cluster of relationships wish to contact people in another cluster but do not have established and time-tested links across the gap, they will honor the demands of a broker. (Hannerz 1980: 190)

Mau-mauing, in essence, is promising to be a broker between groups, but not necessarily having all the contacts that you present yourself as having. A broker can get you access to groups with whom you have no personal contacts. In the search for information, goods, or support, the broker is the key network linkage that makes contact possible. Mau-mauing is a type of brokerage that relies on the holes in the network to manipulate others. The lack of contacts between groups means that there is no way to check the veracity of the claims made by those who present themselves as representatives of the other group. Mau-mauers know that the lack of density between groups means that there is an opportunity to use duplicity to their own advantage. Being the only ties between two groups often confers inordinate power on that connection.

But the exploitation of the lack of ties between groups can go both ways. Hannerz also tells us that

the decision-making bureaucrats do not want to make themselves too accessible to mau-mauing. Hence enter the flak catcher. The job of the flak catcher in the bureaucracy is to receive people making demands, suffer hostility and humiliation, and not make commitments – to make it clear to the visitors, on the contrary, that he is in no position to commit his superiors or the bureaucracy as a whole to any line of action. In other words, to decrease reachability. The flak catcher, too, is a kind of broker, since he stands at the nexus between the public and the real holders of power and channels contacts between them. (1980: 191)

Hannerz reminds us that there may be people in a network who are specifically trying to prevent you from gaining access to others and it could also be that some people are promising access that they can't – or won't – deliver. People with real power may be insulated from others. Just because network ties exist does not mean that they will be used indiscriminately.

Moreover, there is also this issue of what type of network strategy an actor decides to pursue. Some types of strategies are better for some purposes than others. For example, Hannerz (1980: 170–1) also summarizes Mayer's (1966) study of bringing in the vote in an election campaign in the town of Dewas, in the Indian state of Madhya Pradesh. The two different candidates for the seat used two different types of network strategies to bring in voters. The Congress candidate used a strategy of mobilizing the ties of all sorts between long chains of people, like a chain letter – an "each one teach one" soft campaign – to mobilize support for himself. The Jan Singh candidate, on the other hand, ran a "hard" campaign where he put himself into direct contact with as many supporters as possible before the election day. The support that he built was stronger and likely to be more lasting than the indirect contact that the Congress candidate could muster. But the reach of the "soft" campaign was greater than could be possible with the "hard" strategy and, on election day, the Congress candidate won.

The candidates here chose different types of network strategies to pursue, with different outcomes. The strategies which actors pursue in mobilizing their ties matters.

The Search for an Abortionist

Within social networks, there are issues of access, there are issues of agency, and there are issues of trust. We can see these coming together in Nancy Howell Lee's (1969) study of American women searching for abortions in the 1960s – before abortion was legal in the USA. Lee got information from interviews and questionnaires from 114 women who had gotten abortions. These women were operating under many constraints. First, they were under a time limit – they only had a few weeks (usually around six) from the time they confirmed they were pregnant until it was effectively too late to seek an abortion. Moreover, both the woman seeking an abortion and the person providing that abortion were attempting to keep their activity quiet and hidden in order to avoid a confrontation with the law – this was, after all, an illegal activity. On top of that, the social stigma related to having an abortion was such that the abortion seeker was not likely to broadcast her desires widely. Women often hid their search for an abortionist from family members (especially ones from an older generation), people in authority (such as bosses), and so on. There were often constraints related to access (although some women traveled long distances – even internationally – to receive abortions) and to finances to pay for the service. Finally, there was the very important dimension of trust. Illegal abortions were dangerous procedures which could and did result in serious medical consequences, up to and including death, for the women who received them. Finding an abortionist whom they could trust not to botch the procedure and kill them was a high priority and a significant constraint on the women.

The women searched for abortionists in a variety of ways. Only two of the 114 women knew of an abortionist and went directly to him. Another two women induced the abortion themselves. The remaining 110 women had to actively search for an abortionist, often using their networks of relationships to help them. Lee provides narratives of the women's search strategies in which we can see the role played by network ties. For example, Lee quotes one woman's story of her search:

> I told this girl at school I was worried, and she lent me her car and told me about a doctor in town who was supposed to be sympathetic. I went to him for a pregnancy test and I had to go back again to get the results, and I asked him what I could do but he said I would have to get married or something. So I didn't push it. When the test was positive I called my girl friend (in another city) and told her I was coming to stay with her and she should try to find out anything she could. When I got there she had found out about two people, one guy in the city from her roommate and one out of town from the mother of a friend of ours. We made an appointment to see the guy in the city and we went there, but it was so depressing that I had an examination and said I would come back but I never did. In the

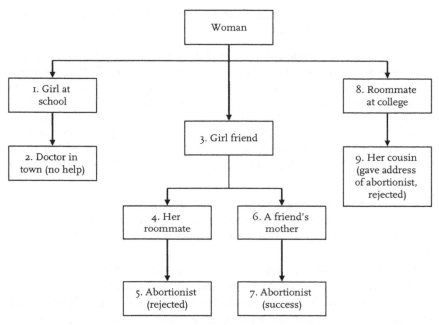

Figure 3.5 Sociogram of a search for an abortionist (Lee 1969: 65, used by permission)

meantime my roommate from college heard about another doctor in the city from her cousin. First we went to the doctor who was out of town. We called up and made an appointment, and went to see him. (1969: 64–5)

The woman chose this doctor and ended her search there. The sociogram of this search which Lee constructed is presented in figure 3.5.

We can see in this example how the woman searching for an abortion actively used her social networks to gain indirect contacts with others who might help her. This is in many ways similar to the "soft" campaign used by the successful Congress Party candidate in Mayer's study. The woman activated several chains reaching out into different parts of her social world in an attempt to find not only a doctor who would perform the abortion, but also one whom she trusted and felt secure with. The mean chain length of the study participants was 2.83; the median chain length was 2.0. The shortness of these chains is important because short chain lengths are associated with trust, which was very important for both parties involved.

The vast majority of the women whom Lee studied, however, ended up with no choices about the abortionist they used because they only ever found one. Lee found much differential access to abortionists. Lee writes that the

> crucial factor in determining the kind of care received is the connections or channels one is able to locate and use within the four-to-ten-week period between the recognition of pregnancy and the time when abortion becomes difficult and dangerous. The problem for the woman is to find a person who links her, however distantly, to the referral network of an abortionist. Beyond that immediate goal, she naturally wishes to find a point of linkage not just to any abortionist but to the one who is most competent, conveniently located, inexpensive, and considerate. (1969: 155)

Lee notes that although some of the women displayed skill and ingenuity in conducting their searches, the more important factor in determining their degree of success was the structure of their personal networks.

Lee argues that the type of network surrounding the woman seeking an abortion would have had an enormous impact on the information available to her and, therefore, on the life choices that she made. Lee looks at three types of networks: "traditional" – which are dense networks of long-standing ties, much like the type of network that Bott found surrounding the Ns; "bachelor" – more loosely knit networks of women who have moved away from their family home and community, much like the dispersed networks that Bott found around those couples who had moved away from their family homes and had joint conjugal roles; and networks surrounding women who participated in abortion-law reform groups and, therefore, incorporated the issue of abortion into their daily lives. The density of the first two networks is an important factor in determining what information and what actions were available to the women in those networks.

Lee writes that a

> traditional network is one which is continuous over the lifetime of its central figure, is based primarily on kinship and geography, and includes people at all stages of the life cycle. ... A traditional network can be relatively open or closed to information about abortion. A woman living in such a social situation may find it easy or difficult to terminate a pregnancy. The point is not that traditional networks restrict the availability of information about abortion, but that a woman who has such a network will have little ability to control whether she receives a great deal of information or no information. (1969: 157)

That is, in these types of worlds, the availability of information about abortion was a feature of the network in which a woman was embedded. If a woman was in a dense, traditional network that had abortion information in it, she would not have had to search for it. If she was in a dense, traditional network that did not have abortion information in it, she would either never have got the information or would have had to leave her network and find some way of entering another network in order to find the information. This is what women were doing when they turned to doctors in the phone book, making repeated appointments with random doctors in the hopes that one of them would help.

In the more dispersed or cosmopolitan networks, however, a search had to be carried out. In order to be successful, that search had to be able to reach outside of the small, dense world in which the woman was embedded and gain information through ties to other worlds. Lee discusses the "inbreeding" of groups, by which she means that people are often tied to groups which have high **in-group density**. But a woman who was connected to several of these inbred groups had access to large amounts of information that may have been useful to her. In discussing one woman who had access to several different densely knit groups, Lee notes that "[w]hile there was inbreeding within each of these groups, there was no overlap, other than herself, linking the people from these different contexts" (1969: 158). This gave the abortion seekers some flexibility in their searches. If one group could provide no useful information, the woman could then turn to another group and find different – and possibly more useful – information from this different set of contacts.

Lee gives an example of how the high in-group density, coupled with a lack of ties to other networks, means that most of the women she studied had no choice about which abortionist they used, even when there was open communication and a great desire among the network members to offer help and information. One example narrative shows the lack of fresh information that comes into a dense, closed-off network:

> I asked several close college friends – all gave me the name and address of a doctor from their friends. From all, separately asked, I got the same name and address. My mother volunteered to help – she asked her friends who had any experience with it. They gave her the same name and address that I had gotten from my friends (one of them had been to him

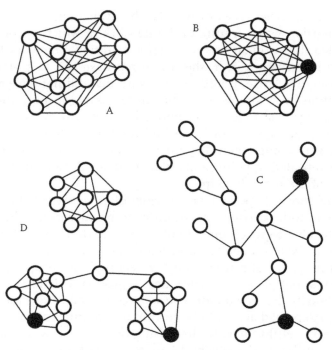

Figure 3.6 Sociograms of abortion-searchers' networks

four times). All assured her that he was a competent doctor and abortion-ist. (1969: 159)

As Lee points out (1969: 159), the woman was successful in her search, but she had absolutely no choice in the doctor she used. Her highly dense network had a tie to one provider, whose name was given to her repeatedly, but they had no connections with any outside information. Should that one doctor have been unacceptable for any reason, the woman would have had no options at all.

The sociograms in figure 3.6 represent different types of networks that surrounded the women searching for abortions. Darkened circles represent an abortionist. Sociogram A represents a traditional network with no information about an abortionist – the search would not work without the searcher leaving the network. Sociogram B represents a traditional network with information about an abor-tionist – in this case the search was largely unnecessary because the searcher already had the information that she needed. Sociogram C represents the bachelor network – search strategies came into play here and there may have been a choice of abortionists for the searcher. Sociogram D represents a woman with access to several non-overlapping traditional networks – search strategies came into play here as well and there may have been a choice of abortionists.

We can see that individuals had agency in activating networks to their advantage. Some search strategies, like some political campaign strategies, were more successful than others. But in this example, as in the other examples in this chapter, we also see that while communities can provide individuals with many resources, the shape and density of the community surrounding the individual matter in determining what resources are available to the community members and what resources may be out of reach. The "Closer Look" section below will discuss network density in more detail so that we can see how to measure it, how to compare densities across networks, and how to interpret different densities.

Density is a facet of cohesion; cohesive groups have a high density of ties among the members. This means not only that the network members are in contact with each other, but also that beliefs, attitudes, and information can be easily shared among the members. As Collins (1988) reminds us, this allows for the sense of community to emerge. For this reason, density is a basic building block of community. Without those dense interpersonal ties connecting them to each other, individuals in a given location are just that – an unconnected assortment of people who happen to be in proximity to each other, like a crowd waiting for a bus. Connections make a community out of individuals when density creates support and mutual obligation among them, when it allows ideas and information to be shared by the members of the group, and when it allows the group to emerge as an entity in itself.

A closer look: density

Networks have different degrees of density. Density is a measure of the number of ties in the network divided by the number of ties that are *possible* in the network. A four-person network (such as in figure 3.7) has 12 possible ties. If "N" stands for the number of nodes in a network, the total number of ties is $N(N - 1)$. So a four-person network has $4(4 - 1) = 4 \times 3 = 12$ possible ties. Notice that these are unidirectional ties – that is, we count the tie from A to B as one tie and the tie from B to A as another tie. If we weren't taking direction

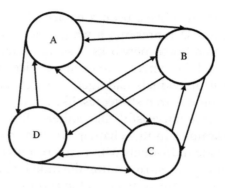

Figure 3.7 Full density

into account, there would only be six possible ties. Figure 3.7 shows a network with full density.

N(N − 1) gives us the total number of ties that are possible in the network, but very few real-life networks have nodes that are as completely connected to each other as they can be. The number of ties that *actually* exist divided by the number of ties that *could possibly* exist is the proportion of ties in the network – that is, the density of the network. The formula for calculating the density is

$$2a/N(N − 1)$$

where "a" is the count of the actual number of ties in the network. The "a" is multiplied by 2 to compensate for the unidirectionality inherent in the N(N − 1) measure used to calculate the total number of ties possible. Because of this, we can calculate density based on a count of the number of ties present in the network without worrying about directionality. If we want to include directionality in our calculation, we simply remove the 2 from the formula. In the sociogram in figure 3.8, there are seven nodes and nine ties (which are presented without direction). So the density of the network is 2 × 9/7 × 6 = 18/42 = 0.43.

If the data in the sociogram in figure 3.8 were to be presented in matrix form, it would look like table 3.2.

In the matrix, we can count 18 1s (representing the ties) out of 42 total cells. If we divide 18 by 42 (the actual number of ties by the possible number of ties) we get 0.43 – the same density that we had calculated using the formula above, 2a/N(N − 1). We do not have to double our count of actual ties because the matrix reports both ties, for example, E

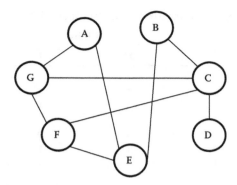

Figure 3.8 Example of density in a sociogram

to F tie and the F to E tie. We don't have to calculate the $N(N-1)$ figure because we have counted the actual number of possible cells.

We are not allowing the actors in this network to have ties with themselves. We thus have left the cells along the main diagonal blank. If we did want to allow the actors to have ties with themselves, those values would go in the cells along the main diagonal and the total number of cells would be 49 instead of 42.

In this type of calculation, the highest density that is possible is 1, which would happen when there are the same number of actual ties as there are possible ties. A density of 0 would mean that there are no ties between any of the actors in the network. A density of 0.5 would mean that there are half the number of actual ties that would be possible. It is possible, however, to have densities greater than 1. As an example, let's look at a matrix made up of individuals belonging to clubs, shown in table 3.3.

If we multiply this matrix by its transpose (as explained in the "Closer Look" section of chapter 2), the person-by-person matrix in table 3.4 is the result.

Table 3.2 Matrix translation of figure 3.8

	A	B	C	D	E	F	G
A		0	0	0	1	0	1
B	0		1	0	1	0	0
C	0	1		1	0	1	1
D	0	0	1		0	0	0
E	1	1	0	0		1	0
F	0	0	1	0	1		1
G	1	0	1	0	0	1	

Table 3.3 Person-by-group matrix of club memberships

	Clubs			
	G	H	I	J
Members				
A	1	0	1	1
B	1	1	1	0
C	1	1	1	1
D	1	1	0	1
E	0	1	1	1
F	1	1	1	1

Remember that in this matrix, the main diagonal cell entries tell us the number of clubs to which the person belongs and the off-diagonal cell entries tell us how many clubs the two actors are in together. The density of this matrix (if we exclude the main diagonal) is 2.6667. If we include the values along the main diagonal, it is 2.7778. These figures are easy to calculate directly from the matrix, but if we want to use the density formula to calculate them, we must remember to take into account not only the number of ties, but also a measure of their intensity. The relationship between F and C, who share four club memberships together, for example, must be treated differently from the relationship between A and D, who only share two memberships together. One way of looking at cell values that are greater than 1 might be to see the values as measures of tie strength. In this type of example, the *multiplexity* of the ties is captured in the matrix. A real-life example of this would be Davis et al.'s data on club women, which we saw in chapter 2.

Rather than looking at the multiplexity of ties, we could also use the cell values to measure the intensity of a relationship. In a matrix of affection, we could code ties that indicate "liking" as a 1, ties that indicated "liking very much" as a 2, and ties that indicate "loving" as

Table 3.4 Person-by-person matrix of club memberships

	A	B	C	D	E	F
A	3	2	3	2	2	3
B	2	3	3	2	2	3
C	3	3	4	3	3	4
D	2	2	3	3	2	3
E	2	2	3	2	3	3
F	3	3	4	3	3	4

a 3, for example. All of these cell values will have an impact on the density that we calculate for the matrix.

This leads to an obvious question: what do these different density values actually *mean*? Density is relative. We can talk about the density of one matrix being higher or lower than the density of another, and in that comparative context, density can help us understand the structures of the networks. For example, look at the matrices of the networks of the workers in the tailor shop that Kapferer (1972) studied. (These are given in the pre-loaded UCINET data files called "kaptail".) Tables 3.5 and 3.6 are the matrices of social relationships among the workers at two times – just before an unsuccessful strike in table 3.5 and just before a successful strike in table 3.6. Notice that the density for the first matrix is 0.2132 and for the second is 0.3009 – that is, the network of social relationships was denser before the successful strike than it was before the unsuccessful one. This *comparison* allows us to build or to test hypotheses about the correlation between network density and social action.

In the "Closer Look" section of chapter 6, we will see how we can calculate the densities of different parts of the network so that we can compare the densities within and between groups in the network.

Calculating density in UCINET6

To calculate density in UCINET, click on "Network" at the top of the page and then choose "Cohesion" from the dropdown menu. Choose "Density" and then "Density Overall." Either enter the name of the matrix whose density you would like to calculate in the "Network Dataset" window or choose a dataset from the list by clicking on the ". . ." button. Note that you can choose whether or not you would like to use the values along the main diagonal in the calculations. Then click "OK."

If you choose the Kapferer data, you will get densities for four matrices – two matrices of "sociational" (i.e., social) ties at two different times (KAPFTS1 and KAPFTS2) and two matrices of "instrumental" (i.e., work-related) ties at two different times (KAPFTI1 and KAPFTI2). The densities for these matrices are 0.2132, 0.3009, 0.0735, and 0.0992 respectively. Notice that the sociational ties are more dense than the instrumental ties in both cases and that the ties at time 2 (preceding the successful strike) are more dense than the ties at time 1 (preceding the unsuccessful strike) in both cases. In

Table 3.5 Matrix of social relations among Kapferer's tailors at time 1 (Borgatti et al. 2002, used by permission)

Matrix #1: KAPFTS1

	1 K	2 N	3 A	4 S	5 C	6 D	7 N	8 M	9 C	10 C	11 L	12 Z	13 H	14 L	15 N	16 C	17 E	18 P	19 M	20 S	21 K	22 Z	23 B	24 I	25 M	26 A	27 K	28 M	29 J	30 J	31 W	32 H	33 C	34 M	35 C	36 K	37 A	38 C	39 M
1 KAMWEFU	–	0	1	1	0	1	0	0	0	0	1	0	0	0	1	1	0	1	0	0	0	0	0	0	0	0	0	0	0	0	0	0	0	0	0	0	0	0	0
2 NKUMBULA	0	–	1	1	0	1	0	0	0	0	1	0	0	0	1	1	0	1	0	0	0	0	0	0	0	0	0	0	0	0	0	0	0	0	0	0	0	0	0
3 ABRAHAM	1	1	–	1	0	0	1	1	0	0	1	1	1	1	1	1	1	1	0	0	0	0	0	0	0	0	0	0	0	0	0	0	0	0	0	0	0	0	0
4 SEAMS	1	1	1	–	0	0	1	1	1	0	1	1	1	1	1	1	1	1	0	0	0	0	0	0	0	0	0	0	0	0	0	0	0	0	0	0	0	0	0
5 CHIPATA	0	0	0	0	–	0	0	0	0	0	1	0	0	0	0	0	1	0	1	0	0	1	0	0	0	0	0	0	0	0	0	0	0	0	0	0	0	0	0
6 DONALD	1	1	0	0	0	–	0	0	0	0	1	0	0	0	1	0	1	0	0	0	0	0	0	0	0	0	0	0	0	0	0	0	0	0	0	0	0	0	0
7 NKOLOYA	0	0	1	1	0	0	–	0	0	0	1	0	1	0	0	0	1	0	0	0	0	0	0	0	0	0	0	0	0	0	0	0	0	0	0	0	0	0	0
8 MATEO	0	0	1	1	0	0	0	–	0	0	1	0	1	0	0	0	1	0	0	0	0	0	0	0	0	0	0	0	0	0	0	0	0	0	0	0	0	0	0
9 CHILWA	0	0	0	1	0	0	0	0	–	0	1	0	1	0	0	0	1	0	0	0	0	0	0	0	0	0	0	0	0	0	0	0	0	0	0	0	0	0	0
10 CHIPALO	1	0	0	0	0	0	0	0	0	–	1	0	1	0	0	0	0	0	0	0	0	0	0	1	0	0	1	0	0	1	0	0	0	0	0	0	0	0	0
11 LYASHI	1	1	1	1	1	1	1	1	1	1	–	0	1	1	1	1	1	1	0	0	0	0	1	1	0	0	0	0	0	0	0	0	0	0	0	0	0	0	0
12 ZULU	0	0	1	1	0	0	0	0	0	0	0	–	1	0	0	0	1	0	0	1	0	1	0	0	0	0	0	0	0	0	0	0	0	0	0	0	0	0	0
13 HASTINGS	0	0	1	1	0	0	1	1	1	1	1	1	–	1	0	0	1	0	0	0	0	0	0	0	0	0	0	1	0	0	1	0	0	0	0	0	0	0	0
14 LWANGA	0	0	1	1	0	0	0	0	0	0	1	0	1	–	0	0	0	0	0	0	0	0	0	0	0	0	0	0	0	0	0	1	0	0	0	0	0	0	0
15 NYIRENDA	0	0	1	1	0	1	0	0	0	0	1	0	0	0	–	1	1	0	0	0	0	0	0	0	0	0	0	0	0	0	0	0	0	0	1	0	0	0	0
16 CHISOKONE	0	1	1	1	0	1	0	0	0	0	1	0	0	0	1	–	1	1	0	0	1	0	0	0	0	0	0	0	0	0	1	0	0	1	1	0	0	0	0
17 ENOCH	0	0	1	1	1	1	1	1	1	0	1	1	1	0	1	1	–	0	0	1	1	0	1	0	0	1	0	0	0	0	0	0	0	0	0	0	0	0	0
18 PAULOS	0	0	0	0	0	0	0	0	0	0	1	0	0	0	0	0	0	–	0	0	0	0	0	0	0	0	0	0	0	0	0	0	0	0	0	0	0	0	0

```
 0 0 0 0 0 0 0 0 0 0 1 1 0 1 0 1 1 0 0 0 0
 0 0 0 0 0 0 0 0 0 1 0 1 1 0 1 0 1 0 1 0 0
 0 0 0 0 0 0 0 0 0 0 1 0 1 0 1 0 1 0 1 1 0
 0 0 0 0 0 0 0 0 0 0 1 0 1 1 1 0 1 1 0 1 0
 0 0 0 0 0 0 1 0 0 1 0 0 1 1 1 0 1 0 1 0 0
 1 0 0 0 0 0 1 0 0 1 0 0 1 1 0 0 1 1 1 1 1
 1 0 0 0 0 0 0 1 0 0 1 1 0 1 1 0 0 1 1 1 0 1
 1 0 1 0 0 0 1 0 1 0 0 0 1 0 0 0 1 1 1 1 1
 0 0 0 0 0 1 0 0 0 0 1 0 1 0 0 1 1 1 1 0 0 0
 1 0 0 0 0 0 0 0 0 0 0 0 1 1 0 1 0 1 0 1 1 1
 1 0 1 0 0 0 1 0 0 0 0 0 0 1 0 1 0 1 0 1 1
 0 0 0 0 1 1 0 0 1 0 0 0 1 0 1 0 1 0 0 1 0
 0 1 0 0 1 0 0 0 0 1 0 0 0 0 0 1 0 1 0 0 0
 0 0 0 0 0 0 0 0 0 0 0 0 1 0 0 1 0 0 0 0 0
 0 0 0 0 0 0 0 0 0 0 1 1 0 0 1 0 0 0 0 0 0
 1 0 1 0 1 0 0 0 0 1 0 0 1 1 0 1 0 0 0 0 0
 1 0 1 1 0 1 0 0 1 1 0 0 0 0 0 0 0 0 0 0 0
 0 0 0 0 1 0 1 1 0 0 0 0 0 0 0 0 0 0 0 0 0
 1 0 0 0 1 1 0 0 0 0 0 0 0 0 0 0 0 0 0 0 0
 0 0 0 0 0 0 0 1 0 0 0 0 0 0 0 0 0 0 0 0 0
 0 0 1 0 1 1 1 0 0 0 0 1 1 0 1 1 1 0 0 0 0
 1 0 0 0 0 1 1 0 0 1 0 0 1 0 0 1 0 0 0 0 0
 0 0 0 0 0 1 1 0 0 0 0 0 0 0 0 0 0 0 0 0 0
 1 1 0 1 0 0 1 1 1 1 0 0 1 1 1 1 0 1 0 0 1 0
 1 1 0 0 0 1 0 0 0 0 1 0 0 0 0 0 0 0 0 0 0
 1 1 0 0 0 0 1 0 0 0 0 1 0 0 1 0 1 0 0 0 0
 0 0 0 0 0 0 1 0 0 0 0 1 0 1 0 0 1 0 0 0 0
 1 1 0 1 0 0 0 0 0 0 0 0 1 0 0 1 0 1 0 0 0
 0 1 0 0 0 0 0 1 0 0 0 0 0 1 0 0 0 0 0 0 0
 0 0 1 0 0 0 0 0 0 0 0 0 0 1 0 0 0 0 0 0 0
 0 0 0 0 0 0 0 0 0 0 0 0 1 0 0 0 0 0 0 0 0
 1 0 1 0 0 0 0 0 0 0 0 0 0 0 1 0 0 0 0 0 0
 0 1 1 0 0 0 0 0 0 0 0 0 0 0 0 0 0 0 0 0 0
```

19 MUKUBWA
20 SIGN
21 KALAMBA
22 ZAKEYO
23 BEN
24 IBRAHIM
25 MESHAK
26 ADRIAN
27 KALUNDWE
28 MPUNDU
29 JOHN
30 JOSEPH
31 WILLIAM
32 HENRY
33 CHOBE
34 MUBANGA
35 CHRISTIAN
36 KALONGA
37 ANGEL
38 CHILUFYA
39 MABANGE

DENSITY: 0.2132

Table 3.6 Matrix of social relations among Kapferer's tailors at time 2 (Borgatti et al. 2002, used by permission)

Matrix #2: KAPFTS2

	1 K	2 N	3 A	4 S	5 C	6 D	7 N	8 M	9 C	10 C	11 L	12 Z	13 H	14 L	15 N	16 C	17 E	18 P	19 M	20 S	21 K	22 Z	23 B	24 I	25 M	26 A	27 K	28 M	29 J	30 J	31 W	32 H	33 C	34 M	35 C	36 K	37 A	38 C	39 M
1 KAMWEFU	0	1	1	0	1	0	0	0	1	0	1	1	1	1	1	1	1	1	1	0	0	0	0	1	0	0	1	0	1	0	1	0	0	0	0	0	0	0	0
2 NKUMBULA	1	0	1	0	1	0	0	1	0	0	1	1	1	1	1	1	1	1	1	0	0	0	0	1	0	1	0	0	1	0	0	0	0	0	0	0	0	0	0
3 ABRAHAM	1	1	0	0	0	1	0	0	1	1	1	1	1	1	1	1	1	1	1	1	0	0	0	1	0	0	0	0	0	0	0	0	0	0	0	0	0	0	0
4 SEAMS	0	0	0	0	0	0	0	1	0	0	1	1	1	0	0	0	0	0	0	0	0	0	0	0	0	0	0	0	0	0	0	0	0	0	0	0	0	0	0
5 CHIPATA	1	1	0	0	0	0	0	0	1	1	1	1	1	1	0	0	0	0	0	0	0	0	0	1	0	1	0	1	0	0	0	0	0	0	0	0	0	0	0
6 DONALD	0	0	1	0	0	0	0	0	0	0	1	1	0	1	0	1	0	0	0	0	0	0	0	0	0	0	0	0	0	0	0	0	0	0	0	0	0	0	0
7 NKOLOYA	0	0	1	0	1	0	0	0	1	1	1	1	1	1	1	1	1	1	1	0	0	0	0	1	0	0	1	0	1	0	0	0	0	0	0	0	0	0	0
8 MATEO	0	1	0	1	0	0	0	0	0	0	1	1	0	0	0	0	0	0	0	1	0	0	0	0	0	1	0	0	0	0	0	0	0	0	0	0	0	0	0
9 CHILWA	1	0	1	0	1	0	0	0	0	1	1	1	1	1	1	1	1	1	1	0	0	0	0	1	0	1	0	1	0	0	0	0	0	0	0	0	0	0	0
10 CHIPALO	0	0	1	0	1	1	1	0	1	0	1	1	1	1	0	0	0	0	0	0	0	0	1	0	1	0	1	0	1	0	0	0	0	0	0	0	0	0	0
11 LYASHI	1	1	1	1	1	1	1	1	1	1	0	1	1	1	0	0	1	0	0	1	0	1	0	1	1	1	0	1	0	0	0	0	0	0	0	1	0	0	1
12 ZULU	1	1	1	1	1	0	0	1	1	1	1	0	1	0	0	1	0	1	0	1	0	0	0	1	1	1	0	1	0	0	0	0	0	0	0	0	0	0	0
13 HASTINGS	1	1	1	0	1	0	0	0	1	1	1	1	0	1	0	0	1	0	0	1	0	0	1	0	1	1	0	1	0	0	0	0	0	0	0	0	1	0	0
14 LWANGA	1	1	1	0	1	1	0	0	1	1	1	0	1	0	0	0	0	0	0	1	1	0	1	0	1	1	0	1	0	0	0	1	0	1	0	0	0	0	0
15 NYIRENDA	0	0	0	0	0	0	1	0	0	0	1	0	0	0	0	1	1	1	0	1	0	0	0	0	0	0	1	0	1	0	1	0	1	0	0	0	0	0	1
16 CHISOKONE	1	1	1	0	1	1	1	0	1	1	1	1	1	1	1	0	1	0	1	1	1	1	0	1	1	0	1	1	0	0	0	1	0	1	1	0	0	0	0
17 ENOCH	0	0	0	0	0	0	0	0	0	0	1	0	0	0	1	1	0	0	0	0	0	0	0	0	0	0	1	0	1	0	0	0	0	0	0	0	0	0	0
18 PAULOS	1	0	0	0	0	0	0	0	0	0	1	0	0	1	0	1	1	0	0	1	0	0	0	1	0	0	1	0	1	0	0	0	0	0	0	0	0	0	0

```
I O O O O O I O I O O O I O O O I O I I I O O O
O I O O O I I O O O O I I O I O I I O I O I O O
O O O O O I O I O O O O I O I O I O I O O O I O
O O O O O O I O O O O O I O I I O I I I O O I I
O O O O O O O I O I O I I I I O O I O I O I I I
I I O O O I I I I O I O I I I I I O I I I I I O
I I O O O O O I O O O I O I O O O I O I I O O I
I O I O O I I I I O O I I O O O I I I I I I O I
O O I O O O O O O O I I I O O I I O I I I O O O
I O I O O I I O O O O O O I O I O I I O I I I O
I O I I I O O O O O O O I I I I I O O O I I O I
I O O I I O O O O I O O O I O O O I O O O I I O
I O I O O O O O O O O I O I I O O O O O O O O O
I O O I O O I O I O O O I O I O I O O O O O O O
I O O I O O I O I O O O I O I O I O O O O O O I
I I I O O O I O O O O O I O I O I O O O O I I O
O O O I O O O O O I I O O O O O O O O O O O O O
I O O O O I O O I O O I O O O O O O O O O O O O
I O O O O I O I O I O I I I O O O O O O O O O O
O O O O O I O O O O O O O O O O O O O O I O O
O O I I O I I I I I I I O I I I O O O O O I
O O I O O I I I O I O O O O O O O O O O O O
I I O O O O I O O O O O O O O O O O O O O O
I I O I O I O I I O O O I I I O I I I I O O O
I I O I I O I I O O O I I O O I O O O I I O O
I I O I I I O I I O O I I O O O I O O O I I O O
I I O I I O I I O O O O I O O O O I I I O O O
I O I O O I O I O O O O O O O O O O O O O O
O O I O O I O I O O O O I O O O O O O O O O
O O I O O I O O O O O O O O O O O O O O O O
I I O O O O I O O O O O O O O O O O O O O O
I O O O O I O O O O O O O O O O O O O O O O
I O O O O O O I O O O O O O O O O O O O O O
O O O O O I I O O O O O O O O O O O O I O O
O O O O O I O O O O O O O O O O O O O O O O
O I I O O I I O O O O O O O O O O O O O O O
O O O O O I I O O O O O O O O O O O O O O O
O I O O O I O O O O O O O O O O O O O O O O
O O O O O O O O O O O O O O O O O O O O O O
```

19 MUKUBWA
20 SIGN
21 KALAMBA
22 ZAKEYO
23 BEN
24 IBRAHIM
25 MESHAK
26 ADRIAN
27 KALUNDWE
28 MPUNDU
29 JOHN
30 JOSEPH
31 WILLIAM
32 HENRY
33 CHOBE
34 MUBANGA
35 CHRISTIAN
36 KALONGA
37 ANGEL
38 CHILUFYA
39 MABANGE

DENSITY: 0.3009

some ways, this finding parallels Genovese's arguments that successful slave revolts were more likely to happen in situations where the
density of ties among the slaves was relatively high, especially when
that was coupled with a relatively low density among the slave owners
because of schisms within that group. High density allows groups
to form a collective identity and perhaps to engage in more effective
collective action.

4 How do communities shape identity?

Inherent in Simmel's arguments about duality is the notion that while we make communities, communities also make us. How do communities make us? How do the social networks which surround us shape our identities and mold us as individuals?

We can start to answer this question by looking at Louis Wirth's classic study of Jews in Chicago in the early twentieth century. *The Ghetto*, published in 1928, is an example of the "Chicago School" of sociology, which emphasized urban sociology, especially as it was related to issues of stratification and social status. By looking at the shapes of the social networks in which the Chicago Jews were embedded, we can see the impact of those networks on identity formation among the individuals in this community.

Community and ethnicity in Chicago

In the early twentieth century, the workings of American society were of great interest to social scientists owing to the variety of rapid social changes occurring on several fronts. First, there was massive immigration into the United States from all over the world, especially from Southern and Eastern Europe. The Immigration Restriction Act of 1924 was one response by the US government to try to limit the entry of immigrants from those countries into the United States, and a eugenics movement centered on fears of Southern and Eastern Europeans (especially Jews) was in full flower (Gould 1996). Second, industrialization was proceeding apace in the USA with the advent of Henry Ford's assembly-line manufacture of the automobile (itself a factor in the rapid social change in the USA). This meant a concomitant urbanization. Third, modernization was shaking up some of the cultural foundations of the formerly mostly agrarian and rural social world. Movies had been introduced, morals were changing, and money – following the end of World War I – was flowing in abundance. The fourth significant change that was occurring in the USA at the time was the end of the idea of "endless open space." The end of this idea was profound for the American psyche. Fears about the detrimental effects of living in cities bubbled through the culture (Fischer 1984).

All of these changes led to concerns about how the country could maintain a national identity, how social cohesion could function, and how communal life could continue to operate. How, for example, could a former resident of a Ukrainian *shetl* or a Polish ghetto live in the same world as F. Scott Fitzgerald's flappers or the Boston Brahmins? What would become of their children? What would become of the cities they inhabited? Wirth addressed some of these issues by looking to see *empirically* what was going on in the Jewish ghetto in Chicago.

Wirth was working from the concentric zone model of urban land use that was developed by his University of Chicago colleagues Robert Park, Ernest Burgess, and R. D. McKenzie. In this model, cities were built in concentric rings around a central business district (CBD), with immigrants and other low-status workers clustered in the inner zones of the city where they could be within walking distance of places of employment. These were not very desirable locations for living (owing in large part to the pollution associated with the factories at which the immigrants could find entry-level labor), and as families moved up the social ladder (often in successive generations), they also moved further out in the zones until they finally reached the outermost, suburban residential zone. The relatively newly arrived Jewish immigrants that Wirth studied were still concentrated in the ghetto that was within walking distance of the industrial jobs that they could get. "The older and richer inhabitants," Wirth noted, "seem anxious to move away as rapidly as they can afford it. They make room for newly arrived immigrants" (1928: 197).

Owned mostly by absentee landlords, the ghetto into which the Jews moved was over-crowded and dilapidated, hemmed in by industrial sites and the pollution and noise that industry generated. But it had the advantages of low rents and convenience to work. Most residents saw it as only a temporary dwelling place – a stop along the way to achieving the American dream of upward mobility. Moreover, Wirth notes that "The ghetto is pre-eminently a cultural community" (1928: 201).

The importation of old world customs helped to create a cohesive cultural community in the ghetto. The viability of these customs in the new world, however, was dependent in many ways on the "weight of numbers." Wirth argues that the "one and a half million Jews in the city of New York, through their very numbers, constitute more of an independent community than do the Jews of Chicago. The active and autonomous life of a community of such size is bound to result in the greater persistence of its cultural traits in the midst of disintegrating influences" (1928: 203–4). The importance of having a critical mass of community members, as we will see, can be viewed in network analytical terms.

The synagogue was the central institution in the ghetto for maintaining the cohesion of the cultural community. Indeed, the synagogue served many functions in the ghetto: it disseminated news, adjudicated disputes among the community members, provided social services for members, helped settle in newcomers, and in general kept "the spirit of Judaism" (1928: 209) alive. Perhaps one of the most important functions of the synagogue was to stop assimilation of the Jews into the larger non-Jewish society. Wirth quoted from an editorial in the local orthodox paper to back up this claim:

> If a Jew in the *Diaspora* ceases to observe the Rabbinical laws and ordinances, he is likely to intermarry; is likely to assimilate with Gentiles and to disappear as a Jew. . . . Reform is a political proposition because it abolishes and destroys the forms of Jewish life with the object of bringing about the destruction of the Jewish people by ultimate assimilation. . . . Orthodoxy means, in the final analysis, the will to live as a Jew, while Reform means the will to die as a *Goy*.

Intermarriages with spouses outside of the faith, while relatively rare, were considered "serious symptoms of community disintegration" (1928: 211).

Given the information that Wirth provides us, we can construct a network picture of the ghetto in the first generation of immigration. There would have been dense ties organized around the synagogue as well as dense ties among family members, among residents who had migrated from the same areas in Europe, among residents who worked together, and among residents who shared space in the same cramped public spaces (such as shopping from the same street vendors). A shared language (Yiddish) and several newspapers active in the ghetto would also have encouraged the formation of ties. And, of course, the Jewish residents were living in one concentrated area of the city, near the CBD,

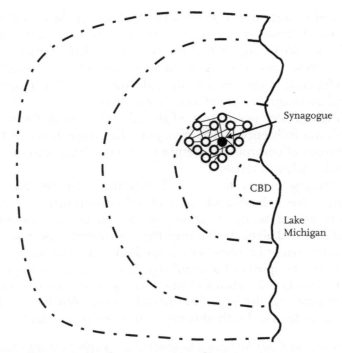

Figure 4.1 Chicago in the first generation of immigration

and were not yet spread out to the surrounding concentric zones. Thus the picture that emerges might look something like figure 4.1.

Two interesting points arise from Wirth's discussion of the ghetto as a cultural community. The first is the connection between inter-marriage and the disappearance of the Jews as a people. The second is the injunction to strictly respect Orthodox laws as the important key to preventing assimilation. Both of these tie in with the weight of numbers that Wirth recognized as crucial to the cultural survival of the ghetto. Looking at this insight from the perspective of network analysis helps us see how the weight of numbers of Jews in the Chicago ghetto and the types of ties among them – and between other groups – play a key role in identity formation.

Minorities, majorities, and the weight of numbers

Rytina and Morgan (1982) develop a quantitative method for ana-lyzing the impact of **out-group tie** formation on the possibility for

Table 4.1 Tie accounts table when ethnicity is not relevant

From:	To: Minority	Majority	
Minority	4,000	36,000	= 40,000
Majority	36,000	324,000	= 360,000

internal cohesion among minority groups surrounded by numerical majorities. How, these authors ask, can small groups maintain their cultural identity in the face of overwhelming numbers of outsiders? Rytina and Morgan find three things: first, a small group can maintain its cohesion if it has a very large number of social ties per person – that is, if it is a *gregarious* group. Second, a small group can maintain its cohesion if it is substantially isolated from contact with the larger group – that is, if it is *segregated*. And third, a small group can maintain its cohesion if its members have so many contacts and the group size is small enough that lots of in-group ties are possible even if there are some out-group ties. In other words, a small group can maintain its cohesion if it has a high in-group density – that is, if it is *saturated*. These three conditions are often met by powerful elites, such as old boy networks or corporate directorate interlocks. We, however, want to look at the flip-side of the problem – what happens to small populations when they *don't* meet these criteria?

Rytina and Morgan use a tie accounts table to analyze the various configurations of in-group and out-group network ties. First, let's understand how the tie accounts table works before we return to the situation of the Jews in Chicago. For our example, imagine a small college with 2,000 students of whom 200 are of one ethnic group (called Minority) and the other 1,800 are of another ethnic group (called Majority). Let's further assume that all the students have about the same number of active friendship ties – say 200. We could set up a two-by-two table to show the distribution of those ties in the population. The table would look like table 4.1. The numbers in each cell of the table would indicate the number of ties going from the group in the row to the group in the column. Ties going from Minority members to other Minority members or from Majority members to other Majority members are *in-group ties*. Ties going from Minority members to Majority members or ties going from Majority members to Minority members are *out-group ties*.

For our first example, suppose that ethnicity had no effect whatsoever on the students' choices of friends. In that case, since 10 percent of the total student body are in the Minority category and 90 percent of the total student body are in the Majority category, 10 percent of the ties of each category of student should go to Minority students and 90 percent to Majority students. There are 200 Minority students with 200 ties each, so as a group the Minority students have 40,000 (200 × 200 = 40,000) ties to give away, of which 10 percent (4000) should go to other Minority students and the remaining 90 percent (36,000) to Majority students. Similarly, there are 1,800 Majority students with 200 ties each, so the Majority students have 360,000 (1,800 × 200 = 360,000) ties all together to give away, 10 percent (36,000) to Minority students and the remaining 90 percent (324,000) to the Majority students. The tie accounts table in this situation, then, would look like table 4.1.

Notice that the number of Majority to Minority ties is equal to the number of Minority to Majority ties. We can now calculate the salience of ethnicity for friendship formation at this college, using the formula that Rytina and Morgan give us (1982: 97):

$$I = 1 - k$$

$$k_I = (1 - IN_I/T_I) / (1 - n_I/N)$$

where I is the index of salience, IN_I is the number of in-group ties for group 1, T_I is the total number of ties for group 1, n_I is the population of group 1 and N is the total population. So using our Minority students as group 1, IN_I would be 4,000, T_I would be 40,000, n_I would be 200, and N would be 2,000. Plugging these numbers into the formula for k_I would give us:

$$k_I = (1 - 4,000/40,000) / (1 - 200/2,000)$$
$$= (1 - .1) / (1 - .1) = .9/.9 = 1$$

Then the salience, I, would be

$$I = 1 - k$$

or

$$I = 1 - 1 = 0$$

Table 4.2 Tie accounts table with complete segregation

To:	Minority	Majority	
From:			
Minority	40,000	0	= 40,000
Majority	0	360,000	= 360,000

So we get the result here that the salience of ethnicity for this population in choosing their friendships is 0, which is exactly what we had set it up to be.

Let's look now at the situation where the students are completely segregated with regard to ethnicity in forming their friendships. In that case, the tie accounts table would look like table 4.2.

(Note that again the number of out-group ties – Majority to Minority and Minority to Majority – is equal.) Filling in the numbers for the formulas for salience, then:

$$I = 1 - k$$

$$k_I = (1 - IN_I/T_I) / (1 - n_I/N)$$

$$k_I = (1 - 40,000/40,000) / (1 - 200/2,000)$$
$$= (1 - 1) / (1 - .1) = 0/.9 = 0$$

and, therefore:

$$I = 1 - 0 = 1$$

So ethnicity is completely salient in this example, just as we had intended it to be.

It is interesting to watch what happens inside the cells of the tie accounts table as the members of this population make choices that lie between these two extremes. For this, instead of looking at the salience of the category of ethnicity in forming friendships, we will instead look at the percentage of in-group ties as a proxy for saturation, which is one of the three necessities for maintaining group cohesion. In the example of complete segregation in table 4.2, the percentage of in-group ties (Minority to Minority or Majority to

Table 4.3 Majority members each having two Minority ties

	To: Minority	Majority	
From: Minority	36,400	3,600	= 40,000
Majority	3,600	356,400	= 360,000

Majority) is 100. Now suppose each Majority person decides to make two Minority friends. Because there are 1,800 Majority students, the total number of ties going from the Majority to the Minority ends up being 3,600. Knowing this we can fill in all the rest of the numbers so that we get table 4.3.

Because the Majority students spend 3,600 of their total 360,000 ties on Minority students, they only have 356,400 ties left to give to other Majority students. Because the Minority students are reciprocating those 3,600 ties to Majority students, they only have 36,400 ties left from their original 40,000 to go to their fellow Minority students. By dividing the numbers in this table by the total number of ties possible for each of these groups, we get the in-group and out-group tie percentages in table 4.4.

The percentage of in-group ties for the Minority members is 91 while the percentage of in-group ties for the Majority members is 99. The percentage of in-group ties declines much more significantly for the Minority students than for the Majority students precisely because there are a smaller number of them. The 200 Minority students have

Table 4.4 In-group and out-group tie percentages for Majority members each having two Minority ties

	To: Minority	Majority	
From: Minority	91%	9%	= 100%
Majority	1%	99%	= 100%

Table 4.5 Majority members each having 10 minority ties

	To:		
	Minority	Majority	
From: Minority	22,000	18,000	= 40,000
Majority	18,000	342,000	= 360,000

to "absorb" the ties sent out by the 1,800 Majority students. While the 1,800 Majority students are sending out two out-group ties each, because there are far fewer Minority students to receive those ties, each of them has to make 18 (3,600/200 = 18) out-group ties, which is 9 percent of their total number of friendship ties available. The Majority members, meanwhile, have only made 1 percent out-group ties.

Suppose instead of making just two out-group ties, however, each of the Majority members had decided to make 10 ties with Minority members. Now the tie accounts table would look like table 4.5, and the percentages of in-group and out-group ties in this situation would look like table 4.6.

As we can see, the percentage of in-group ties for the Majority is still 95 – barely affected by the outgoing ties – while the percentage of in-group ties for the Minority has precipitously declined. Almost half of their ties now are to those outside their group. If we take it one step further and the Majority students each make 20 Minority friends, the table of percentages would look like table 4.7.

Table 4.6 In-group and out-group tie percentages for Majority members each having 10 minority ties

	To:		
	Minority	Majority	
From: Minority	55%	45%	= 100%
Majority	5%	95%	= 100%

Table 4.7 In-group and out-group tie percentages for Majority members each having 20 minority ties

	To: Minority	Majority	
From: Minority	10%	90%	= 100%
Majority	10%	90%	= 100%

By this point, the percentage of in-group ties of the Majority has been only slightly affected by their out-group friendships, but because the Minority members are numerically so much smaller than the Majority members, they have been completely overwhelmed by out-group ties. Only 10 percent of their ties can go to other Minority members. The logic of Rytina and Morgan's model tells us that if a group that is in the numerical minority in a community cannot maintain some segregation, their ability to maintain saturation is severely compromised. The minority group could conceivably compensate for this by being extraordinarily gregarious (that is, by increasing the average number of ties per person for members of the group), but there are often limits to that. Humans only have the time and energy to maintain so many ties – and increasing that number by too much will inevitably lead to a decrease in the strength of those ties that are maintained. Without segregation, saturation and gregariousness, the minority group has little chance of maintaining any kind of group cohesion.

Keeping this in mind, we can return to the discussion of Jews in the Chicago ghetto.

Assimilation in Chicago

The smallness of the ghetto world was matched by the strength of the ties between the residents. "The ghetto is a complete world, but it is a small and a narrow world. . . . Not only do the *Landsleute* [people from the same area] belong to the same synagogue, but as a rule they engage in similar vocations, become partners in business, live in the same neighborhood, and intermarry within their own group" (Wirth 1928: 222–3). These are extremely strong multiplex ties. There are many factors which cause this overlapping of dense multiplex ties, including the institutions in the area – not only the synagogue, but also the numerous shops which cater only to the Jewish clientele, the bathhouse, the Yiddish theatre and newspapers, not to mention the cafés, restaurants, and bookstores which functioned as gathering places for discussion. The result of this density of ties, however, leads to a uniformity of ideas, much like Gemeinschaft or mechanical solidarity. (The "Closer Look" section of this chapter uses balance theory as a more explicitly network analytical way of explaining this uniformity.) The ghetto community could not last in this state forever, though. Movement out of the ghetto had already started even in the first generation.

There is a generational aspect to the tie structure in the Chicago ghetto – it was the children (that is, the second generation) who were falling away from the synagogue and who were intermarrying. What forces were pushing them this way?

One of the first answers that presents itself is the role of the structure of public schooling in the lives of young people. According to Wirth (1928: 218), children's education was highly valued by the Jewish community in the ghetto. But as the children move through the grades from elementary school through high school, the structure of the American educational system, with schools increasing in size and in the area from which they draw their students as the students get older, children from the ghetto are put into contact with children from further and further outside their immediate neighborhood as they progress through the system. Their formerly narrow social interactions are inevitably broadened.

Moreover, as first-generation Jewish merchants began to achieve financial success, many of them moved their families farther away from the center of the city and into nicer neighborhoods. This process accelerated in the second generation. Wirth notes that most often "it is the children who discover the ghetto for their parents. They go to school; they work in the stores and offices in the loop; they make friends; they go to dances, and the girls are seen home by escorts; they are mobile, and the world of the ghetto begins to shrink, then to bore, and finally to disgust" (1928: 242–3).

The dilapidated area further deteriorates and other ethnic groups move in looking for cheap accommodations. Furthermore, Wirth argues, as they acquire sufficient wealth to do so, the Jewish residents are now looking to flee their low-status identities as ghetto-dwellers.

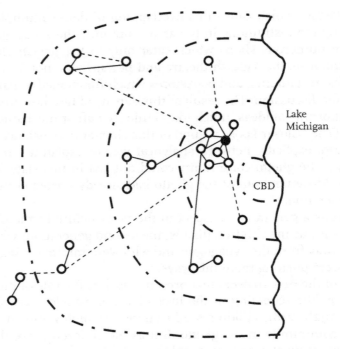

Figure 4.2 Chicago after residential movement

Wirth writes that "the Jew is not so much running away from the area because it is a slum, nor is he fleeing from the Negroes; but he is fleeing from his fellow-Jews who remain in the ghetto. From the ghetto he drifts to Lawndale, where he hopes to acquire status, or where at least his status as a ghetto Jew will be forgotten" (1928: 246).

Figure 4.2 gives us an idea of how this outward movement and the concomitant loosening of ties it causes would look.

Thinking about the ways in which Rytina and Morgan discuss the importance of segregation and saturation for maintaining a cohesive identity for a small group surrounded by a larger group, we can see how this movement out would have begun to affect the identity of the former ghetto residents. Especially as the children began to intermarry (a sure sign of the breakdown of segregation) the minority Jews would be overwhelmed by ties from others, especially those that lived in the far-flung neighborhoods in the zones further away from the center of the city. The social networks of the Jews would no longer be either segregated or saturated with ties to other Jews. As a consequence, the cohesive Jewish culture that had been fostered in the ghetto would begin to deteriorate. As ties are formed with others of different ideologies, cultures, political positions, etc., the attitudes and dispositions of the far-flung Jews would also begin to reflect the new multicultural society around them. All sorts of ties – friendship, business, acquaintances, even kinship ties as intermarriage occurs – would no longer be strictly relegated to other Jews. Soon the unique Jewish identity would be lost.

Interestingly, Wirth argues that as the first wave of Jews migrates out of the ghetto, they are soon followed by a second, less assimilated wave of Jews who move into those far-flung neighborhoods that their former ghetto neighbors have already colonized. "In their attempt to flee from the ghetto, [they] have found that the ghetto has followed them to their new quarters" (Wirth 1928: 254–5). This in turn prompts a further wave of movement as the first wave of ghetto expatriates moves once again.

Geographic movement and weakening social ties go hand in hand. As the minority members come increasingly into contact with the majority, their ability to maintain subcultural cohesiveness degrades. As we have seen before, there are two sides to this. On the one hand, tight communities leave little room for creating deviant identities. On the other hand, Wirth makes an interesting point about the discovery of one's ethnic identity through comparison with different others only once one has left the ghetto. "As long as he remains in the ghetto the Jew seldom becomes conscious of his inferior status. He emerges from the ghetto and finds himself surrounded by a freer but a less comfortable and less homely and familiar world" (Wirth 1928: 261). The response to this among the Chicago area Jews in the early part of the twentieth century was re-ethnicization. Wirth notes that the revival of anti-Semitism in the United States provided "the impetus of external pressure" (1928: 271) that pushed the Chicago Jews together into a more cohesive and self-aware group. Rediscovering their Judaism in the face of widespread anti-Semitism caused many of the Jews who were no longer residents of the ghetto to band together in ethnic solidarity in an attempt to keep their culture alive.

It would seem that banding together would be a good thing to do for these immigrants. But that is not necessarily the case. Network analysis shows us that in many ways, success – economic and otherwise – is really fostered by exactly those sorts of weak ties that the leaders of the Jewish community in Chicago most feared as being destructive of their community and their identity. To understand how this is so, we have to begin by looking at one of the most famous of all network studies – Stanley Milgram's "small world studies," the source of the infamous "six degrees of separation."

Small worlds and six degrees of separation

Milgram started with a rather simple observation:

> Almost all of us have had the experience of encountering someone far from home, who, to our surprise, turns out to share a mutual acquaintance with us. This kind of experience occurs with sufficient frequency so that our language even provides a cliché to be uttered at the appropriate moment of recognizing mutual acquaintances. We say, "My, it's a small world." (1967: 61)

Just exactly how small a world is it? We can refine this question in the way that Milgram did: "Given any two people in the world, person X and person Z, how many intermediate acquaintance links are needed before X and Z are connected?" (1967: 62). Milgram decided to find out by using the following method: a target person was selected. In the case we will discuss in most depth here (the Nebraska study), the target person was a Boston stockbroker. Then "starters" were selected from three different populations – a group of blue-chip stockholders in Nebraska (N = 100), a group of "randomly selected" people in Nebraska (N = 96), and a group of "randomly selected" people in Boston (N = 100). Each starter was given a packet which contained basic demographic information about the target person, including his name and occupation. Each starter was asked to pass the packet along to the target (if the starter was personally acquainted with him – none of them was) or to someone that they were personally acquainted with whom they thought might know the target or know someone who knew him. That is, the starters were instructed to begin a chain that they thought might lead the packet to eventually reach the target. Along the way, every person in the chain was given instructions to send a provided postcard back to the researchers so that the progress of the packet could be tracked through the chain. The chain ended either when the packet reached the target person or when someone along the way declined to participate and thus ended the chain. The question was: what would be the average length of the chain?

Before he started the experiment, Milgram polled colleagues to

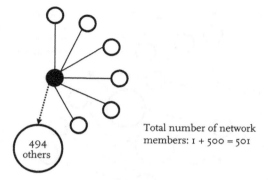

Total number of network
members: 1 + 500 = 501

Figure 4.3 One step away from the starter

see what the estimated number of intermediaries would be. Many people thought the chain would need to be 100 persons or more. As we famously know, though, the average length for the completed chains was only about six. (This number is what we will call the **index of connectivity**.)

This seems at first glance to be a shockingly small number, but from one perspective, it might instead be rather large. How could that be so? Begin by supposing that each person has about 500 acquaintances (a conservative estimate of reality). Their network will look like figure 4.3 at the first step out from the starter. (For obvious reasons, not all 500 ties are individually drawn.)

Now imagine that each of those 500 acquaintances has 500 acquaintances of their own. At two steps out from the starter, the network will look like figure 4.4.

Because each node of the network brings in 500 new acquaintances,

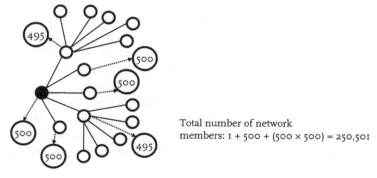

Total number of network
members: 1 + 500 + (500 × 500) = 250,501

Figure 4.4 Two steps away from the starter

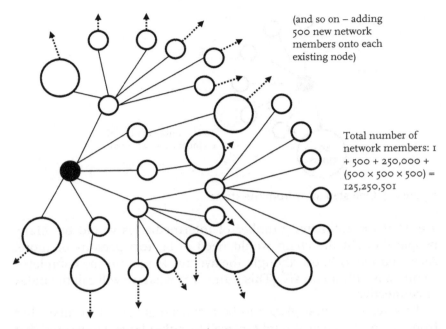

(and so on – adding 500 new network members onto each existing node)

Total number of network members: 1 + 500 + 250,000 + (500 × 500 × 500) = 125,250,501

Figure 4.5 Three steps away from the starter

the size of the network grows exponentially. At the third step out, if the 250,000 people who had been reached at the second step each bring in 500 new acquaintances, the network will look like figure 4.5.

By the fourth step the total will be 62,625,250,501 – more than the entire population of the earth by a factor of about nine. As we can see from these diagrams, if each new member of the network adds 500 more new acquaintances, the network grows rapidly. So if this model is correct, there should really be only three or four steps between any two people in the world, not the six degrees of separation that Milgram found. But of course, it is easy to see that this model is not at all correct. It makes the absurd assumption that each new node in the network brings 500 new acquaintances into the picture. That is not how friendship (or any other kind of relationship) operates. We tend to know the friends of our friends. (This is what balance theory – discussed in the "Closer Look" section of this chapter – tells us.) If a starter who is a friend of mine contacts me as the second step of a chain, I do not know 500 people that the starter doesn't know. Our social circles in all probability overlap at least somewhat – possibly, in fact, they overlap to a very large extent. That means that rather than

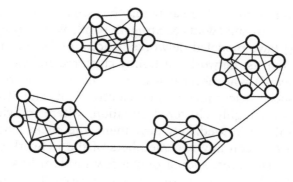

Figure 4.6 Small worlds

growing exponentially, the chains of connections may circle back over and over into the same small group of people. (In chapter 3, we saw this happen with some of the women searching for abortions that Lee studied. Because their chains kept circling around inside the same small group, they were unable to receive fresh information and ended up with no choices about abortion providers.) Instead of looking like an ever-increasing web of relationships stretching out into infinity, ties tend to cluster into small groups of redundant relationships; these small groups are then connected by a few ties which make bridges between the groups. The result would look more like figure 4.6.

Milgram recognized this.

> Finally, when we state there are only five intermediate acquaintances, this connotes a closeness between position of the starting person and the target person. But this is in large measure misleading, a confusion of two entirely different frames of reference. If two persons are five removes apart, they are far apart indeed. Almost anyone in the United States is but a few removes from the President, or from Nelson Rockefeller, but this is true only in terms of a particular mathematical viewpoint and does not, in any practical sense, integrate our lives with that of Nelson Rockefeller. Thus, when we speak of five intermediaries, we are talking about an enormous psychological distance between the starting and target points, a distance which seems small only because we customarily regard "five" as a small manageable quantity. We should think of the two points as being not five persons apart, but "five circles of acquaintances" apart – five "structures" apart. This helps to set it in its proper perspective. (1967: 67)

We could even think of them as being "five small worlds" apart.

Watts and Strogatz (Watts & Strogatz 1998, Watts 1999a, 1999b, 2003, 2004) have modeled networks to account for the **small world structure** – that is, networks of tightly clustered individuals (which they call "caves") who nevertheless have the ability to reach across enormous social spaces relatively efficiently. Watts and Strogatz have found that in a highly clustered situation, where individuals only have ties to those immediately near them, the chain lengths to get information between any two members of the network can indeed be immense. However, adding only a few random links that reach outside of the local area dramatically decreases the average chain length (Watts & Strogatz 1998: 441). We saw this structure before in chapter 3 when we looked at the social networks of slaves in the ante-bellum US south and saw that adding only one or two literate "shortcuts" into the network radically shortened the average chain length for everyone in the system.

Chain length is important because, as Travers and Milgram note (1969: 438), the longer the chain length between the starter and the target, the less likely that the chain will end up being completed at all. That is, if you can't connect with someone pretty quickly, in all likelihood you can't connect with them at all. This means that there is a distinct advantage that accrues to people who have short indices of connectivity. Short chains can be a function either of particular types of search strategies (to navigate your way through the network toward the target) or of particular types of searchers.

In his initial studies of the small world problem, Milgram found that the distribution of the number of intermediaries in the chain was bimodal. In the Nebraska study, Travers and Milgram found that "when the completed chains were divided into those which approached the target through his hometown and those which approached him via Boston business contacts, two distinguishable distributions emerged. The mean of the Sharon [hometown] distribution is 6.1 links, and that of the Boston [business] distribution is 4.6. The difference is significant at a level better than .0005" (Travers & Milgram 1969 431–2). That is, those who used business contacts in the stockbroker world to reach the target had significantly shorter chain lengths. So search strategies matter – or perhaps we could say that those who had access to the resource of ties in the stockbroker world were able to get to the target more quickly. (Again, we can see the connection to Lee's study of women searching for abortions. Some search strategies – particularly those which activated ties to clusters of others who were not in the searcher's immediate close circle of family and friends – were more effective and garnered more information and more choice for the women who used them.)

The social resources available to different types of people are worth exploring. And Milgram tackled part of that problem in his next set of small world experiments. Korte and Milgram (1970) explored how the small world phenomenon operated once they began to take race into account. Using white male starters, Korte and Milgram directed the chains to white and African-American targets. The authors found that "[m]ean chain length was surprisingly consistent with earlier studies, and while the completed Negro-target chains were slightly longer than white-target chains, the difference was not significant. The completed white-target chains were characterized by a mean of 5.5 intermediaries; for the Negro-target chains that were completed, a mean of 5.9 intermediaries" (1970: 104). However, there were some interesting and important differences that emerged from the study. The first was that "[w]hile 88 of the 270 white-target chains (33%) got through to the target, only 35 (13%) of the Negro-target chains were successful" (1970: 103). So although it seems that there is no great difference in the average chain length between white and black targets, the white targets were two and a half times more likely to be reached at all.

A more dramatic finding, however, had to do with not race, but social class. Successful chains were disproportionately much more likely to involve people of higher socio-economic status. When looking at the penultimate link in complete chains, Korte and Milgram found that

> An additional terminal effect was the status-descent of the chain, regardless of target race, as final contact was made with the target. The target typically occupied a lower status than that of the person who forged the final link – for example, of all instances of chain completion, 27% involved cases of professional status targets, while the final contact person was of professional status in 63% of these instances. . . . The gatekeepers, white senders and Negro recipients who served as points of contact and acquaintanceship, in both races were predominantly males of professional status. . . Managers, officials, and sales-clerical personnel were also represented, while lower- and working-class gatekeepers were almost non-existent. (1970: 105)

Korte and Milgram note that chains tend to run down after about five jumps and that, therefore, efficiency is important in using network chains to reach the target. And high-status people are much more efficient at passing along the information to the target. The authors hypothesize that "lower-status peers may be separated by physical and institutional barriers, and passage between peers is often possible only through higher-status intermediaries, who have better cover of the *total* setting or institution" (1970: 107, emphasis in original). So short chains have distinct advantages over longer chains and high-status people tend to have shorter chains than do low-status people.

But what does all this have to do with communities and the way they operate?

"The strength of weak ties"

We can understand the relevance of the small world experiments to community studies by looking at one of the formative pieces of network literature, Granovetter's "The strength of weak ties" (1973), in which Granovetter explores a classic piece of urban sociology, Gans's *The Urban Villagers: Group and Class in the Life of Italian-Americans* (1962), from an explicitly network analytical perspective.

Granovetter begins by looking at balance theory. In brief, balance theory tells us that if an actor, A, is strongly tied to both B and C, it is extremely likely that B and C are, sooner or later, going to be tied to each other (1973: 1363). Granovetter argues that because of this, bridge ties between cliques are always weak ties (1973: 1364). Weak ties may not necessarily be bridges, but Granovetter argues that bridges will be weak. This is because if two actors share a strong tie, they will draw in their other strong relations and will eventually form a clique. The only way, therefore, that people in different cliques can be connected is through weak ties that do not have the strength to draw together all the "friends of friends."

But these weak ties have the advantage that they can operate like the "shortcuts" we saw with the literate slaves in chapter 3. By bridging the otherwise distant cliques, they can radically shorten the average chain length that information has to travel to reach distant members of the system, making the transmission of information more efficient. Bridge ties are those ties that, by leaving the environment of the strictly local area, radically decrease the average tie length between any two members of the network by providing a shortcut among the far-flung cliques. Granovetter's insight was that "[i]ntuitively speaking, this means that whatever is to be diffused can reach a larger number of people, and traverse greater social distance (i.e., path length), when passed through weak ties rather than strong" (1973: 1366). Weak ties not only connect communities to the world outside their immediate neighborhood, they also make chains of connections short and efficient enough to reach their targets.

In reviewing the data from the Korte and Milgram study, Granovetter found that when trying to cross racial lines, chains were twice as likely to be completed when the transition from a white sender to a black receiver happened between "acquaintances" (weak ties) rather than through "friends" (strong ties).

> Ties in the [strong sector of ego's personal network] tend to be people who not only know one another, but who also have few contacts not tied to ego as well. In the "weak" sector, however, not only will ego's contacts not be tied to one another, but they *will* be tied to individuals not tied to ego. Indirect contacts are thus typically reached through ties in this sector. (Granovetter 1973: 1370)

Granovetter argues that people with few ties will be "encapsulated" inside their own small groups (Watts [2003] calls this the "caveman-world") and will be unable to get information from outside that group – much like the women Lee studied who had no choices about abortionists because they had no ties outside their own clique (see chapter 3). Granovetter writes that "those to whom we are weakly tied are more likely to move in circles different from our own and will thus have access to information different from that we receive" (1973: 371).

This is the "strength of weak ties" argument: weak ties – because they are more likely than strong ties to be connected to socially distant (or at least disparate) groups from the ones we typically inhabit – can give us new, fresh, and important information that is not already known to us. We get access to resources that would otherwise have been unavailable to us through weak ties. Our strong ties can give us much social support, etc., but they cannot connect us to distant social worlds because they are so embedded in our own social world.

These weak ties, like the connections between literate slaves, dramatically reduce the overall average chain length in a network. Those ties to socially distant others are vitally important because unless chain lengths are fairly short, the usefulness of the chain is rather minimal. As Granovetter points out (1973: 1372), hearing information at fifth hand is no better than getting that same information from a public source. Information that changes hands many times degrades into uselessness.

The disadvantages of strong communities

Granovetter's discussion of Gans's *The Urban Villagers* (1962) hinges on the distinction between strong and weak ties. Gans's description of the community is one of social cohesion – strong ties – and Granovetter's contention is that precisely the lack of weak ties was the community's undoing. Faced with the prospect of an "urban renewal" project that would destroy their homes, the residents of the West End, although tightly tied together, were unable to activate the weak ties that might have saved their community. In the end, the neighborhood was bulldozed under by city authorities and the former residents scattered to all parts of the city.

Gans characterizes the West End as a "peer group society" where most of the connections that people have with each other, despite the fact that they live in a demographically varied urban area, are within the same peer group. Gans writes that "the various ethnic groups, the bohemians, transients, and others could live together side by side without much difficulty, since each was responsive to totally different reference groups" (1962: 15). Groups were segregated by religion, nationality and ethnicity, and social class. Ties within these groups were strong, but there were very few weak ties bridging the different groups.

Looking at gender and family relations in the West End also reminds us that strong ties to one group are often balanced by a separation from other groups. This is why the West End could have so many close ties and still be so segmented. With regard to the peer group life, Gans found that on first becoming married,

> a couple leaves its peer groups, but after a short time, often following the arrival of the first child, they both re-enter peer group life. Among action-seeking West Enders, the man may return to his corner, and the woman to her girl friends. But most often – especially in the routine-seeking working class – a new peer group is formed, consisting of family members and a few friends of each spouse. This group meets after working hours for long evenings of sociability. Although the members of the group are of both sexes, the normal tendency is for the men and women to split up, the men in one room and the women in another. (1962: 38–9)

This is, of course, very reminiscent of the traditional families that Bott studied (discussed in chapter 3).

Although Gans calls this a "new" peer group, it is still made up of people who have known each other for a very long time. "In the West End, friendship ties seem to be formed mainly in childhood and adolescence, and many of them last throughout life" (Gans 1962: 39). This is a picture of a community with many strong multiplex ties gathered together into densely knit groups, but with deep gulfs between those groups. This segmentation is further advanced by the search for the anonymity (as opposed to privacy) that many West Enders value. Gans tells us that

> they have little interest in the type of privacy demanded by middle-class families. While they do want to be left alone, they are not averse to the aural or visual closeness of their neighbors. ... As one West Ender put it: "I like the noise people make. In summer, people have their windows open, and everyone can hear everyone else, but nobody cares what anybody is saying; they leave their neighbors alone. In the suburbs, people are nosier; when a car comes up the street, all the windows go up to see who is visiting whom." (1962: 20–1)

Given the situation of peer group closeness coupled with physical closeness, it is easy to see how outsiders (and even insiders) could mistakenly believe that the West End was a cohesive neighborhood. The West End seemed to be closely knit with high density – and in some ways it was exactly that. But it is precisely the strength of those close ties that meant the West End could be fragmented – so fragmented that when the very existence of the neighborhood was threatened by redevelopment, the residents were incapable of coming together to save their world.

Granovetter argues that the maintenance of the strong ties which the West Enders cherished took up so much of their time and energy that they had few social resources left with which to build weak ties – or more precisely, with which to build bridge ties. Granovetter argues that

> two common sources of weak ties, formal organizations and work settings, did not provide them for the West End; organization membership was almost nil ([Gans 1962] pp. 104–7) and few worked within the area itself, so ties formed at work were not relevant to the community (p. 122). Nevertheless, in a community marked by geographic immobility and lifelong friendships (p. 19) it strains credulity to suppose that each person

would not have known a great many others, so that there would have been *some* weak ties. The question is whether such ties were bridges. If *none* were, then the community would be fragmented in exactly the same way as described above, except that the cliques would then contain weak as well as strong ties. . . . Such a pattern is made plausible by the lack of ways in the West End to *develop* weak ties other than by meeting friends of friends (where "friend" includes relatives) – in which case the new tie is automatically not a bridge. (1973: 1375, emphasis in original)

Again, we see the role of balance theory where people become new friends with people already tied to their old friends, but don't often break out of their cliques to form bridges to other small worlds.

The problem with having so many strong ties in the West End was that it meant that the residents were lacking in weak ties – or at least they were lacking in weak ties that were also bridge ties. Thinking about Rytina and Morgan and the tie accounts table can help us understand why this would be so. Each in-group in the West End maintained its cultural cohesion and distinctiveness only to the degree that they were able to focus their ties inward and to exclude ties with those in the out-groups. Out-group ties are bridge ties. Precisely because of the demographic variety that the urban setting of the West End provided, every group in it was a minority, holding on to its identity by limiting out-group ties. Ultimately, this doomed the West End to oblivion.

The residents of the West End were unable to cohere in order to resist redevelopment. The segmented nature of the West End community shaped the identities of the residents. In this way they were perhaps more successful than the Jews of the Chicago ghetto who watched their children become increasingly assimilated in the outside culture. The West Enders maintained their strong in-group ties, but the very strength of those ties and the inflexible nature of the identities it produced ultimately doomed the neighborhood. Without the weak ties that would have knit the various factions in the West End into one cohesive whole, the area was never able to come together to effectively resist outside forces. Granovetter argues that "weak ties, often denounced as generative of alienation . . . are here seen as indispensible to individuals' opportunities and to their integration into communities; strong ties, breeding local cohesion, lead to overall fragmentation" (1973: 1378).

Moreover, without the weak ties that bridged the various groups in the West End, the residents lacked the trust in leaders and also lacked the knowledge they needed of the city government to effectively organize to keep their neighborhood from redevelopment. Like some of the women in Lee's study of abortion seekers (see chapter 3), the different peer groups in the West End were trapped in their own small "caves" (to use Watts's [2003] term). Women whose cave included an abortionist were able to get an abortion, but had no choice among different providers. Women whose cave did not include an abortionist were stymied in their search. The residents of the West End, trapped in small groups that had no access to the city politicians and managers, were likewise stymied in their attempts to get information or exercise agency. The strong ties which they had built through the investment of so much time and energy could not provide the efficient access to sources of power that they needed. The strength of weak ties is that they provide bridges across cliques and allow trustworthy information to circulate more widely and efficiently.

The residents of the West End had achieved the "urban village" that social theorists like Tönnies valorized and, like the leaders of the Jewish community in Chicago, they tried to preserve it. The strong ties among residents allowed them to maintain their ethnic and peer group identities without interference from the outside culture. Ironically, this led, in the end, to the destruction of the West End. It was completely demolished in 1959 to make way for luxury apartment houses.

A closer look: balance

"Any friend of yours is a friend of mine." Why? For balance.

Balance theory was developed by Heider (1946, 1958) and extended by others (most notably Cartwright & Harary 1956, Newcomb 1961, 1981) to explain how individuals attempt to structure their relations with others so as to avoid emotional or cognitive dissonance in their sets of relations. That is, we prefer to make friends, for example, with people who share our dispositions, and we feel uncomfortable with people who don't. Cartwright and Harary (1956) then extended and developed this into the theory of **structural balance** (Wasserman & Faust 1994: 221). The idea in structural balance is that in an entire system, all relations will tend toward agreement and away from cognitive dissonance. So, for example, if two people like each other, they will agree on their opinions of others (either liking or disliking that

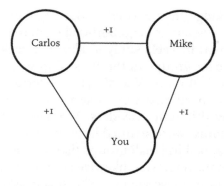

Figure 4.7 A balanced triad

other). Or, if two people dislike each other, they will disagree on their opinions about others. This will then extend through the system to organize it into cliques of people with positive dispositions toward each other and negative dispositions toward others. Let's see how this works.

A dyad is a group of two actors. It is the simplest social form. (Note that in order to be a dyad, the actors must have some type of relationship to each other – two random strangers with no connection to each other are not a dyad; they are just two individuals.) A **triad** is the next most complex form and it is much more complicated in terms of the ways that it can behave. Actors in triads tend to, over time, arrange themselves so as to be balanced. But what is a balanced triad as opposed to an unbalanced one?

An easy way to get the idea of balance is to look at a friendship group. Suppose, for example, that you develop a friendship with someone named Carlos. Carlos probably already has some friends. You are now more likely to meet those friends than you were before you knew Carlos. You may like those new friends. Your friendship with Carlos gives you some reason to have a positive feeling toward Carlos's friends. If you are in a positive friendship relationship with Carlos and you are also in a positive friendship relationship with his friend Mike, then you are in a balanced triad. Figure 4.7 is a sociogram of a balanced triad. We can denote the positive ties by labeling them with a +1.

But suppose you *don't* like Mike. We can denote the negative tie by labeling it with a −1. Figure 4.8 shows the triad that results.

This triad is unbalanced. We can see this when we think about

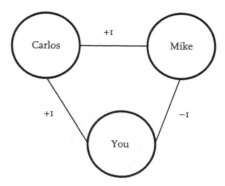

Figure 4.8 An unbalanced triad

the relationships involved – especially the stress that this will put on Carlos. He is now in the situation of having two friends who dislike each other. Carlos and Mike do not share the same disposition toward you (Carlos likes you and Mike does not), and you and Carlos do not share the same disposition toward Mike. Carlos is placed in a state of cognitive dissonance and will, on many occasions, be torn between two competing loyalties. Whom should he invite to his birthday dinner? To share the great summer sublet he finds? To go with him to the movies?

Unbalanced triads tend to be unstable. Over time, because of the interpersonal difficulties that arise, unbalanced triads tend to resolve themselves into balanced triads. There are a couple of ways that this can happen. You and Mike may decide to bury the hatchet and become friends. This will bring the triad back to the balanced position that was depicted in figure 4.7. Or Carlos may find that he has to choose between his two relationships. If he chooses you, the triad that results will once again be balanced, but now in a different way. Instead of sharing a disposition of friendliness toward Mike, as in figure 4.7, you and Carlos will share a disposition of dislike toward Mike, as depicted in figure 4.9.

In figure 4.9, all the cognitive dissonance has now been solved. You and Carolos both dislike Mike and he dislikes both of you. In fact, you and Carlos may be drawn even more tightly together through the bond of your mutual dislike of Mike.

The extension of this **interpersonal balance** into structural balance involves following out the chains of relations between the members of the original triad and other actors in the system. Suppose, for

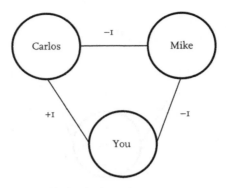

Figure 4.9 Another type of balanced triad

example, that we start with the balanced triad between you, Carlos, and Mike in figure 4.9 and we add others to the network. Imagine that Mike has a friend, Reza. Given that there is dislike between you and Mike and between Carlos and Mike, how will Reza have to feel about you and about Carlos in order for the triads to be balanced? Figure 4.10 shows this extended network with all triads balanced.

Imagine further that Carlos has a friend, Sam. What type of relations would Sam have to have with Reza, with Mike, and with you to keep the triads balanced? Figure 4.11 shows this. Notice that the balanced triad of positive ties between you, Carlos, and Mike is separated by negative ties from the Mike–Reza pair.

If we work out balanced triads for a larger system, we end up with pictures like the sociogram in figure 4.12 where groups of positively tied actors are separated from each other by gulfs of negative ties.

Over time, the negative ties may possibly weaken as people in

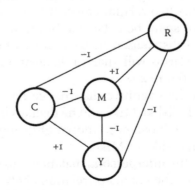

Figure 4.10 Extended balanced network

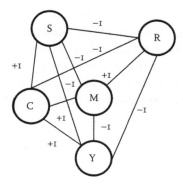

Figure 4.11 Extended balanced network

negative relationships avoid contact and interaction with each other, so that eventually those dyads will fade away or the ties between them become too weak to matter much in terms of personal cognition. In this situation, we will end up with the type of social world depicted in figure 4.6, from our earlier discussion of the small world problem.

One final point to make about structurally balanced networks is that they point out the high social costs that an actor may incur by deviating from the norms and mores of the clique in which she is embedded. Changing a tie from positive to negative not only affects the two actors involved in the immediate relationship, but also has ripple effects throughout the system. In order to re-establish balance, a whole series of connected ties may have to be reoriented. We often see this process happen when romantic partners split up and the extended group of friends has to readjust the tenor of their relations

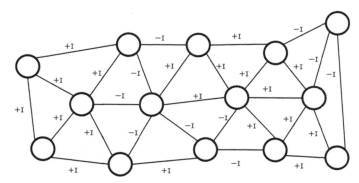

Figure 4.12 A balanced network

not only with the former couple, but perhaps even with the other members of the immediate network. Balance theory is one way to explain the social pressure that individuals may feel not to "rock the boat" among their associates. Being at odds with others can lead to a larger split in the group. In the next chapter, we will look at communities that become fractured and some of the results of those splits.

5 What happens when communities become fractured?

Communities may shape identity, foster conformity, and function as urban villages, but that certainly does not mean that all communities are harmonious conclaves of like-minded members. Throughout history, we can see communities splinter, sometimes in spectacularly vicious ways. In this chapter, we will examine two related questions: what causes a community to turn on some of its members? And what determines which particular members are singled out?

The Salem witch trials of 1692, in which hundreds of people were accused of witchcraft and 19 men and women were executed, hold perennial fascination for Americans. What caused this unusual outburst among the supposedly sober-minded Puritans? Explanations for the witchcraft accusations abound, ranging from the psychological (Starkey 1949) to the social (Erikson 1966) to even biological explanations involving mass poisoning (Caporael 1976, Spanos & Gottlieb 1976). A network analysis of the incident, though, shows that the mystery is not as mysterious as it might seem.

Witchcraft in Salem

The town of Salem was founded on the edge of the Massachusetts Bay in 1626 by devout Puritans. Salem was a busy seaport and the cod fishing off the coast was abundant and profitable. Salem was one of the very first fishing stations established in the new world, and by the mid-sixteenth century more than half of the fish eaten in Europe was North American-produced cod (Kurlansky 1997: 51). The result of this, Kurlansky writes, was that "New Englanders were becoming a commercial people, independent and prosperous . . . [They] were growing rich on free-trade capitalism. Theirs was a cult of the individual, with *commerce becoming almost a New England religion*" (1997:

75, emphasis added). The usurping of one religion by another played an important role in the later events in Salem. Bailyn documents how the New England fisheries "could become the basis of a thriving colonial economy," but only for those colonists who had easy access to the coast, the towns, the roads, and the harbors (1955: 5).

Along with commercial fishing and participation in the Atlantic trade, the beginnings of mercantile capitalism were also appearing in Salem and many residents were beginning to prosper economically. In 1672, however, the settlement split into Salem Town, along the coast, and Salem Village, a more inland settlement that relied on farming as its economic backbone. But while the sea off the coast of Salem teemed with cod, the farming land was stony and the growing season was short. Merchants, traders, craftsmen, and fishermen of Salem Town prospered under the beginnings of mercantile capitalism, but the farmers of Salem Village continued to eke out a meager and precarious existence. A division between the two began to grow.

This was no "live-and-let-live" community, and the different modes of life being pursued by the different segments of Salem society could not simply peacefully coexist. Miller documents the communal nature of Puritan life and of Puritan ideology:

> The lone horseman, the single trapper, the solitary hunter was not a figure of the Puritan frontier. . . . Neither were the individualistic business man, the shopkeeper who seized every opportunity to enlarge his profits, the speculator who contrived to gain wealth at the expense of his fellows, neither were these typical figures of the original Puritan society. . . . There was no questioning that men who would not serve the purposes of society should be whipped into line. The objectives were clear and unmistakable; any one's disinclination to dedicate himself to them was obviously so much recalcitrancy and depravity. (1964: 143)

The merchants of seventeenth-century Salem walked a fine line between fulfilling their calling in the role in which God had seen fit to place them and violating the very foundation of Puritan ethos by fulfilling that role *too* well, becoming rich as a result. The merchants were caught in a bind – damned if they did and damned if they didn't – in this case, literally so.

As the seventeenth century went on, the merchants facing this dilemma began more and more to solve it by resisting the strict theological control of their business affairs by traditionalist ministers. In this, Bailyn says, "lay the seeds of change" (1955: 16). There were increasing ideological tensions because of the development of trade, not the least of which was that trade often necessitated sustained contact with the outside (non-Puritan) world – a world that was viewed with suspicion and hostility on account of its sinful and possibly contaminating influence. The view of contact with outsiders as being polluting and possibly dangerous was similar to the orthodox Jews' in Chicago three centuries later attempting to deter assimilation to mainstream society by trying to limit contact with outsiders. We can see in Salem how the division of labor (separating farmers from merchants) was weakening the collective conscience, much to the dismay of some in the community.

Bailyn (1955: 20–1) notes that the Puritans were especially leery of trade with regard to its *moral* dangers. Not only did trade tempt men to exploit others for their own individual gain, but by its very nature it also threw the traders into contact with outsiders – with those who did not necessarily share the traditional Puritan ideology and might therefore prove to be a corrupting influence on those with whom they came in contact.

Inevitably, those trade relationships began to have their effect. Ties with outsiders facilitated economic success and also began to have the effect of diluting the Puritan culture. The towns and villages of seventeenth-century New England began to change as social mobility and social freedom began slowly to replace the Puritan virtues of stability, order, and discipline (Bailyn 1955: 139).

Not everyone around Salem was equally affected by these changing economic fortunes and the changing social mores with which they went hand in hand. A split developed in the community between those oriented toward the new capitalist order (centered in Salem Town) and those defending the traditional Puritan ideals (centered in Salem Village). Increasingly, the new merchant class began to achieve power and political prominence and the more traditionally oriented farmers began to suffer from relative deprivation, as their way of life was not only less economically remunerative but also began to be less culturally hegemonic. Boyer and Nissenbaum note that "the prosperity of the Town had polarized the distribution of its wealth and propelled into a position of clear dominance a single group of men: the merchants" (1974: 87).

Against this shift, traditional Puritan ministers began to fight back, emphasizing a theological argument that God had placed each person in the place in society where he or she was meant to stay and that to violate that order was to violate the will of God. Particularly odious to

the traditionalist ministers was the pursuit of wealth through trade
(Starkey 1949: 77). "Instead of devotion to a life of the spirit they saw
only a mad pursuit of gain by a people rotten with the sin of pride. . . .
At trade and its propagators they hurled their bitterest invective, for in
them lay one of the deep roots of malignancy" (Bailyn 1955: 139–40).

Meanwhile, as this social revolution was emerging, the
Massachusetts Bay Colony was simultaneously undergoing a political crisis. The charter granted to the Puritan colonists by the English
king had been revoked, the English governor of the colony had been
overthrown in a coup, and the colonists were living in enormous
uncertainty with regard to their political and economic futures until
the new governor arrived from England, bringing with him the
new charter. Land titles issued under the old charter were invalid,
contracts of all types were up in the air, and court cases could not
be legally tried until the new charter arrived from England. The
Reverend Increase Mather had been in England since 1688 trying
to negotiate the terms of the new charter and until he returned (in
the spring of 1692) the colonists lived under the cloud of dreadful
uncertainty. By the early 1690s, rumors bubbled through the colonies
that the new charter would not invest political power exclusively with
the Puritan Elect, but give power more broadly to the population of
merchants and tradesmen whom the traditionalist Puritans despised
and feared.

On a smaller, more personal scale, the inhabitants of Salem were
also facing uncertainty over their own economic futures. As Erikson
writes,

> the original settlers had measured their achievements on a yardstick
> which no longer seemed to have the same sharp relevance. New England
> had been built by people who believed that God personally supervised
> every flicker of life on earth according to a plan beyond human compre-
> hension, and in undertaking the expedition to America they were placing
> themselves entirely in God's hands. These were men whose doctrine
> prepared them to accept defeat gracefully, whose sense of piety depended
> upon an occasional moment of failure, hardship, even tragedy. Yet by the
> end of the [seventeenth] century, the Puritan planters could look around
> them and count an impressive number of accomplishments. Here was no
> record of erratic providence; here was a record of solid human enterprise,
> and with this realization, . . . the settlers moved from a "sense of mystery"
> to a "consciousness of mastery," from a helpless reliance on fate to a
> firm confidence in their own abilities. This shift helped clear the way for

the appearance of the shrewd, practical, self-reliant Yankee as a figure in American history, but in the meantime it left the third generation of settlers with no clear definition of the status they held as the chosen children of God. (1966: 156–7)

This social upheaval would play a critical role in the events in Salem in 1692.

Geography would also matter. Salem Town and the eastern part of Salem Village had access to the coast and the docks which played such an important role in trade. The western part of Salem Village, on the other hand, had less access to the coast and was mostly rocky and difficult farmland. In the emerging competitive economic system of mercantile capitalism, as those in Salem Town or close to it prospered while those in the inland areas of Salem Village floundered, the Puritans in 1692 were facing a world of great uncertainty on two levels: with regard to the future of the colony and with regard to their own personal futures.

Into this volatile situation came the man who would inflame the accusations of witchcraft. In 1688, the Reverend Samuel Parris arrived in Salem and the next year the Salem Village Church was formed with Parris as its minister. Parris was a polarizing figure from the very beginning of his tenure as the Village pastor. A failed businessman himself, he seemed to hold a grudge against the more successful of his parishioners and oriented himself, in terms of theology, stringently toward the traditional Puritan residents of Salem Village, particularly those living in the western half of the Village, farthest away from the corrupting influence of the town – and farthest away also from the economic opportunities centered on the seaport.

While no one person could be completely responsible for the Salem witchcraft hysteria, Boyer and Nissenbaum (1974: 163) document the extent to which Parris, and the social network surrounding him, played a key role in shaping the town's social structure so as to provide fertile ground for the tragic events of 1692. Parris galvanized the traditionalist Puritans around the anti-capitalist ideology.

As the pastor of the Salem Village (as opposed to the Salem Town) church, Parris strongly sided with the poor, the traditionally oriented Puritans, and the village-oriented members of the community. He was the moral center of the fight against the changes that were rippling through the community. From competing 1695 petitions to have Parris either removed from his post or retained in it, combined with data gathered from the Village tax records, Boyer and Nissenbaum found a division in the community with regard to feelings about Parris that was correlated with wealth. The pro-Parris faction was much less wealthy than the anti-Parris faction. Boyer and Nissenbaum's data shows that "the richest men in the Village opposed Parris by a margin of better than two-to-one, while the poorest supported him in almost precisely the same proportion" (1974: 82).

And it was in Parris's own household that the witchcraft accusations first emerged. In the winter of 1691–2, Parris's nine-year-old daughter, Elizabeth, and eleven-year-old niece, Abigail Williams, along with a small number of other girls, had been spending time with Parris's Barbados-born slave, Tituba, listening to the tales of magic and divination that she had brought with her from her homeland. As the winter wore on, the girls eventually began experimenting with magic themselves, creating a type of crystal ball from an egg white suspended in water for the purposes of fortune-telling. Importantly, given the economic turmoil which pervaded Salem society, Boyer and Nissenbaum point out that the girls' concern "came to focus on that point where curiosity about future love merged with curiosity about future status: the nature of their own marriage, 'what trade their sweethearts should be of'" (1974: 1).

In January 1692, the girls began to exhibit strange behaviors, "fits." The girls made animal sounds, crawled under furniture, screamed as if they were in pain, shook with seizures, babbled incoherently, threw things, acted as if they were flying, and engaged in all manner of violent and confusing actions. The initial response to the girls' behaviors seems to have been perplexity, but in mid-February the "diagnosis" of them began to emerge: the girls were being "afflicted" by witchcraft.

Boyer and Nissenbaum note that "the afflictions were beginning to spread ('plague-like,' as Parris later put it) beyond the minister's house; soon they would come to affect about seven or eight other girls as well, ranging in age from twelve to nineteen, and including three from the household of Thomas Putnam, Jr." (1974: 3). Putnam was one of Parris's staunchest allies and defenders – and one of the villagers whose fortunes had been negatively affected by the social flux inherent in the new economic order advancing in Salem.

The first three women accused of being the witches in question were the typical powerless and marginal people who might be expected to fall victim to these kinds of actions.

Three better candidates could not have been found if all the gossips in New England had met to make the nominations. The first, understandably, was Tituba herself, a woman who had grown up among the rich colors and imaginative legends of Barbados and who was probably acquainted with some form of voodoo. The second, Sarah Good, was a proper hag of a witch if Salem Village had ever seen one. With a pipe clenched in her leathery face she wandered around the countryside neglecting her children and begging from others, and on more than one occasion the old crone had been overheard muttering threats against her neighbors when she was in an unusually sour humor. Sarah Osburne, the third suspect, had a higher social standing than either of her alleged accomplices, but she had been involved in a local scandal a year or two earlier when a man moved into her house some months before becoming her husband. (Erikson 1966: 143)

As Boyer and Nissenbaum (1974: 32) document, however, by March a new type of accused witch was emerging – wives of prosperous freeholders, wealthy ship owners, a Harvard-educated minister, elected town officials, some of the most prominent people in Massachusetts. That is, after the first few accusations, the daughters of the relatively downwardly mobile Salem Village residents turned their accusations against precisely those people who represented the new order, those who had prospered under the rise of mercantile capitalism. The witchcraft accusations initially followed the fairly typical pattern of focusing on the marginal and disadvantaged, but quickly changed course and moved steadily up the social scale.

As Boyer and Nissenbaum document, the witchcraft accusations came from one side of the factional split in the town and were directed against the other side. The accusers, aligned with the Village pastor, Parris, and with one of the most traditionally Puritan – and economically and socially aggrieved – families, the Putnams, directed their accusations against the more prosperous, town-oriented faction organized around the wealthy Porter family.

Maps of Salem Village put together by Boyer and Nissenbaum from contemporary records show the locations of the residences of the people who were accused of witchcraft and of both their accusers and their defenders. Maps also show the locations of the residences of those signing the pro- and anti-Parris petitions. These maps give us a picture of the geographic split in the town. First, the accusers were concentrated largely in the western part of the village, most distant from the influence of Salem Town and most isolated from the economic and social opportunities provided by proximity to the town and the growing mercantile capitalism there. Most of the accused witches and the defenders of those accused, on the other hand, were concentrated in the eastern part of the Village nearest to Salem Town, especially along the prosperous Ipswich Road, and even over the boundary into the Town proper.

Second, it is clear that the pro-Parris areas of the Village were also those that produced the accusers while the anti-Parris areas of the Village were where those targeted as witches lived and where their defenders also resided. Boyer and Nissenbaum found that the "petitioners who lived nearest Salem Town (or, in a few cases, just over the Village line in the Town) opposed Parris by a ratio of six-to-one. Those whose houses were in the northwestern half of the Village, most remote from the Town, *supported* Parris by a ratio of better than four to one" (1974: 83).

Boyer and Nissenbaum (1974: 69) argue that the divisions in the Village between the increasingly impoverished traditionalists and the rising mercantile capitalists already existed before the witchcraft hysteria of 1692. It was that split in the community that explained the virulence of the accusations and the strange direction they took – going ever higher on the social scale. "To understand this intensity, we must recognize the fact – self-evident to the men and women of Salem Village – that what was going on was not simply a personal quarrel, an economic dispute, or even a struggle for power, but a mortal conflict involving the very nature of the community itself" (Boyer & Nissenbaum 1974: 103).

Using the same pro- and anti-Parris petitions from 1695 discussed earlier, as well as numerous town records, to map out the social network ties among the villagers, Boyer and Nissenbaum constructed a sociogram of some of the accused witches and their defenders. As we can see from figure 5.1, the accused were tied together through bonds of kinship, friendship, and business. But the structure was also vulnerable. If we take the sociogram provided by Boyer and Nissenbaum and transform the data into a matrix, we can discern an interesting pattern. Table 5.1 is the matrix translation of Boyer and Nissenbaum's sociogram, organized into structurally equivalent blocks. Structural equivalence is the subject of the "Closer Look" section of the next chapter, but for right now we can just say that nodes which have the same types of ties to the same other nodes are structurally equivalent. If you look at the matrix in table 5.1, you can

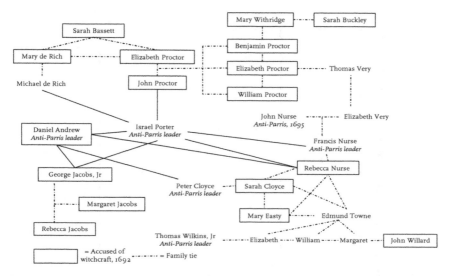

Figure 5.1 An anti-Parris network (Reprinted by permission of the publisher from *Salem Possessed: The Social Origins of Witchcraft* by Paul Boyer and Stephen Nissenbaum, p. 184, Cambridge, Mass.: Harvard University Press, Copyright © 1974 by the President and Fellows of Harvard College.)

see how the members of the four structurally equivalent blocks have somewhat similar patterns of relations to the other individuals in their group. In this case we can see four groups with somewhat high in-group density and very few out-group ties. (This is a symmetric person-by-person matrix so that the rows and columns are the same people in the same order. The main diagonal is blank because the individuals do not have ties to themselves.)

Table 5.2 gives the densities inside each of the areas of the matrix in table 5.1. We can see, for example, that the in-group density of the first group of structurally equivalent actors (Sarah Bassett, Mary de Rich, and Michael de Rich) is 0.667, meaning that about two-thirds of the possible ties among the members of this groups have in fact been made. (While Mary and Sarah are tied to each other and Mary and Michael are tied to each other, Sarah and Michael do not have a tie.) We can also see, for example, that this group has only two out-group ties with the second group (for a density of 0.083), only one out-group tie with the third group (for a density of 0.026) and no out-group ties with the fourth group (for a density of 0.000). In fact, we can see by looking down the main diagonal of the density matrix in

Table 5.1 Matrix translation of Salem witchcraft sociogram

	S	M	M	E	J	B	S	M	T	E	W	I	E	J	F	R	E	M	S	P	D	G	R	M	T	E	W	M	J
SarahBassett		I		I																									
MaryDeRich	I			I																									
MichaelDeRich		I		I							I																		
ElizabethProctor	I	I		I	I		I			I																			
JohnProctor				I	I	I	I		I	I	I			I															
BenjaminProctor				I	I	I		I	I	I																			
SarahBuckley						I				I																			
MaryWithridge				I	I						I																		
ThomasVery				I	I	I			I		I																		
ElizabethProctor				I	I	I		I		I																			
WilliamProctor				I	I	I				I	I																		
IsraelPorter		I						I							I						I								
ElizabethVery													I		I														
JohnNurse													I		I						I								

FrancisNurse
RebeccaNurse
EdmundTowne
MaryEasty
SarahCloyce
PeterCloyce
DanielAndrew
GeorgeJacobsJr
RebeccaJacobs
MargaretJacobs

ThomasWilkinsJr
ElizabethWilkins
WilliamTowne
MargaretTowne
JohnWillard

Table 5.2 Density matrix for Salem witchcraft

	1	2	3	4
1	0.667	0.083	0.026	0.000
2	0.083	0.464	0.019	0.000
3	0.026	0.019	0.269	0.015
4	0.000	0.000	0.015	0.400

table 5.2 that the in-group densities for all of these groups are much higher than any of the out-group densities. If we make a sociogram of these groups (rather than of the individual people in the groups) we end up with a picture like that shown in figure 5.2. There are internal ties within each group but very few or non-existent ties between the groups. (We will discuss exactly how group membership is determined in chapter 6.)

Although the network overall is fully connected, it is not a strongly integrated whole. Like the urban villagers in the West End or the white opposition to the Montgomery bus boycott (see chapter 3), the accused witches in Salem had strong ties that were concentrated mostly within their particular groups, but had little integration across the entire network. The social structure of the accused witches and their defenders might have been vulnerable to attack precisely because the individualistic ideology of the newly minted merchant class prevented them from organizing into a unified resistance.

Boyer and Nissenbaum paint a compelling picture of the witchcraft accusations as the result of a schism in the community between the new mercantile capitalists (represented by the Porter family) and the traditionalist farmers who felt left behind and who felt insecure

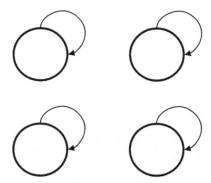

Figure 5.2 Group sociogram of Salem witches

about their futures (represented by the Parris and Putnam families). Witchcraft was a convenient finger to point at the other faction. The accusations began in the Parris household and quickly spread to the Putnam household. Boyer and Nissenbaum point out that "Ann Putnam, the twelve-year-old daughter of Thomas Putnam, Jr., was by far the most active of the afflicted girls, and a total of eight members of the family, drawn from all three of its branches, were involved in the prosecution of no fewer than forty-six accused witches" (1974: 103). The witchcraft accusations were an attempt by an increasingly marginalized faction in the Village to reassert the fading dominance of the traditional Puritan hierarchy.

Looking at the sociogram of the accused witches and their defenders in figure 5.1, however, shows one particularly glaring exception to Boyer and Nissenbaum's contention that the Salem witchcraft hysteria was an attack by one faction in the community against another. If this contention is correct, why was Israel Porter never accused? He was at the center of the anti-Parris network, was one of its leaders, and was one of the wealthiest men in Salem, the epitome of the new breed of men who were coming to dominate the political, economic, and cultural order in the village. And yet, unlike his close friend John Proctor, Israel Porter was never accused of witchcraft. Why not?

Boyer and Nissenbaum (1974: 188) propose one solution to this riddle. They argue that local deference to the most powerful man in the Village ran so deep as to protect him, at any rate, from accusations. Perhaps if the witchcraft scare had continued longer, even Israel Porter himself might have had the girls' fingers pointed at him. Certainly the picture presented in figure 5.1 gives an indication that the sharks were circling. But if we analyze more carefully the sociogram presented in figure 5.1, an interesting issue emerges: centrality.

As the "Closer Look" section of this chapter explains in greater detail, there are different ways of being central to a network. For instance, one could have a great number of ties in the network (**degree centrality**), one could be within a small number of steps of everyone else in the network (**closeness centrality**) or one could be a connecter among different nodes in the network (**betweenness centrality**). If we calculate these different types of centrality for the group of actors in the "anti-Parris network," we see that the person with the highest degree of centrality was Rebecca Nurse, who was accused of witchcraft and executed in 1692. In fact, of those in the network who were in the top six degree centrality scores (that is, having the greatest number of ties in the network), five of them (all but Israel Porter) were accused on witchcraft in 1692. Of the top eleven, all but two were accused. Overall, 59 percent of the people in the network were accused of witchcraft, but of the top six degree centrality scorers, 83 percent were accused, and of the top eleven degree centrality scorers, 82 percent were accused. It seems that having lots of connections in the network did not protect you from being accused of witchcraft – quite the opposite.

It is notable, however, that when we look at different types of centrality, the person at the very top in both betweenness centrality (being the connection between different people or groups of people in the network) and closeness centrality (being within very few jumps of everyone else in the network) was Israel Porter, the man who was never accused of witchcraft while those all around him were being attacked. In fact, of the top five betweenness centrality scorers, only 40 percent were accused – as opposed to 59 percent in the general population. Being the bridge between people or groups of people seems to have acted as a deterrent to being accused of witchcraft.

Closeness centrality is more ambiguous. Again, Israel Porter was the top scorer in closeness centrality and was not accused, but of the top five closeness centrality scorers, 60 percent were accused (about the same as the average population) and of the top six closeness centrality scorers, 50 percent were accused. The strengths, weaknesses, and advantages of the different types of centrality are discussed in greater detail in the "Closer Look" section below. For the moment, we can merely note that Israel Porter had a structurally very powerful position in the network because of his centrality so that even when the accusers were targeting those who had prospered under the new system, he remained immune.

As the witchcraft hysteria came to an end in the fall of 1692, it seems likely that it was the girls' overreaching into parts of the social structure that should have been immune that played a key role in the demise of their power. Starkey writes that

[m]ore than protest was causing the collapse of prosecution. The voice of reason had after all been lifted long before, but until now it had been a voice crying in the wilderness. That it was heeded at last was due to the fact that the devil had now progressed to the stage of total war. Literally no one was safe. No degree of eminence insured one against accusation. Recently the girls had cried out on the spirited Lady Phips, who in the absence of her husband had the daring to sign a release for one prisoner

personally known to her. All very well for the judges to tell the girls that they had made a mistake, as they had done when Willard was accused, but when they had done this just so many times, the line between mistaken and true accusation became obliterated. (1949: 219)

An analysis of the social networks in Salem at the end of the seventeenth century seems to indicate that the witchcraft hysteria there was a war of the defenders of traditional Puritan ways against the rise of mercantile capitalism and its agents. The accusers were on the losing side of history, even if for a moment they had seemed to be winning the battle.

The witchcraft hysteria happened with such virulence in Salem because the town was already divided into factions and the accusations provided those who were in a socially vulnerable position in the social structure with a weapon to try to increase their own status and the status of those in their group. The "us vs. them" social network structure that already existed in the town was the reason for the witchcraft hysteria. It was only an expression of the already extant social structural divisions. Strangely enough this same dynamic played out in almost the same geographic area three centuries later.

Arson and the Indochinese in East Boston

In the 1980s, a series of suspicious fires burned down the homes of several families of Indochinese refugees in East Boston. "On May 7, 1983, two twelve-year-old boys set fire to a six-family duplex at 404 Meridian Street ... The fire destroyed the house, the historic neighborhood settlement house next door, and damaged four houses across the street. Sixteen families were left homeless, all but one of them Vietnamese" (Feinberg 1985: 46–7). Further fires occurred on September 10, 1983; January 22, 1984; February 18, 1984; and March 31, 1984. All of the fires affected the Indochinese refuges who had recently relocated to the area.

> In ten months, 32 Indochinese families were left homeless as a result of fire. If each family had between three and five people, about 100 to 150 refugees were displaced. If the estimate of about 1200 Indochinese in East Boston is accurate, then 8 to 15 percent of the Indochinese population in East Boston was burned out in ten months. A similar proportion of East Boston as a whole would equal three to five thousand peop' (Feinberg 1985: 47)

The arson in East Boston was in many ways a modern-day witch-hunt and the community structure that facilitated the fires was remarkably similar to the social structure in Salem.

Like Salem in the seventeenth century, East Boston, a mostly working-class area adjacent to Logan Airport, was undergoing change. A decline in local industry meant that many residents were now commuting outside the area to work, and court-ordered busing to integrate schools meant that many children were attending schools away from their own neighborhoods. Both of these developments put pressure on the local community to shore up the solidarity of network ties that might otherwise have weakened. Most importantly, gentrification was occurring and this meant that the old neighborhoods were being infiltrated by young professionals and minorities. Local residents often perceived themselves and their way of life as being under attack by outsiders, and on a few occasions, there had been violent racial disturbances in the area (Feinberg 1985). Although the residents of East Boston were as physically proximate to each other as they had always been, the *cohesion* of the community was weakening.

In the early 1980s approximately 1,000 Vietnamese and 200 Cambodian refugees settled in the area. Shortly after, the fires began to break out. Long-time residents of East Boston blamed the fires on the Indochinese refugees themselves, claiming that the refugees were careless, negligent, and ignorant of how to use modern appliances – especially kitchen stoves. The long-time residents claimed that the Indochinese were dangerous to live near and to have in the community.

In discussing the fires and the Indochinese with the long-time residents of the area, Feinberg found that the residents used language to describe the refugees that could easily have been applied by the traditionalist Puritans to their rising mercantile capitalist neighbors: "the refugees are a threat, they live differently than others, they need to be taught how to live properly, they do not value the same things we do" (1985: 49).

The fires were concentrated mostly in the Meridian Street neighborhood of East Boston. Feinberg looked at three different theories to explain racism – the interest, contact, and neighborhood decline theories (Feinberg 1985: 2–5) – and found that none of them could explain the variation in active racism – arson – among the three neighborhoods. Instead, Feinberg argues that it is the differing social structures of the neighborhoods that account for the differences among them with regard to the level of arson directed against the Indochinese. Each neighborhood had a similar number of Indochinese residing within it, each had approximately equivalent socio-economic status, but the social networks of the neighborhoods were profoundly different.

In Meridian Street, where the majority of the fires occurred, Feinberg (1985: 85–7) found a divide between two groups of residents: the "Churchers" and the "Toughs." The Toughs had lived in the area for decades or even generations. Their social network was large and dense with many multiplex ties built up from kinship relations, work relations, friendships, joint organizational memberships, and all types of chance meetings and encounters in the neighborhood over the course of many years. As long-time residents of the area, the Toughs were particularly hostile to what they saw as invasion from outsiders, especially the gentrifying newcomers who had preceded the settlement of the refugees in the area. Once the Indochinese arrived, the Toughs adopted hostile and resentful attitudes toward them. About the Toughs, Feinberg writes that informal

> mechanisms restrict Toughs from either forming ties with the Indochinese or Churchers, or adopting similar attitudes to those of the Churchers. One male Tough who was invited to a neighborhood barbecue between the refugees and their neighbors, said, "They breed cats and skin them. They had this barbecue and invited all the neighbors. They were real nice. I wouldn't go. People were telling us: You going to eat that food?" The resident, who said he was probably going to go until he talked to his neighbors, shows the social control mechanism by which these networks and groups maintain their solidarity. (1985: 91–2)

The other faction in the Meridian Street area was the Churchers, who were somewhat new to the area, having moved into East Boston within the last ten years before the arrival of the Indochinese. Mostly members of the local Lutheran church and affiliated with the Southeast Asian Refugee Task Force, the Churchers were tolerant and even welcoming to the Indochinese. Although their network was not quite so dense as the network of the Toughs, the Churchers were still an integrated group. They had kinship, friendship, and neighbor ties. Some of the women got together to participate in a regular clay-crafting class in a neighbor's house. And, of course, they were drawn together by participation in the Lutheran church.

Feinberg found that the Churchers were also drawn together by a shared dislike of the Toughs. "Not only are the crystallizing effects of

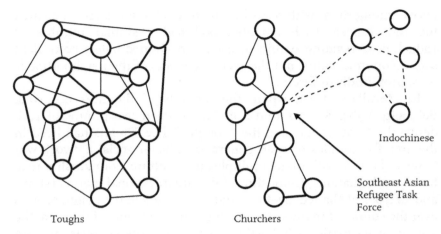

Figure 5.3 Meridian Street

the task force responsible for the Churchers' sympathetic attitudes, but also the presence of the Toughs themselves. The Churchers define themselves largely in opposition to the Toughs and their views" (Feinberg 1985: 89). That is, because the Toughs were so hostile to the Indochinese, the Churchers, who disliked the Toughs, were *more likely* to be supportive of the refugees. This makes perfect sense from the perspective of balance theory, which states that a shared dislike can draw two members of a triad closer together.

Between the Churchers and the Toughs, even before the Indochinese arrived, there was a gulf of negative feeling, resentment, and hostility where each group defined itself in opposition to the other. Feinberg calls the social structure of the Meridian Street area a "divided network" (1985: 135). It was in this neighborhood that the vast majority of the arson against the Indochinese took place. Figure 5.3 is a sociogram of the Meridian Street neighborhood.

The second neighborhood that Feinberg investigated was Princeton Street, which he describes as a "fragmented network" (1985: 135). There was much greater residential mobility in and out of the neighborhood than there had been on Meridian Street and many of the residents were relatively new to the area. Partly because of this, there was no division between factions on Princeton Street as there had been on Meridian Street. In fact, there seemed to be very few ties between the residents at all. The one institution in the area that had drawn the residents somewhat into contact, a dry cleaner's run by a

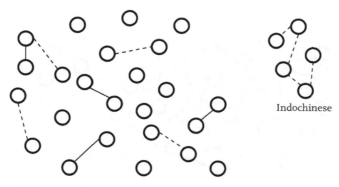

Indochinese

Figure 5.4 Princeton Street

man named Jimmy Dee, had closed up just as the Indochinese were starting to move into the area. Feinberg found a few dyads and triads, but overall, the residents of this area were disconnected from their neighbors except in the most casual ways. Figure 5.4 is a graphic representation of this structure.

The Princeton Street residents had as many racist opinions and attitudes toward the Indochinese as did the Toughs, but Feinberg found that this racism remained passive – all talk, no arson. The explanation that Feinberg puts forward for the difference from Meridian Street is not based on the individual attributes and attitudes of the residents of Princeton Street, but rests instead on the difference in social structure in the neighborhood.

> The social network in the Princeton area is fragmented, as compared with that of the Toughs. Because of this, there is no unified opposition to the Indochinese; even if the racism became active in one small fragment or clique, it would not spread to and mobilize other cliques. Furthermore, no outside institution is perceived as penetrating the neighborhood on the refugees' behalf. The crystallizing effect of a clear internal enemy does not exist: there is no group of Churchers. (Feinberg 1985: 125)

The third area that Feinberg investigated was Jeffries Point. He described this area as having "an aura of still being 'tight', not having changed as much as other areas of East Boston, of retaining its old neighborhood feeling" (1985: 125). Like the Toughs in Meridian Street, the residents of Jeffries Point had lived in the neighborhood for many years and had a dense network of multiplex ties. Especially important were the large numbers of organizations, such as the Catholic church and various social clubs, that drew the residents

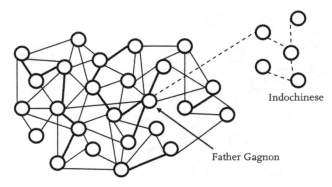

Figure 5.5 Jeffries Point

together. Missing from Jeffries Point, however, was any oppositional group, such as the Churchers in Meridian Street. The neighborhood was one cohesive whole. Figure 5.5 shows this social structure.

Feinberg found that although the residents of Jeffries Point were passively racist, they were nevertheless quite accepting and even sometimes generous and welcoming to the Indochinese. Part of this could be attributed to the presence of Father Gagnon, the local Catholic priest, who was an integrated part of the neighborhood network and saw it as his responsibility and Christian duty to provide help to the Indochinese in getting settled. As an "insider" in the dense local network at Jeffries Point, Father Gagnon's generally tolerant attitude toward the refugees had an enormous impact on the attitudes of the other members of the network. In this case, balance theory tells us that we should expect the attitudes in this tightly knit social world to be in agreement for the most part.

But an important part of the difference between Jeffries Point and Meridian Street was even more explicitly structural. There was passive racism in all three areas. Why did Meridian Street have so much more active racism? First, as in Salem, there was already an "us vs. them" situation. The Indochinese moving in gave the Toughs a good reason to show their hatred of the Churchers. They did this indirectly through attacks on weaker and less well-defended members of the community who acted as scapegoats for the larger issues at play. Again, this has similarities to Salem, where the attacks focused on those not quite as powerful as Israel Porter.

The Churchers and the Toughs both had formed their attitudes in opposition to each other. Again, we can see how the situation was similar to that of Salem in 1692. There was antagonism from the more traditionally minded toward those who seemed to be outsiders with regard to their ideology – those who pursued a new vision of what the community should be in the future. In both cases, the virulence of the situation was because the actors were fighting (sometimes actually to the death) over the identity of the community and over their own identities as they were connected with their place in the social hierarchy. In both cases there was a struggle over the power to define the terms by which status would be assigned. In both cases, those on the losing side of that battle resorted to violence against their opponents. But also in both situations, the weaker members of the group were targeted as proxies for the real targets who were too powerful to come under direct assault themselves. In both situations, the fragmented community structure resulted in violence directed at one group by the other.

As a final example of a fragmented community, we can turn to the extreme instance of social atomization in a community when it was faced with extraordinary pressures – Nazi Germany. Allen (1984) gives a detailed history of the Nazi seizure of power in one town in central Germany, but the process he documents occurred repeatedly throughout Germany during the 1920s and 1930s.

Isolation and atomization in Germany

One common question about Nazism is why there was so little protest from the German people about Nazi policies and programs. Or the flip-side of that: how could something so horrible have happened in a modern, civilized country? How could horrors on such a large scale affect so many lives with so little reaction or resistance? What Allen shows us in his study of Northeim, one small German town, is that the answer to that question is a structural answer.

Allen starts by pointing out some of the pre-Nazi cleavages that existed in Northeim as well as some of the organizations that drew people together, painting a picture of the social network structure of the town. First, there were cleavages among the townspeople based on: politics (right wing vs. left wing), social class (workers vs. the bourgeoisie), employment (stable government workers – especially civil servants – and small business people vs. unstable seasonal workers), and length of residence (newcomers vs. old timers). As in Salem and East Boston, there were divisions that had existed long before any crisis made them suddenly salient. As with the urban villagers of the West End, these cleavages were not problematic until outside pressures made them so.

The town also had some unifying features, such as the political dominance of the SPD (Social Democrats) and the numerous social clubs. Club life was vibrant in Northeim and there was a plethora of all types (military, sports, political, choral, drinking clubs, etc.), which were segregated by social class, however.

Allen tells us that "[f]or Northeimers who were neither workers nor Socialists, the real social cohesion was supplied by clubs. There is a proverb: 'Two Germans, a discussion; three Germans, a club.' This was almost true of Northeim where, in 1930, there were no fewer than 161 separate clubs, an average of about one for every sixty persons in the town" (1984: 17). These clubs included sports clubs, occupational associations, religious and charitable societies, veterans' clubs and hobby groups. Almost all of the clubs were separated along class lines so that there would be different clubs for workers and for the middle class. One of the most important features of these clubs was the closeness and mutual trust that the members had with each other. Conversation was free-flowing among people who had known each other for a long time and could rely on each other.

This was the starting point for the entrance of the Nazis. The town was organized by all of the clubs and other associations, but was fragmented because these organizations did not cross class lines – or integrate community members into any type of cohesive whole. If we were to draw a sociogram of the town of Northeim, it would look very similar to the one we drew for the Salem anti-Parris network – cliques with internal cohesion, but relatively few connections among them. As we saw in Salem, this type of structure makes communities vulnerable.

Also like Salem at the end of the seventeenth century, Northeim found itself in a period of great uncertainty as the world economy began to collapse. It was this that allowed the Nazis to begin to gain a foothold in the town. Following the collapse of the New York Stock Exchange, the middle class in Northeim, although not immediately negatively affected themselves, began to entertain not only enormous fears about their own futures, but also radical solutions for those fears.

Businessmen whose own enterprises were doing well worried about the general situation in Germany. Banks that had no difficulty collecting on loans began to reduce all credit allotments. Only the workers were directly hurt, but the rest of the townspeople, haunted by the tense faces of the unemployed, asked themselves, "Am I next?" "When will it end?" Because there were no clear answers, desperation grew. In this situation, the voice of the Nazi began to be heard. (Allen 1984: 24–5)

The fear of the effects of the Depression was more motivating than were the real effects. We can see the fear itself as an expression of the extant cleavages in the town. If the people in the town had had more actual contact with the seasonal workers who were first to experience the effects of the Depression, they would have known the reality rather than letting themselves imagine the worst. Further, the fear that the middle class had of the revolutionary left wing led directly to the formation of the first Nazi cell, which was middle class and staunchly anti-communist.

Organized in 1922, the first Nazi cell in Northeim was a tiny group made up mostly of middle-class young men. One of the key members was Wilhelm Spannaus, a 35-year-old bookseller who had connections all over the town. As with Father Gagnon in Jeffries Point (but much more malignantly), Spannaus's connections in the town meant that his ideas could spread more easily throughout the network than would have been possible for the ideas of outsiders.

Wilhelm Spannaus came from an old Northeim family; his father owned the town's first bookstore. ... Wilhelm Spannaus was exceedingly well liked in Northeim. A spare, lively man, he was gentle and kindly, friendly to everyone yet thoughtful and reserved enough to hold people's respect. His bookstore was the intellectual center of the town, for he was acquainted with many of the writers and poets the town admired, and he was chairman of the Northeim Lecture Society. In addition, he was a prominent member of the Lutheran church. "Wilhelm Spannaus bears a heavy burden, for it was mainly his example that led many people to join the NSDAP," remarked one Northeimer. "People said, 'If he's in it, it must be all right.'" (Allen 1984: 32–3)

Spannaus's central position in the Northeim network was crucial to the initial success of Nazism. Because he had ties which bridged many different groups in the town, knew many people, and had relations that reached to all parts of the community – that is, he had high betweenness, degree, and closeness centrality – he could disseminate his ideas widely and they were accepted as trustworthy by those who came in contact with them. It seems as though chance and luck

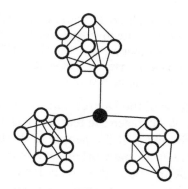

Figure 5.6 High betweenness centrality coupled with group marginality

helped out the Nazis here, yet this was somehow happening all over Germany. This is because there is a structural reason to explain all of this – it was structure, not luck, which was activating this process.

After the initial group of middle-class men formed the first Nazi cell, the next wave of members came from a much more marginalized population. Many of those who voted for the Nazis in the September, 1930, elections, for example, had not bothered to vote in previous elections, even though they were not newly qualified voters. This makes sense from a network analytical perspective. One of the interesting implications of balance theory is that marginal people – those disconnected from the influences that percolate through structurally balanced networks – would be more likely to hold extreme views. They are not very likely, though, to be able to spread those views to others, precisely because they are so disconnected. There is, however, one type of centrality that is both marginal to cliques and still central to networks; people with high betweenness centrality scores can be both marginal and central. High betweenness centrality is often found when people connect different social groups by being in none of the groups very deeply. The bookseller Wilhelm Spannaus may have been placed in just such a structural position as depicted in figure 5.6. The darkened node has high betweenness centrality since it connects the three separate cliques, but it is marginal to all of them.

Once the Nazis had gained a foothold in Northeim, the next step was to work on consolidating their power. Fear was still the key ingredient in this phase, which occurred in the first few months after Hitler was appointed chancellor. And the reality was that Northeimers had much to fear. The Nazis, once they had gained some power, began a program of intimidation and physical violence against the German citizenry. There were searches of people's homes and seizures of any weapons (like hunting rifles) that were discovered. And Northeimers feared being sent to concentration camps, including one that was located very close to the outskirts of the town. Street violence was on the increase and it seemed to many Northeimers that it was only a random chance whether they would fall victim to it or not. But the ruthless and arbitrary nature of the terror increased its effectiveness. Allen argues that " if Northeimers came to believe implicitly that they might expect no mercy from their new Nazi rulers, then later terrorism would not be needed. The initial investment of terror would multiply itself through rumor and social reinforcement until opposition would be looked upon as wholly futile" (1984: 184).

One of the most important effects of this was the breakdown in trust. No one knew who would inform on whom in order to save his own skin from the Nazi persecution. Rumors flew through the town regarding who might or might not be an informer, but without precise information, the rumors only added to the general atmosphere of fear. The further effect of the breakdown of trust was the end of social group life. Fearing that their former friends and comrades might now be Nazi informers, Northeimers felt it was safer to stay at home and the conviviality of the social clubs withered.

This fits with Hannah Arendt's observation in *The Origins of Totalitarianism*: "It has frequently been observed that terror can rule absolutely only over men who are isolated against each other and that, therefore, one of the primary concerns of all tyrannical government is to bring this isolation about. Isolation may be the beginning of terror; it certainly is its most fertile ground; it always is its result" (1973: 474).

An important part of this isolation, Arendt argues, is the destruction of public life.

> Totalitarian government, like all tyrannies, certainly could not exist without destroying the public realm of life, that is, without destroying, by isolating men, their political capacities. But totalitarian domination as a form of government is new in that it is not content with this isolation and destroys private life as well. It bases itself on loneliness, on the experience of not belonging to the world at all, which is among the most radical and desperate experiences of man. (1973: 475)

As public life in Northeim disappeared under the cloud of distrust and fear, the citizens there became isolated and atomized, unable to trust each other enough to organize any resistance to the Nazis. It became, Allen writes, "every man for himself" (1984: 191).

Now we start to see why there was never any protest against the slow infiltration of the Nazis. Allen asks:

> What was the Northeimer Social Democrat to do? Rebel? Even if one had weapons, whom was one to shoot? Policemen? Every Nazi (including those you went to grade school with)? And when? Which one of the various small acts exactly tipped the scale toward a dictatorship? And who was to rebel with you, since the factor of distrust entered in? And what then? Was Northeim to declare itself an independent entity within Germany? (1984: 200)

The infiltration of the clubs was the most important aspect in controlling the whole society and in stifling all dissent. Eventually, all the clubs in Northeim were taken over by the Nazis and reorganized so that independent groups ceased to exist. From the summer of 1933 on, all clubs became official parts of the Nazi system. Rather than the profusion of shooting clubs, drinking clubs, choral societies, and so on that had characterized the gregarious social life in the town, now all clubs were officially organized and overseen by the Nazi government officials. Under this system, the trust and free flow of discussion that had formerly characterized these gatherings quickly withered away. "What was the value of getting together with others to talk if you had to be careful about what you said? Thus to a great extent the individual was atomized. By the process of *Gleichschaltung* [reorganization of the clubs under Nazi control] individuals had a choice: solitude or mass relationship via some Nazi organization" (Allen 1984: 232). Meetings still happened in Northeim. In the winter of 1938–9, for example, there was an average of one meeting every three days (Allen 1984: 283), but these were not the convivial gatherings of old friends that had characterized pre-Nazi Northeim. Instead, they were organized by the local Nazi government and attendance was mandatory. Local group leaders checked to see that Northeimers attended meetings, but also saw to it that informal socializing was kept to a minimum.

The new structure of Northeim was built on the fragmented nature of the pre-Nazi community, but carried the fragmentation to the furthest point – the point where every individual was isolated from every other one. Now the structure, built on distrust and fear, looked like figure 5.7. Like the residents of Princeton Street that Feinberg

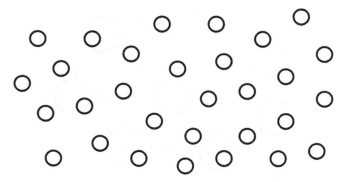

Figure 5.7 Northeim after the Nazi seizure of power – atomized and isolated

studied, the residents of Northeim were structurally unable to act on their feelings or desires, no matter what those were.

This structure, which characterized the third phase of the Nazi seizure of power, was eminently suited to totalitarian domination. While fear still played a role in organizing the community, the over-riding sentiment now, according to Allen, was apathy. Now that attendance at Nazi events was compulsory, enthusiasm for them dwindled. Moreover, the sheer number of meetings meant that Northeimers had little time left (even if they had inclination) for any other types of gatherings. Through atomization and isolation of individuals, the Nazis aimed to routinize apathy and mindless compliance. Exhausted and alone, the Northeimers no longer had any means to resist the Nazi government.

As we have seen, communities can be fragmented along many lines. In Salem, East Boston, and Northeim, the divisions that already existed within the communities were the dry kindling that burst into flames once a spark – such as the arrival of the Indochinese refugees – touched off the volatile mixture of ignorance, fear, and resentment. In communities where the social networks were split into differ-ent camps and where, as a result, an "us vs. them" mindset already permeated the area, the situation was ripe for attacks on scapegoats – "witches," foreigners, minorities, or any other vulnerable group that could be demonized by those looking to gain, regain, or hold onto power. The results can be tragic.

The fragmented structure of the communities, moreover, could also mean that people of good will were powerless to resist the actions that they saw occurring around them. Looking at figure 5.7, we can

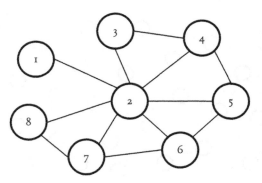

Figure 5.8 Degree centrality

see that because the network is no longer connected, there can be no actors who have any type of centrality. Central actors are important for organizing social groups. They often play a key role in organizing resistance and other types of social movements. In the next chapter, we will see how social movements, including those aimed at resistance, can be successfully organized at the community level.

A closer look: centrality

Centrality is a feature that individual nodes in a network can have to a greater or lesser extent. That is, an actor may be very central to a network or may be very marginal. Actors may also have different types of centrality. Three types that we have discussed in this chapter are degree centrality, closeness centrality, and betweenness centrality.

Degree centrality is a measure of the number of direct ties that a node has with others in the network. The nodes that are the most central are those that have the most of these ties. In figure 5.8, node 2 has a degree centrality score of 7.00 while node 1 has a score of 1.00. Because the size of the network obviously has a direct impact on the degree centrality score (bigger networks offer more possibilities of others to whom the actor may be connected), we can normalize the degree centrality score so that we can compare across networks by dividing by the size of the network. If a network has N members then each node in that network has a possibility of being connected to N − 1 others. If we call the number of others to whom the node is actually connected D, then D/N − 1 is the normalized measure of degree centrality – the number of actual direct connections divided by

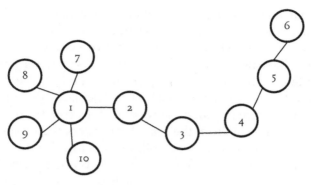

Figure 5.9 Closeness centrality

the number of possible direct connections. (UCINET then multiplies this number by 100 to interpret a fraction as a percentage.) In figure 5.8, node 2 has a normalized degree centrality score of 100.00, while node 1 has a score of 14.286.

Degree centrality is a measure of direct ties in the network, but indirect ties also matter. An obvious example is the study of the transmission of diseases such as STDs (sexually transmitted diseases). A node in a network of sexually active people would be very interested in knowing the health status of those to whom he or she is indirectly connected through shared sexual partners. Not only disease, but also information, ideas, power, influence, and so on are spread through networks by means of indirect ties. Closeness centrality is concerned with these types of ties. It is a measure of how close, on average, each network member is to every other member of the network. That is, how many jumps from node to node would it take, on average, for a node to reach every other node in the network?

In order to calculate the closeness centrality score for each node, we first need to define "**geodesic**." The shortest path between any two members of a network is called a geodesic. In figure 5.9, the length of the geodesic between node 1 and node 2 is 1. The length of the geodesic between node 6 and node 2 is 4.

The idea with closeness centrality is that nodes that have lots of short geodesics (or, more accurately, whose average geodesic length is small) are relatively close to the rest of the network while nodes that have lots of long geodesics (or whose average geodesic length is large) are relatively distant from the rest of the network. We compute the closeness centrality score for each node by summing the geodesics between that node and all of the others in the network. The higher that number, the *farther* the node is from the rest of the nodes in the network. In UCINET, we are given two scores – Farness and Normalized Closeness. To read the Farness score, remember that large numbers mean farther away from others. In the sociogram presented in figure 5.9, using UCINET to calculate the score, we find that the farness score for node 1 is 19 while the score for node 6 is 39. Node 6 is farther away from the rest of the others than node 1 is. The normalized closeness score (controlling as before for the size of the network) for node 1 is 47.368 while for node 6 it is 23.077. Node 1 is closer to the rest of the nodes than node 6 is.

There are a couple of caveats when computing closeness centrality scores. First, they only work if the network is fully connected. That is, every node of the network must be accessible from every other node through network ties. For example, if the tie between nodes 5 and 6 did not exist, there would be no way to calculate the distance of the geodesic between node 6 and any other node in the network. The number of steps that it would take to reach node 6 from any other node would be infinite. While it is easy to see on a small sociogram like this whether or not the network is fully connected, if you are inputting a matrix into a network analysis computer program in order to calculate centrality scores, it is a good idea to make certain that the network is fully connected first. The second caveat is that these examples are for symmetric matrices. If instead the ties had direction, we would have two closeness scores for each node – one for each direction.

A third type of centrality – betweenness centrality – looks at each node's position in the network with regard to the ways in which that node is the link between other nodes. If we look at figure 5.10, we can see that node 5 is the link between two different cliques in the network. Because of this position as the link, node 5 is of interest. It may, for example, act as a gateway for information between the two cliques and therefore command a certain amount of power. Or it may be in a unique position to meld ideas from both cliques into a new, creative synthesis. Node 5 is surrounded by what Burt (1992, 2004) calls "**structural holes.**" These are gaps in the network – ties that could exist between nodes but do not. Nodes that are surrounded by structural holes and have high betweenness scores can often occupy a brokering position in the network that gives them a lot of power.

For each node, the betweenness score is the sum of all of the

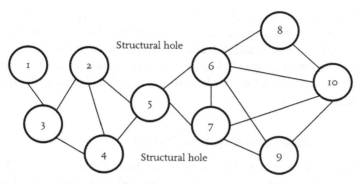

Figure 5.10 Betweenness centrality

geodesics that pass through that node. The more geodesics (short-est paths between other nodes in the network) that pass through the node, the higher its betweenness centrality score. As with closeness centrality, this score is obviously dependent on the size of the network and can also be standardized so as to compare scores across networks. Using UCINET to calculate the betweenness scores of figure 5.10, we find that node 5 has an unstandardized betweenness centrality score of 20.0, while node 1, of course, has a betweenness centrality score of 0.0. All geodesics connecting nodes on the left side of the network with nodes on the right side of the network must pass through node 5. No geodesics pass through node 1. The higher the score, the greater the betweenness centrality.

Each of these three types of centrality measures a different type of power, a different type of resource, and a different type of position in the network. In figure 5.11, node G has the highest betweenness

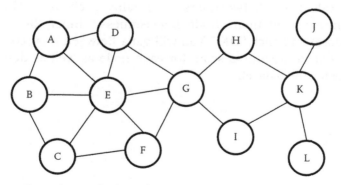

Figure 5.11 Centrality – who has it?

centrality and the highest closeness centrality, but node E has the highest degree centrality. Node K has fairly high betweenness because it is the link between nodes J and L and the rest of the network and also has the third highest degree centrality, after G and E, but has quite low closeness centrality because it is rather far away from most of the other nodes.

How to calculate centrality in UCINET6

Calculating these types of individual centrality scores in UCINET is very straightforward. Once you have entered your data into a matrix and saved it, click on "Network" at the top of the page and then choose "Centrality and Power" from the dropdown menu.

To calculate degree centrality, choose "Degree" and enter the name of your dataset. Decide if you want UCINET to treat the data as symmetric and whether or not to include the values along the main diagonal. Then click "OK." You will get both unnormalized and normalized scores for each node as well as descriptive statistics for the dataset.

To calculate closeness centrality, choose "Closeness," enter the name of your dataset and then click "OK." You will get both a Farness score (the higher the score, the farther away the node is from other nodes in the network) and a normalized Closeness score (the higher the score, the closer the node is to other nodes in the network). If the ties are directional, you will get two Farness and two Closeness scores, one for each direction. You will also get descriptive statistics for the dataset. If the network is not fully connected, you will get a message alerting you to that.

To calculate betweenness centrality, choose "Freeman Betweenness" and then "Node Betweenness." Enter the name of your dataset and click "OK." You will get a Betweenness score and a normalized Betweenness score for each node as well as descriptive statistics for the dataset.

6 How do communities mobilize for collective action and social movements?

There are many different types of collective behavior and social movements – from riots to peaceful protests, letter-writing campaigns, fads, fashions, setting up self-help groups, revolutions, and on and on. In this chapter, we will look at several different types of social movements and collective behavior to see how the structure of the communities played a role in organizing and shaping them. What are the structural characteristics of communities that engage in collective behavior? What types of network structures facilitate successful social movements?

Riots in Washington

Anthropologist Ulf Hannerz's *Soulside: Inquiries into Ghetto Culture and Community* (1969) is a study of the Washington, DC, ghetto based on participant observation in the community for two years – from August 1966 to July 1968. In April 1968, when Hannerz had been living in the community for 21 months, Dr. Martin Luther King, Jr., was killed by an assassin in Memphis, Tennessee, and the Washington ghetto erupted into violent riots as a response. Hannerz, by that time deeply embedded in the community, was therefore uniquely positioned to observe up close as the riots unfolded.

Hannerz's ethnography gives us the chance to look at the network attributes of the setting before the riots and to see how those attributes played a role in facilitating and shaping the riots. We will look specifically at ways in which the community was drawn together and ways in which it was divided. We will also examine ways in which the community was attached to the "outside" world and ways in which it was separated from it.

Hannerz was based in the Winston Street neighborhood of Washington's African-American low-income ghetto. Within the Winston Street neighborhood itself, a vibrant communal life was facilitated by a variety of commercial establishments.

> At the corners of Winston Street and the surrounding streets are small business establishments: groceries, liquor stores, carry-out food shops, variety stores, laundromats, shoeshine shops, barber shops, beauty salons; all very modest in appearance. ... The carry-outs, the barber shops, and the shoeshine shops serve not only their manifest function but are also the hangouts, the centers of sociability, of teenagers and adult men. (Hannerz 1969: 19)

These institutions of daily life provided a place for the small-scale interactions, the day-to-day exchanges, the informal give-and-take of network building to take place. Social life was built around the interactions that took place in a wide variety of venues.

Few of these businesses, however, were owned by blacks, although they often had black employees. And in some cases, the informal sociability was tempered by a certain cautiousness with regard to some topics of conversation. Hannerz quotes one of his informants who commented, "You know, nowadays if I see somebody in the barbershop I don't know I keep my mouth shut if somebody starts talking about politics. You never can tell if there's a Muslim or one of those black power people in there and they might jump you if you say something they don't like. I keep my mouth shut" (1969: 28–9). Although these small businesses provided an opportunity for socializing, they were not protected enclaves free from all dissent or safe from all outsiders.

Many of the small businesses were, in fact, de facto segregated along subcultural lines. Different bars, for example, were frequented by different age groups and by different categories of other patrons. "Other bars have become established in the public knowledge as hangouts for more specialized clienteles: gamblers, 'gorillas', homosexuals. Those ghetto dwellers who do not belong to such categories will usually avoid such places. There grows up an identification between people and the places where they hang out, and nobody would want to get an unearned stigma attached to himself" (Hannerz 1969: 31). With regard to network structure, the segregation of the

Table 6.1 Matrix of bar ties

```
| x x x x x
| x x x x
| x  x x x
| x x  x x
| x x x x x
|        x x x x x
|        x x x x x
|        x  x x x
|        x x    x
|        x x x x
|                 x x x  x
|                 x x  x x
|                 x x x x x
|                  x x x x
|                 x x  x
```

bars means that ties are built within the different segments of the
community, but not between segments. People in the bars become
structurally similar to each other in that they share the same patterns
of ties with the same others and lack ties of casual sociability with
those who do not patronize their same hangouts. But this is only
one dimension of the types of ties that the ghetto residents have with
each other. If we looked at *this one type* of relation in matrix form, it
might look something like table 6.1, which shows the general pattern
of ties which might exist between the members of the segmented bar
culture.

But ties made in bars were not, of course, the only types of ties
that existed in the ghetto. Much like the Jewish ghetto in Chicago
decades earlier (see chapter 4), the Washington ghetto was also in
many ways a community of immigrants who were drawn to the area
by previously existing social and kinship ties – ties that continued to
operate once the newcomers were settled into the ghetto (at least in
the first generation). According to Hannerz (1969: 25), about half of
the adults in the ghetto were born in either North or South Carolina.
A smaller fraction came from Maryland and Virginia, with only about
a third of the residents actually born in the District of Columbia. Ties
to their home states were maintained by many of the residents, who
visited back and forth with relatives still living there, and by a steady
trickle of newcomers from the south who migrated to Washington
and relied on their kin already in the area to help them get settled.

Kinship ties drew ghetto residents together, as did more informal ties of shared place of origin. These ties also connected the ghetto residents to the outside world – especially the outside world of the African-American community still living in the south.

Younger residents, though, had less strong identification and less strong ties to the places from which their parents came, or from which they themselves came at young ages. Increasingly, the younger generation was made up of people who considered Washington their home and who felt little cultural or social connection with their rural relatives. The structure of the school system, as in the Jewish ghetto in Chicago, also pulled the children increasingly out of the immediate neighborhood as they advanced from elementary to junior high to high school, where they come in contact with other students from a much wider area of the ghetto. So while these differences made a generational divide within the ghetto network, they also built ties of friendship that connected the younger generation more broadly across the whole area.

We see an interesting parallel and contrast to Wirth's study (see chapter 4) when we look at the experiences of those who begin to leave the ghetto. Ghetto residents who had done well economically and moved their families to better areas of the city often found themselves isolated from their new neighbors by racial prejudice directed against them by their new neighbors. Hannerz observes that for this and other reasons, ghetto residents tended to remain in the neighborhood, even when they might have relocated. "[O]n the whole," he writes, "the ghetto remains in many ways a community to itself without extensive ties of personal friendship with people in other parts of the city" (1969: 25). For most ghetto residents, the only outsiders with whom they regularly interacted were landlords, bosses, and the police – whites in positions of authority, often abusively so.

This meant that the pattern of ties was such that ghetto residents were more likely to have ties with people two or three states away than they were with people across town. There was no indiscriminate tie building of gregarious actors making numerous out-group ties, but instead in-group tie building with others who shared attributes similar to their own. These ties could stretch all over the ghetto.

> The Winston Street neighborhood is not a world to itself. As a neighborhood, it has its own web of social relations, but it is also a part of larger entities. . . . [Residents] have their interests spread out over the ghetto.

Table 6.2 Matrix of strong and weak ties

```
| x x x x x x   x        x
| x x x x x   x   x          x
| x   x x x                x
| x x   x x   x
| x x x x x        x        x
|     x     x x x x x   x        x
| x         x x x x x       x
|     x   x   x x x   x       x
| x           x x   x       x
|     x       x x x x
| x             x     x x x   x
|   x   x     x       x x   x x
|     x           x     x x x x x
|       x   x           x x x x
| x     x       x       x x   x
```

They may have lived somewhere else in it before, and they have friends and kinsmen scattered over it with whom they get together more or less frequently. They also make use of a number of ghetto locales which are outside their own neighborhood. The setting for their life in the community is thus wider than just the few blocks closest to home. (Hannerz 1969: 27)

Space and place played an important role in organizing social relations in the neighborhood. Areas like front stoops and street corners provided spaces for congregating and socializing for some groups – and were avoided as much as possible by other people for exactly that reason. Drinking, fights, and other loud and disturbing behavior that occurred in these public gathering places annoyed more quiet-minded residents and discouraged them from frequenting those places if they could at all avoid them – sometimes out of fear for their personal safety. As with the bars, some public places brought certain groups together and simultaneously separated those groups from others in the neighborhood. In terms of the structure of ties, we can see that although there were tight-knit cliques based on some types of relations (such as regularly drinking at the same bar), there were more widely dispersed webs when we look at other types of ties (such as kinship). Unlike the urban villagers of the West End of Boston (see chapter 4), this world had both strong ties within groups and a web of weak ties that stretched all over the ghetto and even outside it to a number of other southern states. Table 6.2 is an expansion of a matrix of ties in table 6.1 once we take into account the variety of relations that spanned the ghetto.

There were almost no *positive* ties between blacks and whites, however. "In the Winston Street neighborhood, at least, many more conversations about grievances dwell on white-owned businesses and the police; probably this is so because these are continuously present, represented by 'real people', on ghetto territory" (Hannerz 1969: 160). Black ghetto residents had no interaction with whites outside of those with whom they came into contact within a context of exploitation in the ghetto. "In his state of isolation from mainstream society, a ghetto dweller may well view institutionalized segregation as a direct expression of average white personal prejudice" (Hannerz 1969: 166). The resident of the ghetto had little other experience to counteract the idea that all whites were oppressors.

When there were interactions between whites and blacks, they were usually negative – but for the most part they were non-existent. Positive ties were only within the racial groups, both black and white, where information was passed around to shore up negative views of the other group. This network structure strengthened negative attitudes on both sides of the racial divide. And the experiences of the black ghetto-dwellers with white exploiters and oppressors certainly legitimized the negative view that they had of whites in general.

This was the situation when Dr. Martin Luther King was assassinated in April, 1968. Initially community leaders hoped to calm the anger from the ghetto community as the news filtered through the community from radio stations, telephone calls from friends and relations, and face-to-face communication on the streets. Crowds began to gather and local leaders, such as Stokely Carmichael and the popular radio DJ Nighthawk, urged the crowd to remain peaceful in memory of Dr. King. Despite their efforts, some people began breaking store windows and looting. Hannerz quotes one man who had been out on the streets at the time:

> You know, this thing had been building up for a long time, and so when something like this happens you can't just say, "Hey, cool it, it's dangerous." People felt they just got to do something, you know, and I guess most people don't believe too much in marching and that kind of stuff any more. (1969: 173)

That is, the injustices and inequalities to which ghetto residents were subjected had been simmering for years and the isolation that the residents felt from mainstream society gave them little hope that more legitimate and peaceful forms of petitioning for social change would be effective. The urban villager residents of Boston's West End did not realize that they were effectively disconnected from the mainstream society until it was too late and their neighborhood was slated for destruction. The residents of the Washington, DC, ghetto, however, were fully aware of their subordinate status and needed only the trigger event of Dr. King's assassination to unleash years of pent-up anger and resentment.

Residents of the ghetto had wide-ranging networks of both strong and weak ties and had the critical mass of numbers to make them feel safe in rioting and looting. Hannerz notes that a great many of the people who participated in the looting probably would not have done so had not the action been effectively condoned by the mass of people around them – their neighbors, friends, family members, and others whom they knew from the streets. Furthermore, during the first night of the rioting, the numbers of police on the streets were so small as to be ineffectual. Only when the National Guard and federal troops began to arrive the next day did the looting and rioting begin to quiet down. After two days, Hannerz writes, "looting and burning gradually ceased. Soldiers were standing guard outside the stores that were left, but along long stretches of the main business streets only ruins remained" (1969: 175).

Some of the contrasts with the situation in Northeim under the Nazis (see chapter 5) are clear. Unlike in Northeim, where the slow, step-by-step infiltration of the Nazis never provided a decisive moment to spark resistance, the assassination of Dr. King was the event that allowed the ghetto residents to release the pent-up rage that had been building for generations. Moreover, while the residents of Northeim would have had to turn on old friends and school mates whom they had known since childhood, the targets in Washington were white outsiders – or those white insiders who were particularly odious. In fact, ghetto residents scrupulously avoided damage to black-owned businesses. It is also important that although, as in Northeim, the ghetto gathering places – the barber shops, bars, and street corners – were segregated to certain particular groups, they nevertheless did at least exist and the trust that they engendered among their patrons was precisely what the Nazis had stripped from the Northeimers.

In contrast to those of the West End of Boston, the Washington residents had not only strong ties within their particular groups, but also weak ties that spanned the entire area. And while the West Enders perceived the leadership of the movement to block the redevelopment as coming from outside their world and therefore distrusted it, the participants in the Washington riots were very much insiders. Hannerz particularly notes how some participants in the looting would not have done it had they not seen others around them doing the same.

Finally, unlike the Jews in Chicago, the Washington residents were not an isolated minority, but had been the numerical majority in the city for about a decade when the riots took place. While the Jews moved out to nicer neighborhoods and gradually assimilated with mainstream American culture, racial discrimination against the Washington ghetto residents meant that they could not follow the same path. They stayed in the ghetto and maintained solidarity with the other residents there.

The Washington ghetto community rose up in two days of anger following the assassination of Dr. King, but to what degree were these really *urban* riots as opposed to riots that just happened to occur in an urban place? Did the urban setting itself influence the ability of actors to engage in collective movements? Do urban settings in general influence how those collective movements are organized and take shape and proceed? How do the special ways that cities affect the structure of social networks also affect how the social movements in urban situations emerge and proceed? In what ways does the *city-ness* of the situation affect what happens?

Urban revolt in Paris

Roger Gould (1995) looks at the importance of the urban context for the uprising of the Paris Commune in 1871. The Paris Commune has long been categorized as a workers' uprising against the regime of Napoleon III after France's defeat in the Franco-Prussian War, but Gould argues that it was actually an urban revolt facilitated by the ways in which urban networks were transformed and were structured in nineteenth-century Paris. The communal revolution of spring 1871 was, Gould argues, one of urbanites against the state rather than of one social class against another.

Gould's first argument is that the city-dwellers of Paris were forged into a united whole by a shared opposition to the French government, which they saw as having abandoned the city to Bismarck's army in the Franco-Prussian War of 1870–1. This shared opposition meant, Gould argues, a shared position with regard to grievances and with regard to ideology. Balance theory, of course, argues that members of a triad can be brought closer together when they share a mutual disposition to a third party. Gould takes this argument further, though, and argues that the shared position of opposition to the government in Versailles forged the Parisians into structurally equivalent actors. (Structural equivalence is the topic of this chapter's "Closer Look" section.) Gould writes that

> at the core of my argument lies the idea of "structural equivalence" – a relation among pairs of individuals that obtains if they are tied in equivalent ways to equivalent others, regardless of whether they are tied to one another. As anyone who has examined social networks knows, there are multiple ways (none of them perfectly satisfying the formal definition of structural equivalence) of portioning actors in a network into equivalence classes defined in this way – a fact that has proved immensely frustrating for scholars working in this area. But in the realm of social movements, this is precisely the point: mobilizing appeals compete with one another precisely because there are many ways in which people can view their social position relative to others. This is true not only because people linked by a particular set of social relations can be divided into subgroups in a variety of ways that satisfy the equivalence criterion equally well; it is also true because different kinds of social ties are accorded dramatically different amounts of salience from different ideological standpoints. The issue of conflicting loyalties (between friend and kin, family and employer, nation and church) is resolved as much through the ranking of the relations within which these loyalties are expressed as through a ranking of the actors implicated in these relations. (1995: 16–17)

It is not only ideology, however, that plays a role in forging structural equivalence – contact is key. It is the actual lived relations – real ties between real people – that allowed the Parisian city-dwellers to recognize their structural equivalence and to act on it. Participants in the Paris Commune risked injury, imprisonment, and even death. Like the participants in the Washington riots, Parisians would only be willing to participate in collective action if they were certain that sufficient numbers of others like themselves were also involved. And, in contrast to the residents of Northeim who were unable to mobilize (see chapter 5), the Parisians needed to have enough network ties formed through groups, clubs, and other informal associations both to get information about possibilities for participation in collective

action and to have a high degree of trust in the validity of that information. Individuals without network ties to others have no way of
forging either social or ideological solidarity strong enough to moti-
vate participation in risky collective action. Those who do have such
ties, however, not only receive information through them, but also, as
we have seen in other instances, use them to develop identities. As
Gould argues,

> critical events can set the stage for mobilization not because they create
> collective identities where none existed before but because they rearrange
> the priority ranking of social identifications that already matter to people
> in varying degrees. ... If events increase the likelihood of collective
> action, it is because they crystallize collective self-understandings – not
> by forging new ones but by attaching new significance to old ones. (1995:
> 19–20)

The role that clubs, associations, committees, and so on play in
facilitating and maintaining the networks that give rise to identities
should not be underestimated. But the memberships of these clubs
and so on, while forming strong ties of trust among the members,
cannot be allowed to remain in isolation. In order for the network
to be effective in mobilizing collective action, it must have not only
strong ties, but also weak ties that form bridges between various
organizations and that reach widely across the city. Gould argues
that it was the *physical* transformation of the city of Paris during the
1850s and 1860s that was responsible for giving the social networks
there the optimal form for revolution. Especially important was the
transformation of the urban space undertaken by Baron Georges
Haussmann.

Haussmann worked in Paris from 1853 to 1870 constructing
a system of wide boulevards that connected all parts of the city.
Outlying towns were incorporated as parts of Paris and the new
system of roads made them easily reachable from the city center.
All together, the number of streets in the city was increased by
almost 20 percent and the average width of the thoroughfares was
doubled (Gould 1995: 73–4). As part of this process, vast numbers
of workers were relocated from the center of the city to outlying
neighborhoods which were much less homogeneous with regard to
class or occupation. This meant that people began to form ties with
members of other groups as they were thrown together (for example,
in neighborhood cafés) with a variety of other Parisians. Finally, the

creation of the great public parks, the Bois de Boulogne and the Bois de Vincennes, was another factor that brought Parisians together for leisure. This "haussmannization" meant that the social networks of Parisians began to spread as ties were formed between members of groups who had formerly been kept rather separate.

As an example of this, Gould examined data about the witnesses present at marriages with regard to their social class and found that people who lived in the peripheral districts of Paris (in contrast to those who still lived in the central districts) had witnesses to their marriages from a variety of classes and occupations. They did show a decided preference for witnesses from their own neighborhood. That is, it was now place of residence, rather than social class or occupation, which tied people together.

Moreover, looking at the character of the social gathering places in the peripheral neighborhoods Gould finds the same phenomenon. The wine shops and cabarets in the peripheral neighborhoods served as meeting places for a mixed clientele of many different types of customers from the neighborhood. Gould argues that because there was not a critical mass of workers in any one particular trade or craft in the peripheral neighborhoods, the cabarets and wine shops instead catered to a wide range of people from many different occupations (1995: 121). This meant that in their leisure hours, Parisians living in the peripheral neighborhoods were now interacting with a broad range of others drawn together by physical proximity rather than occupational solidarity.

In addition, neighborhood meetings flourished in 1868–70. These meetings were on a variety of topics, mostly political in nature, and the attendees were heterogeneous with regard to class and occupation. The attendees were, however, drawn from the immediate or at least nearby neighborhoods. This was another way in which place of residence had become a basis for network building.

Movement out of the center had broken down some of the ties related to class and occupation, and forged ties that crossed these group boundaries. This same process, recall, happened with the Jews in Chicago (see chapter 4). But instead of stopping at the point in the analysis where in-group solidarity and ethnic identity had been damaged, Gould takes us further and looks at how that process opens up the possibility for forging a collective identity with the wider community. This wider collective identity forms the basis for wider collective action.

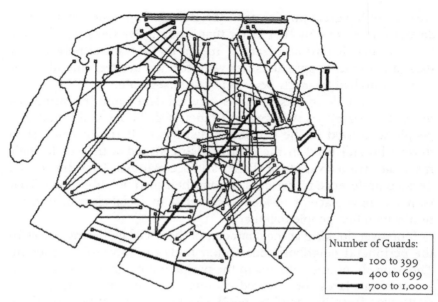

Figure 6.1 Numbers of National Guardsmen serving in legions outside their *arrondissement* of residence, by *arrondissement*: Paris Commune, 1871 (Gould 1991: 724, used by permission)

But how did all these little neighborhoods get tied together into the "city of Paris" during the 1871 Commune? One important factor was the movement of the National Guard. National Guard members were regularly recruited into regiments based outside of their own neighborhoods. Figure 6.1 is Gould's map of the Paris *arrondissements* showing the areas in which the National Guardsmen served and those in which they were residents during the Commune. The lines on the map represent ties between areas made up of the movements of hundreds of men. "The National Guard Federation thus created an organizational framework for a collective self-understanding among militants that was based on neighborhoods, yet citywide in scope" (Gould 1995: 156). As in the Washington, DC, ghetto, residents had strong ties within their own groups, but simultaneously had a larger web of weaker ties that spanned the city. This meant that there was strong social pressure within neighborhoods to ensure that residents participated in the insurgency while at the same time there was a cohesive city-wide organization.

Gould sees this as the result of the urban situation itself.

The shift in patterns of social ties during the urban renovations of 1852–70, the meeting movement and its relationship to the imperial police, and the experience of the siege [by the Prussian army during the Franco-Prussian War of 1870] had all provided the basis for a distinctive collective identity unrelated to class struggle. This identity was that of the urban community, defined and experienced explicitly as a spatially circumscribed and economically diverse collectivity in opposition to the central state authority. (1995: 176)

This opposition to the central state authority placed Communards from all over the city in positions of structural equivalence vis-à-vis the state.

Recruitment into collective action was, Gould argues, based not on individual motives, but rather on appeals to neighborhood solidarity (shored up by strong local ties) and also on the creation of an "insurgent identity." We have seen some of the ways in which communities create identities. These same processes were at work in the Commune of 1871. Individuals were positioned by their network memberships as parts of some groups and as oppositional to other groups. The wide-ranging pattern of ties gave the insurgents reliable information that they were not acting alone, but were part of a larger mobilization of others like themselves – others who shared this new, urban insurgent identity.

Recruiting high-risk activists

The creation of a shared activist identity is one of the key components in recruitment to high-risk activism. And ties to others – social networks – play an important role in shaping those identities. We can see this process at work in McAdam's study (1988) of volunteers to the Freedom Summer, a project sponsored by the Student Non-Violent Coordinating Committee (SNCC) in the summer of 1964 which recruited white college students to go to Mississippi for the summer to try to register black voters. In the atmosphere of racism and violence that permeated the American south, the volunteers were harassed, jailed, beaten, and in June three civil rights workers – Michael Schwerner, James Chaney, and Andrew Goodman – were murdered. How do participants get recruited into such high-cost and high-risk activism?

Participants in the Freedom Summer completed lengthy applications to the program. McAdam used the data from these applications to compare those volunteers who went to Mississippi with those who filled out the application and were accepted for the program, but who nevertheless withdrew before the summer started and did not go to Mississippi. In his analysis, McAdam found that for individuals to reach a point where they were willing to participate in the project involved a long process during which their social networks were slowly transformed so that, as with the Communards, an activist identity and explicitly activist networks eventually dominated the lives of the participants. Social pressure externally from the network of relations and internally from the activist identity combined so that participants were willing to engage in extremely risky and costly activism. McAdam argues that activists developed an activist identity that superseded all other identities because of the social ties that they made before the Summer Project and that were deepened and strengthened during the summer. These networks continued to function, in fact, even years after the end of the project.

The simplest explanation for involvement in a social movement is personal affinity. People who believe in the movement goals get involved; those who don't believe don't join. But as anyone who has ever tried to get others involved in even a simple form of social activism knows, belief does not necessarily always translate into action. From looking at the data of the applicants to the Freedom Summer, McAdam rejects the explanation that those who went were simply more motivated to do so. All of the applicants believed in the civil rights movement and all put in considerable time and effort to apply to the project in the first place. All wrote essays detailing their firm ideological commitment to the cause of racial equality. Why, then, did some participate in the Freedom Summer and some withdraw before it started? It turns out that network ties were an important factor in distinguishing between the two groups. From looking at the information on the applications, McAdam was led to ask: "were there ways in which concrete social ties served to 'pull' people into the project? The answer to this last question would appear to be 'yes'" (1988: 50).

One way that this happened was through prior involvement in less risky and less time-consuming activism. Signing petitions, attending teach-ins, going to marches, and – especially – belonging to campus political groups gave the Freedom Summer participants a network of other activists whose social support, McAdam argues, was decisive in separating participants from withdrawals.

For the vast majority of applicants, then, Freedom Summer did *not* mark their initial foray into the civil rights movement. . . . Extremely risky, time-consuming involvements such as Freedom Summer are almost always preceded by a series of safer, less demanding instances of activism . . . . In effect, people commit themselves to movements in stages, each activity preparing the way for the next. (McAdam 1988: 51)

These previous instances of activism prepared the participants for the next level by embedding them ever more deeply into networks made of activists. As contacts with other activists increased, so did the social pressure to conform to group norms and the social support to act on ideology. McAdam found that "personal ties between applicants were extensive. . . . And their accounts make it clear that these ties were important in their decision to apply to the project. Several even described their decision to apply as more a group than an individual process" (1988: 52).

As with the Paris Communards, these ties encouraged the formation of an "activist" identity. McAdam found that those applicants who had more and stronger ties to other participants were more likely to go to Mississippi. Those applicants, however, who did not have ties to other participants – or who had ties instead to other withdrawals – were more likely to withdraw. McAdam found that "no other item of information on the applications proved to be a better predictor of participation in the project than this" (1988: 63).

There were certainly reasons for even students who were strongly committed ideologically to the civil rights movement to consider backing out from the program, given the risk and cost involved. Social ties made the difference between those who did and those who didn't. McAdam argues that

[i]f one acted alone in applying to the project and remained isolated in the months leading up to the campaign, the social costs of withdrawing from the project would not have been great. On the other hand, the individual who applied in consort with friends or as a movement veteran undoubtedly risked considerable social disapproval for withdrawal. One can also stress a more positive interpretation of the same process. In the months leading up to the summer, well-integrated applicants were no doubt encouraged to make good on their commitment through the reinforcement and sense of strength they derived from other applicants. (1988: 64–5)

Moreover, the experience in Mississippi forged an identity that carried over in the participants' lives long after the end of the summer. These activist identities in turn, McAdam argues, shaped the communities that the individuals then went on to make. McAdam quotes one of the volunteers saying,

> I mean we really came back feeling that . . . [we] had been part of a new world . . . a new community, a new society . . . that was being born and you know all these people . . . and there were networks of people all over the place and . . . you really did feel very much a part of a movement . . . and you really felt you belonged to it. (1988: 137)

McAdam argues that, to preserve those activist identities and the new community that the participants felt they had created, the Freedom Summer participants went on to spark the sixties counterculture in the USA. Following the Freedom Summer, the participants were integral parts of the birth of the women's rights movement, the anti-draft and anti-war movements, the campus free speech movements, the anti-nuclear movement, and other progressive causes. Many of them joined the Peace Corps; many others became professional activists.

Network ties continued to be important after the Freedom Summer. McAdam writes that "Freedom Summer did more than simply radicalize the volunteers. It also put them in contact with any number of other like-minded young people. Thus, the volunteers left Mississippi not only more disposed toward activism, but in a better structural position, by virtue of their links to one another, to act on these inclinations" (1988: 190). The pattern of network connections makes possible effective action for which attitudinal affinity is just not enough. The structure of ties – between individuals and between the groups that those individuals form – can determine the efficacy of large-scale social movements and collective action.

Structuring connections

New York City was hit early and hit hard in the HIV/AIDS epidemic. By the time the Centers for Disease Control released its first report mentioning what would later be known as HIV/AIDS in June 1981, hundreds of New Yorkers had already contracted the disease and many had already died (Shilts 1987). The US government was remarkably unconcerned with the epidemic that seemed at first to affect only the most marginal members of society – gay men, intravenous drug users, and Haitians. It wasn't until February 1986, four months after his Hollywood friend Rock Hudson had died from the disease, that Ronald Reagan, the president of the United States, first mentioned AIDS in an official policy speech. By then, hundreds of thousands more people were infected, 36,058 Americans had been officially diagnosed, and 20,849 Americans were dead (Shilts 1987: 596).

In New York City, dense networks among those groups of people who first came in contact with the disease facilitated the spread of the virus. In his detailed account of the response by the New York community to the HIV/AIDS crisis, Lune writes:

> The city hosts a large, relatively open, relatively politicized gay community and a large, but mostly hidden, population of injecting drug users. The size of the two most vulnerable population categories in the early years of HIV/AIDS provided conditions for the rapid spread of the virus. The density of the social worlds allowed the condition to reach epidemic proportions prior to any significant anti-AIDS mobilization; exposure to HIV spread far more quickly than relevant prevention information. Yet the size and density of the most affected social groups also provided the conditions for an organized response – social networks with active channels for rapid communication, access to resources, activist histories, and a sense of collective social identity that occasionally included an explicit awareness of collective interests. New York City was therefore both the nation's epicenter for HIV/AIDS and the center of collective organizing in its wake. (2007: 7–8)

As we have seen already, though, dense networks, whether they are facilitating the spread of a disease, facilitating the spread of information, or facilitating the organization of collective action, can be inefficient. As long as the dense ties are segregated from the general population into one small group, they will only reach so far. Without weak ties to connect small groups to each other, STDs cannot spread – and neither can the information and organization to try to stop them. Without broad-ranging bridge ties to other groups, the citizens of Northeim were powerless to resist the Nazis (see chapter 5). Because their communities did have those types of ties, however, the Communards were able to organize the insurgency of 1871 and the Freedom Summer participants were drawn to Mississippi.

In the cases of Washington, DC, and Paris, we have also seen how the existence of a clear enemy helped bring together the different constituencies into positions of structural equivalence. (This is, remember, one way to balance a triad.) A similar dynamic was at work in the early years of the AIDS crisis. US government indifference to the crisis forged allies out of a variety of response groups. "Organizing around something often entails organizing against someone . . . . Diverse groups can find unity in their opposition to someone else even in the absence of stronger ties among themselves. . . . [T]he differences between groups within the field are less salient and less precise than the differences between the field of community-based organizations and the institutions of the state or industry" (Lune 2007: 30). Government indifference – and even hostility – to the early victims of the disease induced structural equivalence among those community-based organizations which, despite their different agendas and different constituencies, nevertheless banded together in the fight against AIDS.

The lack of government leadership meant that the original community-based organizations focused on a response to the disease came together in informal networks that were decentralized, but still connected. This decentralized structure, Lune argues, allowed the various organizations more flexibility to respond to their own particular issues and constituencies in ways that they might not have been able to if there had been more central coordination or agenda setting. Given the diversity of the populations who were initially affected by the disease, this flexibility was one of the strengths of the "urban action network" – Lune's terms for the coalition of non-profit community-based organizations which connected as a community in the fight against AIDS.

The urban action network was initially built on the base of informal social networks that already existed in the community. "The post-Stonewall gay community in New York had been active in political, social, and health issues, but it was relatively quiescent just prior to the onset of HIV/AIDS. One activist in the present study called this mobilization base a 'social network with no purpose' on which the 'incredible success of [early] AIDS work' relied" (Lune 2007: 8). These informal social ties that underlay the more formal organizational ties that sprang up meant that the urban action network, like the Washington and Parisian and insurgents, could have strong ties internally within their specific groups, but still be connected by weak ties all across the city. This network structure, which was so effective, was further developed, Lune argues, by the processes of *splitting, outreach,* and *enrollment* (Lune 2007: 152).

Splitting is the division of one organization into two or more. This can happen amicably, when subsets of members of one organization decide to concentrate their efforts on a particular project or direction and form a splinter organization to do so. Or the split can be less friendly and involve animosity among members. In either case, though, weak ties from former associations may still be present and, perhaps more importantly, third party organizations are now likely to be connected to both groups and to form indirect bridge ties between them. As Lune points out, "[s]plitting loosens bonds, but it need not sever them" (2007: 154). These weak ties, of course, are strong in their ability to link the various organizations together.

Outreach and enrollment both involve not the creation of new organizations, but the creation of new ties between already existing organizations. The creation of these ties creates bridges that, Lune argues, span structural holes. As Burt has argued (1992, 2004), spanning structural holes – gaps in the network – is of great benefit to those who manage to do so in terms of both the information that they are likely to receive and the innovative thinking in which they are likely to engage.

This innovative thinking, so crucial to addressing the epidemic that seemed to come from nowhere and to completely baffle medical science, was further enhanced by the marginality of the actors involved. Lune argues that mainstream and established groups were under more pressure to stay within traditional areas of action than were the more marginal groups. (Balance theory again explains why we should expect this to be so.) "The more 'connected' the other organizations were, the less willing they were to pursue controversial agendas" (Lune 2007: 46–7).

The three factors that Lune credits with allowing the innovative solutions to the HIV/AIDS epidemic to emerge were scope, novelty, and slack. Scope "refers to the diversity of the affected populations" (Lune 2007: 150). The diversity of groups affected by the epidemic meant that response organizations had a wide range of others to whom they could turn for support and resources. Novelty refers to the newness of the issues. Because so many of the responses to HIV/ AIDS were novel (such as "treatment activism" and "buyer's clubs" for medicines), Lune argues that the collective actors had more flexibility in finding new ways to organize themselves. "When an issue is new, innovation is encouraged and even required. Interorganizational networking within a policy domain can be more dynamic if there is no preexisting field of work defined around the issue or subsuming the issue" (Lune 2007: 150). Finally, slack refers to the lack of significant organized opposition. Lune argues that this allows the action network and the organization in it to develop as they see fit without having to respond, in perhaps deleterious ways, to hostile outside forces.

These were the key elements that Lune found for the success of the early urban action network around AIDS/HIV. Eventually, the US government was forced to take an active role in the fight against the disease and many of the original community-based response organizations modified their missions or ceased work entirely. However, their innovative organizational strategies left a legacy for future organizing as well as for the structure of the field of AIDS/HIV response. In the next chapter, we will look more broadly at the structures of community which encourage innovation and creativity on a variety of levels.

A closer look: structural equivalence

In their seminal paper, "Structural equivalence of individuals in social networks," Lorrain and White write: "In other words, *a* is structurally equivalent to *b* if *a* relates to every object *x* of *C* in exactly the same way as *b* does. From the point of view of the object of the structure, then, *a* and *b* are absolutely equivalent, they are substitutable" (1971: 63). What does this mean and how can it be useful to us?

Structural equivalence is concerned with an actor's position within the network – that is, with the actor's pattern of relations with others in the population. Nodes (actors) are structurally equivalent if they have the same types of ties to the same others. Figure 6.2 is an example of a friendship network.

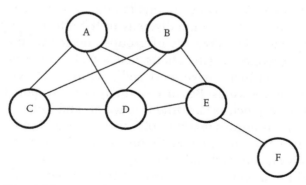

Figure 6.2 Friendship network

Table 6.3 Matrix of figure 6.2

	A	B	C	D	E	F
A		o	I	I	I	o
B	o		I	I	I	o
C	I	I		I	o	o
D	I	I	I		I	o
E	I	I	o	I		I
F	o	o	o	o	I	

A and B are friends with C, D, and E. They have the same ties (friendship) to the same others (C, D, and E). A and B are structurally equivalent. That is, they occupy interchangeable places in the sociogram. If you switched the labels with their names on the circles, it would not change the sociogram at all. C, D, E, and F, however, are not structurally equivalent because each of them has ties to a different set of others.

Inspecting sociograms to look for people with the same ties would be a laborious and error-prone process. The better way to find structural equivalence is to translate the sociogram into a matrix. Table 6.3 is the matrix translation of figure 6.2.

White et al. argue that it is the absence of ties that structures the relations in the network: "First, structural equivalence requires that members of the population be partitioned into distinct sets, each treated homogeneously not only in its internal relations but also in its relations to each other set. Second, the primary indicator of a relation between sets is not the occurrence but the absence of ties between individuals in the sets" (1976: 739).

This means that we can shuffle around the rows and columns of this matrix so as to make sets (known as *blocks*) of all os together (at least as much as possible). One way of doing this is shown in table 6.4. (Zeros have been added along the main diagonal to make

Table 6.4 Reordered friendship matrix

	A	B	D	E	C	F
A	o	o	I	I	I	o
B	o	o	I	I	I	o
D	I	I	o	I	o	I
E	I	I	I	o	o	I
C	I	I	I	o	o	o
F	o	o	o	I	o	o

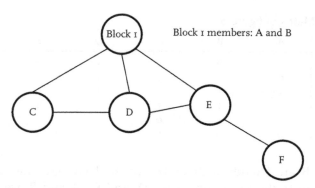

Figure 6.3 Collapsed friendship network

the blocks easier to see.) The nodes that have the same patterns of 1s and 0s (i.e., the same pattern of ties) end up next to each other in the matrix. Structurally equivalent nodes are now grouped together.

Why do we care about structural equivalence? For many reasons, two of which are that it can help in simplifying large sociograms and that it can give us clues about the attitudes and actions of the actors.

Figure 6.3 is the collapsed sociogram of figure 6.2. Those actors who are structurally equivalent – A and B – have been placed together into one block. We call that node block 1 and note that block 1 has two members – A and B. This is a way of simplifying the sociogram so that we can begin to see the structure of the relations. Collapsing the nodes in such a small network as this seems trivial. However, once the networks become larger, reducing the actors to structurally equivalent blocks allows us to picture the social structure of the network more analytically than would be possible with only the massive, unordered sociogram or matrix. Because the structurally equivalent actors share the same patterns of ties, we do not lose any information about the shape of the total network with the collapsed picture. Instead, we gain information about the individual actors involved – specifically, the actors acquire a categorical attribute: block membership. That is, we now know which actors in the network share the same pattern of ties.

Of course, in real life, very few people are *completely* structurally equivalent. No one has *exactly* the same pattern of ties as another person. In reducing a large sociogram, structural analysts have to make decisions about the number of ties that can differ between two nodes for them to still be considered structurally equivalent. Look again at figure 6.2. Do the nodes labeled C, D, and E have patterns of ties that are similar enough to consider them structurally equivalent? What about just C and D? In looking for structural equivalence in real data, we often group together actors that are *more or less* equivalent. Table 6.5 is the matrix of relations from Boyer and Nissenbaum's sociogram of the anti-Parris network in Salem, discussed in chapter 5.

As it stands, the matrix tells us very little. We can reorder the rows and columns, however, to maximize the number of zero blocks. Doing so gives us table 6.6.

Notice that not all of the zero blocks are completely free of all ties, but for the most part they are fairly empty. Table 6.7 gives us the densities of ties within and between the different blocks.

We can turn this density matrix into an **image matrix**. An image matrix uses 1s and 0s to show the relations among the blocks of structurally equivalent actors. Suppose we decided that in order for a block to be considered a zero block, it should be completely empty of ties – that it, it should have a density of 0.000. All other block densities will be coded as 1s. In that case, the image matrix for table 6.7 is shown in table 6.8.

We can now reverse the process by which we create matrices from sociograms and use the image matrix in table 6.8 to create a sociogram, shown in figure 6.4. (Note that we know the members of the individual blocks by reading them from the blocked matrix in Table 6.6.) This is a very highly connected looking network. However, when we look back at the original blocked matrix in table 6.6, we see that this image matrix doesn't capture the reality of the situation in the network very well. Block 3, for example, which appears in figure 6.4 to be connected to all of the other blocks, in reality only has significant in-group ties and a few scattered out-group ties. One way to handle this situation would be to indicate the strength of the connections between different blocks with heavy or dotted lines, for example. Another way to handle the reality of less than perfect zero blocks is to choose a cut-off point higher than 0.000 below which we will consider blocks to be zero blocks, even though they are not perfectly so. The lower we set that cut-off point, the less robust the pattern of ties in a cell of the matrix has to be in order for the cell value to be coded as 1. The higher we set that cut-off point, the more robust the pattern of ties in a cell of the matrix has to be in order for the cell to be coded as 1. In the case of the Salem data, the overall density for the matrix is 0.1133. Suppose we use that as our cut-off point? All cell values lower

Table 6.5 Matrix of the anti-Parris network

		1 SB	2 MD	3 EP	4 MD	5 JP	6 IP	7 SB	8 MW	9 BP	10 EP	11 WP	12 TV	13 EV	14 JN	15 FN	16	17	18	19	20	21	22	23	24	25	26	27	28	29
1	SarahBassett	–	0	1	0	0	0	0	0	0	0	0	0	0	0	0	0	0	0	0	0	0	0	0	0	0	0	0	0	0
2	MaryDeRich	1	–	1	0	0	0	0	0	0	0	0	0	0	0	0	0	0	0	0	0	0	0	0	0	0	0	0	0	0
3	ElizabethProctor	1	1	–	1	0	0	0	0	1	1	1	0	0	0	0	0	0	0	0	0	0	0	0	0	0	0	0	0	0
4	MichaelDeRich	0	1	1	–	1	0	0	0	0	0	0	0	0	0	0	0	0	0	0	0	0	0	0	0	0	0	0	0	0
5	JohnProctor	0	1	0	1	–	1	0	0	1	1	1	0	0	0	1	1	0	0	0	0	0	0	0	0	0	0	0	0	0
6	IsraelPorter	0	0	1	0	1	–	0	0	0	1	0	0	0	0	0	0	0	0	0	0	1	1	0	0	0	0	0	0	0
7	SarahBuckley	0	0	0	1	1	1	–	1	0	0	0	0	0	0	0	0	0	0	0	0	0	0	0	0	0	0	0	0	0
8	MaryWithridge	0	0	0	0	1	0	1	–	1	0	0	0	0	0	0	0	0	0	0	0	0	0	0	0	0	0	0	0	0
9	BenjaminProctor	0	0	1	0	0	0	1	1	–	0	1	1	0	0	0	0	0	0	0	0	0	0	0	0	0	0	0	0	0
10	ElizabethProctor	0	0	1	1	1	1	0	1	0	–	1	0	1	0	0	0	0	0	0	0	0	0	0	0	0	0	0	0	0
11	WilliamProctor	0	0	1	0	1	0	1	0	1	1	–	0	0	1	0	0	0	0	0	0	0	0	0	0	0	0	0	0	0
12	ThomasVery	0	0	1	1	1	0	0	1	0	0	1	–	1	0	0	0	0	0	0	0	0	0	0	0	0	0	0	0	0
13	ElizabethVery	0	0	0	0	1	0	0	0	0	1	0	1	–	0	1	0	0	0	0	0	0	0	0	0	0	0	0	0	0
14	JohnNurse	0	0	0	0	0	1	0	0	0	1	0	0	0	–	1	1	0	0	0	0	0	0	0	0	0	0	0	0	0
15	FrancisNurse	0	0	0	0	0	0	0	0	0	0	0	0	1	1	–	1	0	0	0	0	0	0	0	0	0	0	0	0	0

```
o o o o o o o o o o o o ı o
o o o o o o o o o o o ı o ı
o ı o o o o o o o o ı o ı o
o o o o o o o o o ı o ı o o
o o o o o o o o o ı o o o o
o o o o o o ı o ı o o o o o
o o o o o o ı o ı ı o o o o
o o o o o ı o ı ı o o o o o
ı o o o ı o ı o o o o o o o
o o o ı o ı o o o o o o o o
ı ı ı o ı o o o o o o o o o
ı ı o ı o o o o o o o o o o
ı o ı ı o o o o o o o ı o o
o ı ı ı o ı o o o o o o o o
ı o o o o o o o o o o o o o
ı o o o o o o o o o o o o o
o o o o o o o o o o o o o o
o o o o o o o o o o o o o o
o o o o o o o o o o o o o o
o o o o o o o o o o o o o o
o o o o o o o o o o o o o o
o o o o o o o o o o o o o o
ı o o o o ı ı o o o o o o o
o o o o o o o o o o o o o o
o o o o o o o o o o o o o o
o o o o o o o o o o o o o o
o o o o o o o o o o o o o o
o o o o o o o o o o o o o o
```

16 RebeccaNurse
17 EdmundTowne
18 MaryEasty
19 SarahCloyce
20 PeterCloyce
21 DanielAndrew
22 GeorgeJacobsJr
23 RebeccaJacobs
24 MargaretJacobs
25 ThomasWilkinsJr
26 ElizabethWilkins
27 WilliamTowne
28 MargaretTowne
29 JohnWillard

Table 6.6 Blocked matrix of the anti-Parris network

	1 S	2 M	4 M	3 E	5 J	9 B	7 S	8 M	12 T	10 E	11 W	6 I	13 E	14 J	15 F	16 R	17 E	18 M	19 S	20 P	21 D	22 G	23 R	24 M	25 T	26 E	27 W	28 M	29 J
1 SarahBassett		I	I																										
2 MaryDeRich	I		I																										
4 MichaelDeRich	I	I																											
3 ElizabethProctor					I	I				I	I																		
5 JohnProctor				I		I				I	I																		
9 BenjaminProctor				I	I					I	I																		
7 SarahBuckley								I	I																				
8 MaryWithridge							I		I																				
12 ThomasVery							I	I																					
10 ElizabethProctor				I	I	I					I																		
11 WilliamProctor				I	I	I				I																			
6 IsraelPorter																						I	I						
13 ElizabethVery														I	I	I	I	I											
14 JohnNurse													I		I	I	I	I											
15 FrancisNurse													I	I		I	I	I											

16 RebeccaNurse
17 EdmundTowne
18 MaryEasty
19 SarahCloyce
20 PeterCloyce
21 DanielAndrew
22 GeorgeJacobsJr
23 RebeccaJacobs
24 MargaretJacobs

25 ThomasWilkinsJr
26 ElizabethWilkins
27 WilliamTowne
28 MargaretTowne
29 JohnWillard

Table 6.7 Density matrix

	1	2	3	4
1	0.667	0.083	0.026	0.000
2	0.083	0.464	0.019	0.000
3	0.026	0.019	0.269	0.015
4	0.000	0.000	0.015	0.400

Table 6.8 Image matrix

	1	2	3	4
1	1	1	1	0
2	1	1	1	0
3	1	1	1	1
4	0	0	1	1

than 0.1133 will be coded 0 and all cell values at 0.1133 or higher will be coded 1. In that case, the image matrix we get is presented in table 6.9.

This image matrix seems to be much more true to the original data. The sociogram that we can construct from this appears in figure 6.5.

We could also continue to subdivide the blocks of the original matrix so as to separate out more pure zero blocks. If we continue subdividing the reshuffled matrix of ties in the anti-Parris network, we could, for example, produce the matrix in table 6.10.

The density matrix for table 6.10 is presented in table 6.11.

Making a sociogram of table 6.11 gives us finer detail, but we also risk losing some of the clarity about the overall structure that the

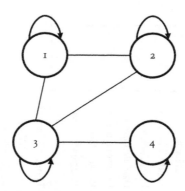

Figure 6.4 Sociogram of image matrix

Table 6.9 Image matrix

	1	2	3	4
1	1	0	0	0
2	0	1	0	0
3	0	0	1	0
4	0	0	0	1

less fine image matrix gave us. As with deciding on a cut-off point for zero blocks, when deciding how far to subdivide, we are always balancing the strengths and weaknesses of the different analyses. It is often helpful to divide matrices in several ways and to set several cut-off points for the image matrix before determining which level of analysis is most useful.

We can now use these reduced matrices to compare structures across networks. By comparing the image matrices of various networks, we can understand why certain actions or attitudes did or did not occur in certain situations. That is, now that we have simplified the network, we can use structural equivalence for its other purpose – helping us to understand the attitudes and actions of the actors in the network. Part of White's great insight about structural equivalence was that structurally equivalent actors share the same *roles* in the network. We can see this in an example of the relations among artists in a small Pacific island (Giuffre 2009). Table 6.12 is the matrix of choices that the artists made when asked who they thought were the best artists on the island. (Numbers are used to identify the actors in order to protect their anonymity.)

Note that many artists choose others who did not choose them

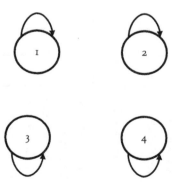

Figure 6.5 Sociogram of image matrix

Table 6.10 Further subdivision of the anti-Parris matrix

	1 S	2 M	4 M	3 E	5 J	9 B	10 E	11 W	12 T	7 S	8 M	6 I	23 R	21 D	22 G	24 M	13 E	18 M	19 S	20 P	14 J	15 F	16 R	17 E	25 T	26 E	27 W	28 M	29 J
1 SarahBassett	1			1																									
2 MaryDeRich	1	1	1	1																									
4 MichaelDeRich			1																										
3 ElizabethProctor				1	1	1	1	1	1																				
5 JohnProctor				1	1	1	1	1	1																				
9 BenjaminProctor				1	1	1	1	1	1																				
10 ElizabethProctor				1	1	1	1	1	1																				
11 WilliamProctor				1	1	1	1	1	1																				
12 ThomasVery				1	1				1								1												
7 SarahBuckley										1	1																		
8 MaryWithridge						1	1			1	1																		
6 IsraelPorter				1								1	1									1	1	1					

23 RebeccaJacobs
21 DanielAndrew
22 GeorgeJacobsJr
24 MargaretJacobs

13 ElizabethVery
18 MaytEasty
19 SarahCloyce
20 PeterCloyce
14 JohnNurse
15 FrancisNurse
16 RebeccaNurse
17 EdmundTowne

25 ThomasWilkinsJr
26 ElizabethWilkins
27 WilliamTowne

28 MargaretTowne
29 JohnWillard

Table 6.11 Density matrix

	1	2	3	4	5	6	7	8
1	1.000	0.500	0.167	0.000	0.000	0.000	0.000	0.000
2	0.500		0.000	0.000	0.200	0.000	0.000	0.000
3	0.167	0.000	0.733	0.083	0.033	0.021	0.000	0.000
4	0.000	0.000	0.083	1.000	0.000	0.000	0.000	0.000
5	0.000	0.200	0.033	0.000	0.600	0.100	0.000	0.000
6	0.000	0.000	0.021	0.000	0.100	0.393	0.042	0.000
7	0.000	0.000	0.000	0.000	0.000	0.042	0.667	0.167
8	0.000	0.000	0.000	0.000	0.000	0.000	0.167	1.000

back. That is, this is not a symmetric matrix. However, the unordered matrix tells us very little. But if we reorder the rows and columns so as to maximize the number of zero blocks, we get the matrix in table 6.13, divided into four blocks of more or less structurally equivalent actors.

The density matrix for this is presented in table 6.14.

The average density for the entire matrix of artists is 0.1579. If we use that number as the cut-off point for constructing the image matrix, we get table 6.15.

Table 6.12 Esteem matrix of Pacific artists

	1	2	3	4	5	6	7	8	9	10	11	12	13	14	15	16	17	18	19
1	0	0	0	0	0	0	1	1	0	0	1	0	0	0	0	0	0	0	0
2	0	0	0	0	1	0	0	0	0	0	1	0	0	0	0	0	0	0	0
3	0	1	0	0	0	1	1	0	0	0	1	0	0	0	0	0	0	0	0
4	0	0	0	0	0	0	1	0	0	0	0	0	1	0	0	0	0	0	0
5	0	1	0	0	0	1	0	0	0	0	1	0	0	0	0	0	0	0	0
6	0	0	0	0	0	0	0	0	0	0	1	0	0	0	0	0	0	0	0
7	0	0	1	0	0	0	0	0	0	1	1	0	0	0	0	0	0	0	0
8	0	1	0	0	1	0	0	0	0	1	0	0	0	0	0	0	0	0	0
9	0	0	1	0	0	0	1	0	0	0	0	0	1	0	1	0	0	0	0
10	0	0	0	0	0	0	1	0	0	0	0	0	0	0	0	0	0	0	0
11	0	1	0	0	1	1	0	0	0	0	0	0	1	0	0	1	0	0	0
12	0	1	0	0	1	1	0	0	0	0	0	1	0	0	0	0	0	0	0
13	0	0	0	0	0	1	1	0	0	1	0	0	0	0	0	0	0	0	0
14	0	0	0	0	1	0	1	0	0	0	1	1	0	0	1	0	0	0	0
15	0	0	0	0	1	0	0	1	0	0	0	1	0	0	0	0	0	0	0
16	0	1	0	0	0	1	0	1	0	0	1	0	0	0	0	0	0	0	0
17	0	0	0	0	0	0	1	0	0	0	0	0	1	0	0	0	0	0	0
18	0	0	0	0	0	0	1	0	0	0	0	0	1	0	0	0	0	0	0
19	0	0	0	0	0	0	0	0	0	0	0	0	0	0	0	0	0	0	1

Table 6.13 Blocked matrix of Pacific artists

	1	19	14	4	9	18	17	3	7	10	13	2	6	5	11	12	8	16	15
1								I							I	I			
19	I																		
14								I					I	I		I			I
4								I		I									
9								I	I	I									I
18								I		I									
17								I		I									
3								I				I	I		I				
7								I	I						I				
10								I											
13								I	I			I							
2													I	I					
6															I				
5												I	I		I				
11												I	I		I	I			I
12												I	I	I	I				
8									I			I	I		I				
16												I	I		I		I		
15															I	I	I		

Table 6.14 Density matrix

	1	2	3	4
1	0.000	0.393	0.107	0.143
2	0.000	0.500	0.313	0.000
3	0.000	0.000	0.750	0.125
4	0.000	0.063	0.625	0.250

Table 6.15 Image matrix

	1	2	3	4
1	0	I	0	0
2	0	I	I	0
3	0	0	I	0
4	0	0	I	I

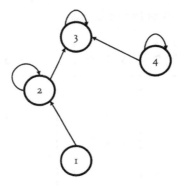

Figure 6.6 Sociogram of image matrix

The sociogram of this image matrix is presented in figure 6.6.

Notice that the lines connecting the nodes have arrows. This is because the ties have direction. Looking at the matrices for this data, we can see that, for example, the members of block 1 esteem the members of block 2, but the compliment is not returned. This is true also for the relation from block 2 to block 3 and from block 4 to block 3. In this situation, we can see a rather clear hierarchy emerge. Moreover, those who occupied structurally equivalent positions in the network also shared attitudes and engaged in similar actions. Artists in block 1 tended to be dissatisfied with the art scene on the island and highly critical of artists in block 3, for example. In general, people in positions of power or dominance in the network may believe that the status quo is right and just and will work toward maintaining it. People in subordinate positions, on the other hand, may believe differently and act to change the status quo. However, their powerless position may make it less likely that they will achieve their program. This is the argument Gould is making with regard to the Parisian citizens in 1871 – they shared a similar position in the network with regard to the government at Versailles and therefore shared similar attitudes and dispositions. In this case, that meant a shared insurgent identity.

How to find structural equivalence with UCINET6

Click "Network" at the top of the page and then choose "Roles & Positions" from the dropdown menu. Choose "Structural" and then "Concor," which is one algorithm for finding structural equivalence.

Choose "Standard" and input your dataset name in the window. An important decision that you will make here is the maximum depth of splits that you want the algorithm to produce in the blocked matrix. The higher the number of splits that you request, the more finely the program will divide the matrix. Once you have decided that number, click "OK" and you will get the output from the program. Scrolling down the screen, you will see a partition diagram showing you how the splits were performed at successive levels, then the blocked matrix like the ones we have been looking at in the examples above, and then the density matrix from which you can construct the image matrix of your choice. Closing that screen will then show you a cluster diagram of the partition of the actors in your matrix.

As you can tell from the number of options that UCINET presents which we have ignored, this only begins to scratch the surface for possibilities of analysis. Explanations going into much further depth can be found in Knoke and Yang (2008), Scott (2000), Lorrain and White (1971), Wasserman and Faust (1994), and White et al. (1976).

7 How do communities foster creativity and innovation?

We tend to think of creativity as an individual attribute – something that some people have more or less of than other people do. But throughout history, we can point to certain communities at certain times – the Golden Age of Athens, Renaissance Florence, Paris in the 1920s, for example – that have experienced an extraordinary outpouring of creativity. Is it just coincidence that large numbers of creative individuals came together at the same place at the same time? Or is it possible that there is something about the community itself that facilitates the creativity of its members? Why do some places at some times provide a locus for creative and innovative thought while other places at other times do not?

Recent research in many disciplines in the social sciences has begun to focus on the importance of social connections for fostering creativity in individuals (e.g., Csikszentmihaly 1996, McLeod et al. 1996, Farrell 2001, Liep 2001). McLeod et al. (1996), for example, find that those who have contact with dissimilar others are more likely to engage in the divergent thinking that is the basis for innovation. By stepping back from these individual-level analyses, we can hypothesize that those communities which have structures that facilitate this type of interaction are more likely to play host to creative cultures than are communities where the social structure inhibits that type of tie formation.

Social networks and innovative thinking

Burt's research on *structural holes* (1992, 2004) investigates how one particular type of structure facilitates innovative thinking. Burt's main claim is that "people who stand near the holes in a social structure are at higher risk of having good ideas" (Burt 2004: 349). What does this mean and why is it so?

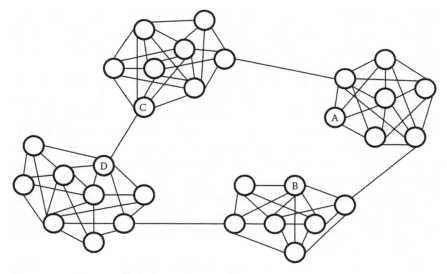

Figure 7.1 Structurally balanced network

Remember that structurally balanced networks resolve into positively tied cliques that are separated from each other by gulfs of negative or (eventually) missing ties. As the negative ties are left to wither away, over time we get a picture of a social structure with which we are now very familiar, seen in figure 7.1. The gaps that exist between these cliques are also consistent with Milgram's findings from the small world studies (see chapter 4).

There is a high degree of homogeneity of ideas, beliefs, and values within the cliques because of the needs of clique members to maintain balance. If there is deviance within the cliques, it is more likely to be in those nodes that are on the edges of the cliques than in those embedded more tightly in the center of the clique – that is, deviance is more likely in those nearest the gaps in the structure. These gaps are structural holes – places in the social structure where ties could exist but do not. Figure 7.1 is filled with structural holes. For example, nodes A and B could have had a tie between the two of them, but they do not. There is a gap – a hole – in the social structure there. "By dint of who is connected to whom, holes exist in the social structure . . . The holes in social structure, or, more simply, structural holes, are disconnections or nonequivalencies between players in the arena" (Burt 1992: 1–2).

Burt argues that those players who manage to bridge the gaps in the social structure – that is, who have ties to other cliques but who are themselves surrounded by structural holes (such as nodes C and D in figure 7.1) – will reap many advantages, including being at higher risk for "good ideas." Why is this so?

Burt quotes John Stuart Mill's (1987 [1848]: 581) opinion that "it is hardly possible to overrate the value . . . of placing human beings in contact with persons dissimilar to themselves, and with modes of thought and action unlike those with which they are familiar. . . . Such communication has always been, and is peculiarly in the present age, one of the primary sources of progress" (Burt 2004: 350). Placing human beings in contact with persons dissimilar to themselves, Burt and Mill argue, facilitates "out of the box" thinking because individuals are now in contact with so many different kinds of boxes. It might be more accurate, instead, to call this type of thinking "out of the cluster."

The clusters are important, as well as the holes between them. It is in the clusters that distinctive information and ideas get formulated. But much like the information about the availability of an abortionist (see chapter 3), which circulated inside some tightly knit cliques but did not cross the boundaries to other cliques, the ideas common inside one cluster are absent from others. "Given greater homogeneity within than between groups, people whose networks bridge the structural holes between groups have earlier access to a broader diversity of information and have experience in translating information across groups" (Burt 2004: 354).

People trapped in the middle of dense cliques don't have this opportunity to synthesize divergent ideas, Burt argues, and, therefore, to innovate. The contradictory – or at least dissimilar – ideas held by the different tightly knit groups provide a source of creative thinking for those who have access to more than one world of thought. The contradictions that arise when an actor brings together two different small worlds are the key to creative thinking. Burt argues that "idea generation at some point involves someone moving knowledge from this group to that, or combining bits of knowledge across groups" (2004: 356).

This contention is supported by much of the literature from psychology, where individual creativity is highly correlated with the ability to entertain contradictory thoughts and to engage in multiple perspectives. This is what McLeod et al. (1996), for example, refer to as "kaleidoscope thinking" – putting together a variety of diverse pieces into a whole.

Burt argues that

> [p]eople with connections across structural holes have early access to diverse, often contradictory, information and interpretations, which gives them a competitive advantage in seeing and developing good ideas. People connected to groups beyond their own can expect to find themselves delivering valuable ideas, seeming to be gifted with creativity. This is not creativity born of genius; it is creativity as an import-export business. An idea mundane in one group can be a valuable insight in another. (2004: 388)

It would seem that this type of creativity would be made more possible by the density and diversity of urban life. In the city, although people may still live in their urban villages, they also rub up against people who inhabit different villages. That means that they are also more likely to find bridges across the structural holes that exist between villages or clusters. But not all cities at all times are hotbeds of creative ferment. What are the particular structural aspects of some communities that make the existence of villages or clusters and the building of bridges across the structural holes between those groups more likely?

The creative context of the city

Florida argues that "creative class" people – those people "whose economic function is to create new ideas, new technology and/or new creative content" (Florida 2002: 8) – are drawn to certain types of communities, specifically to those offering particular types of amenities and particular populations. Florida makes a case that "creativity has always gravitated to specific locations. As the great urbanist Jane Jacobs [1961] pointed out long ago, successful places are multidimensional and diverse – they don't just cater to a single industry or a single demographic group; they are full of stimulation and creative interplay" (2002: 7). That is, Florida argues that creative-class people gravitate toward those communities where they find the things they value – openness, diversity, vibrant street life, and so on. But Burt's argument suggests that the causal arrow may point in the other direction. It may be that the existence of the community-level factors such as diversity and a vibrant street life are themselves what facilitate individual creativity. Perhaps creative individuals are not so much drawn to these places as they are *created* by them – or at least their creativity is facilitated by the social structure in which they find themselves. Florida notes, in fact, that "creativity flourishes best in a unique kind of social environment: one that is stable enough to allow continuity of effort, yet diverse and broad-minded enough to nourish creativity in all its subversive forms" (2002: 35). This description seems very similar to a community of small, supportive groups linked together by bridge ties across structural holes.

The key to this is diversity in the population – diversity of all types. Florida found that the desire for and appreciation of diversity was a "fundamental marker" (2002: 79) of the creative class. It might also be a fundamental generator of it. Not only do creative cities have ethnic and racial diversity, they also offer diversity in the amenities available to residents. Florida found that big-ticket, big-venue events were not appealing to members of the creative class. Instead, they looked for smaller, more fluid, and – most importantly – more *eclectic* activities. "Eclecticism in the form of cultural intermixing, when done right, can be a powerful creative stimulus" (Florida 2002: 185). One way to think of eclecticism is as a new combination of formerly divergent small world ideas. When we look at correspondence analysis in the "Closer Look" section of this chapter, we will see how we can structurally model and analyze these types of connections.

Eclecticism, Florida argues, is facilitated in communities by weak ties.

Putnam [2000] and other social capital theorists favor "strong ties." These are the kinds of relationships we tend to have with family members, close friends and longtime neighbors or coworkers. . . . But weak ties are often more important. . . . Weak ties are critical to the creative environment of a city or region because they allow for rapid entry of new people and rapid absorption of new ideas and are thus critical to the creative process. I am not advocating that we adopt lives composed entirely of weak ties. That would be a lonely and shallow life indeed . . . But most Creative Class people . . . maintain a core of strong ties. They have significant others; they have close friends; they call mom. But their lives are not dominated or dictated by strong ties to the extent that many lives were in the past. . . . Life in modern communities is driven more often and in more aspects by a much larger number of loose ties. . . . Weak ties allow us to mobilize more resources and more possibilities for ourselves and others, and expose us to novel ideas that are the source of creativity. (Florida 2002: 276–7)

Florida is advocating here for the benefits of small, supportive worlds with bridge ties spanning the structural holes between them –

perhaps more bridge ties than existed in the past, but not bridge ties to the exclusion of other types of strong in-group ties.

Institutions in a community can facilitate the creation and maintenance of this social structure. Certain types of amenities in cities draw creative people to communities that possess them, and those creative people in turn reshape the community so as to enhance innovation. In his study of patent holders in the USA (by definition innovative thinkers) Clark (2004), for example, found that young, talented people move to cities rich in certain specific types of amenities. Consistently with Florida's ideas, Clark found that, rather than big venues, "[s]mall amenities may be more important: like cafes which change [the] street life of individual citizens" (2004: 8). These small amenities – cafés, art galleries, local music venues, and so on – Clark argues "are the cheese, or correction, the three star meal, attracting talent. They transform a location into a scene. Sometimes a cool scene" (2004: 5). Clark argues that (2004: 2) young and talented people move to certain communities because they are drawn to the eclectic amenities provided in those communities and then either look for work in that area or start up businesses where they can use their own innovative ideas to their fullest. However, Clark continues, "different people seek distinct amenities. What attracts one person can repel others" (2004: 11). The types of amenities that attract the young and the talented are not the same as those that attract, for example, retirees.

It seems that some of the chief attractions for creative people are venues that facilitate interactions with others – especially diverse others – and that foster eclecticism. This is part of what Oldenburg (1989) means when he discusses the needs of communities to have a variety of "third places."

Home and work are the first two places. But Oldenburg argues that in order for vibrant communal life to exist, we need "third places" – public venues where people can come together without any particular purpose other than to meet and socialize with others. Cafés, taverns, main streets, parks, beauty parlors, and so on can function as third places – just as they did in the Washington ghetto or in Northeim before the Nazis infiltrated them. Oldenburg fears that America – especially in the suburbs – is quickly losing or has already lost many of its third places and, therefore, is losing the sense of community that these places kept alive.

It is not only that in creative communities there are plenty of public places, but also, importantly, that there is a great eclecticism in the types of people who are present in these places. That is, people from many small worlds might come together in them and begin to build the bridge ties that will span structural holes.

> Towns and cities that afford their populations an engaging public life are easy to identify. What urban sociologists refer to as their interstitial spaces are filled with people. The streets and sidewalks, parks and squares, parkways and boulevards are being used by people sitting, standing, and walking. Prominent public space is not reserved for that well-dressed, middle-class crowd that is welcomed at today's shopping malls. The elderly and poor, the ragged and infirm, are interspersed among those looking and doing well. The full spectrum of local humanity is represented. (Oldenburg 1989: 14)

Oldenburg notes that this lively diversity may be viewed negatively by many. "Social reformers as a rule, and planners all too commonly, ignore the importance of neutral ground and the kinds of relationships, interactions, and activities to which it plays host. Reformers have never liked seeing people hanging around on street corners, store porches, front stoops, bars, candy stores, or other public places" (1989: 22–3). This kind of "hanging around" is often seen as a breeding ground for crime and deviance. But innovative thinking is, by definition, deviant from traditional ways of thinking. Clamping down on the promiscuity of interaction which seems a harbinger of crime by clamping down on the places where that interaction could occur may also be inadvertently clamping down on a creative and innovative culture in the community. Instead, Oldenburg argues, communities need these types of places where people can go at any time and find others with whom to interact. "Third places that render the best and fullest service," he writes, "are those to which one may go alone at almost any time of day or evening with assurance that acquaintances will be there. . . . Access to them must be *easy* if they are to survive and serve" (1989: 32).

This picture of a heterogeneous, eclectic, vibrant, and innovation-fostering public life is what Jacobs extolled in her classic work, *The Death and Life of Great American Cities* (1961). Jacobs argued, first and foremost, for a *mixture* of uses in areas of the city with a great diversity of types of businesses, types of residences, public spaces, and types of people inhabiting each area. Jacobs noted how the large numbers of people in urban environments made this possible because a critical mass of patrons could keep small businesses, local music venues, esoteric restaurants, art galleries, mom-and-pop stores, and so on financially afloat.

However, Jacobs notes, simply having the critical mass of people is not enough to insure the diversity and vitality of the community. She writes that

> although cities may fairly be called natural economic generators of diversity and natural economic incubators of new enterprises, this does not mean that cities *automatically* generate diversity just by existing. . . . For our purposes here, the most striking fact to note is the extraordinary unevenness with which cities generate diversity. On the one hand, for example, people who live and work in Boston's North End, or New York's Upper East Side or San Francisco's North Beach-Telegraph Hill, are able to use and enjoy very considerable amounts of diversity and vitality. . . . At the other extreme, huge city settlements of people exist without their presence generating anything much except stagnation and, ultimately, a fatal discontent with the place. It is not that they are a different kind of people, somehow duller or unappreciative of vigor and diversity. Often they include hordes of searchers, trying to sniff out these attributes somewhere, anywhere. Rather, something is wrong with their districts; something is lacking to catalyze a district population's ability to interact economically and help form effective pools of use. (1961: 193–4)

The missing ingredients, Jacobs argues, which are necessary to make a vibrant communal life, are:

> 1. The district, and indeed as many of its internal parts as possible, must serve more than one primary function; preferably more than two. These must insure the presence of people who go outdoors on different schedules and are in the place for different purposes, but who are able to use many facilities in common. 2. Most blocks must be short; that is, streets and opportunities to turn corners must be frequent. 3. The district must mingle buildings that vary in age and condition, including a good proportion of old ones so that they vary in the economic yield they must produce. This mingling must be fairly close-grained. 4. There must be a sufficiently dense concentration of people, for whatever purposes they may be there. This includes dense concentration in the case of people who are there because of residence. (1961: 196–7)

Looking at these four conditions, we can see that Jacobs is arguing for eclecticism of people and purposes combined with the physical space to facilitate bringing the various pieces together. One way to think about this is as McLeod et al.'s "kaleidoscope thinking" on a large scale. Another way to think about this is as a space to facilitate the building of ties that bridge structural holes between small groups or clusters.

Small world structures

The argument that the New Urbanists like Jacobs are making, rephrased in network analytic terms, is that communities become loci of creativity and innovation when their structures include both the small, supportive cliques where unique ideas can be developed and bridge ties across these cliques that allow those ideas to come into contact with each other. This is the "small world" structure (Watts 1999a, 1999b, 2003, Watts and Strogatz 1998). The small world structure is one in which there is clustering among the nodes (more so than in a random network, at least) while there are also bridge ties (like the shortcuts between literate slaves; see chapter 3) that keep the path length between any two nodes relatively short (at least as short as they would be in a random network).

Uzzi and Spiro (2004) investigated whether the financial and critical success of Broadway musicals could be correlated with the small world-ness of the networks of the people involved in them. The idea here is that creative thought – because it is deviant from traditional thought – needs social support from others in order to flourish. But should the ties that provide that support become too overwhelming, creativity would be inhibited. These authors argue that having high clustering – that is, friends of friends who collaborate together on projects are supportive, share resources, and develop group norms of cooperation and collaboration – enhances the performance of the group as a whole. This only works up to a point, though. Too much group support and cohesion can close members off to new experiences and new ideas that come from outside the group. We saw this in chapter 5 among the Toughs on Meridian Street who discouraged individual members of their group from getting to know the Indochinese or attending their barbecue. The strength of weak ties, recall, is that bridge ties outside of the supportive cluster in which an actor is embedded bring in fresh ideas, fresh information, and fresh attitudes that prevent the kind of non-creative "groupthink" typical of tight clusters where the need for balance among the members makes the social risks of entertaining deviant thoughts too high.

Uzzi and Spiro point out that

[f]eelings of obligation and friendship (or revenge) may be so great between past collaborators that they risk becoming an "assistance club" for ineffectual actors in their cluster . . . . Preserving a space for "friends" can further hamper the recruitment of outsiders that possess fresh talent into a cluster . . . Similarly, McPherson et al. . . . argued that tight clusters also promote recruitment by homophily, minimizing diversity and reproducing rather than advancing existing ways of thinking in a network. (2004: 12)

The solution to this is not to destroy the supportive clusters, but to make sure that sufficient bridges to other small clusters are maintained. The groups work best when they are clustered enough to provide collaboration, support, and resource sharing, but not so tightly clustered that they inhibit the members' exposure to outside influences, ideas, and experiences. This intermediate level of small world clustering is what Uzzi and Spiro call the "cradle of creativity."

Uzzi and Spiro looked at a cultural product – Broadway musicals – to see if the small world-ness of the networks which produced them mattered. Can we look instead at a creative community to see whether any of these factors are present? Freiberger and Swaine's detailed history of the beginnings of the personal computer revolution, *Fire in the Valley* (2000), provides us with the wealth of detail that we need to examine network theories in light of empirical examples. Their discussion of the development of the Apple I computer and the founding of the Apple Computer Company highlights the role played by social networks and small world structures.

The Apple example

In 1975, a small group of electronics hobbyists in the San Francisco Bay area put together a flyer to announce meetings for like-minded individuals who might want to get together. It read: "Are you building your own computer? Terminal? T Typewriter? I/O device? Or some other digital black box? Or are you buying time on a time-sharing service? If so, you might like to come to a gathering of people with like-minded interests. Exchange information, swap ideas, talk shop, help work on a project, whatever" (Freiberger & Swaine 2000: 109). Thus began the Homebrew Computer Club – a hotbed of people and ideas that would play a central role in the birth of the personal computer revolution.

The Bay area was home to both Stanford University and the

University of California at Berkeley as well as to the countercultural rebels of the 1960s and 1970s, for whom the sharing of information was an important part of their ethos. This ethos of intellectual generosity and the community-minded spirit that came with it were part of the Homebrew meetings from the very beginning. Freiberger and Swaine write of one early meeting of the group: "As the meeting concluded, one Homebrewer held up an Intel 8008 chip, asked who could use it, and then gave it away. Many of those there that night sensed the opportunities presented by this community spirit" (2000: 120).

It is important to note that the Homebrew meetings were open to everyone – there were no dues and no membership rolls to sign. Instead, the meetings provided the kind of third place conviviality that facilitated network building. Freiberger and Swaine write of the meetings, informally led by Lee Felsenstein:

> First came a mapping session, during which Felsenstein recognized people who quickly proffered their interests, questions, rumors, or plans. . . . A formal presentation followed, generally on someone's latest invention. Finally, there was the Random Access session, in which everyone scrambled around the auditorium to meet others they felt had common interests. The formula worked brilliantly, and numerous companies were formed at the Homebrew meetings. A remarkable amount of information was also exchanged at those meetings. (2000: 122)

As Freiberger and Swaine note, "The Homebrew Computer Club was not merely the spawning ground of Silicon Valley microcomputer companies. It was also the intellectual nutrient in which they first swam" (2000: 124).

One of the early attendees of the Homebrew meetings was a young electronics enthusiast named Steve Wozniak who would design the first Apple computer and start the company with his friend Steve Jobs. Wozniak had grown up deeply embedded in the electronics industry culture of the Silicon Valley and had dreamed of having his own computer for years.

> The Woz was not the only student in Silicon Valley with such a dream. Actually, in some ways he was fairly typical. Many students at Homestead High had parents in the electronics industry. Having grown up with the new technology around them, these kids were not intimidated by it. They were accustomed to watching their parents mess around with oscilloscopes and soldering irons. Homestead High also had teachers

who encouraged their students' interests in technology. Woz may have followed his dream more single-mindedly than the others, but the dream was not his alone. (Freiberger & Swaine 2000: 255)

Moreover, the Homebrew Computer Club meetings further nurtured Wozniak's interests – and strengthened his ties to the world of electronics/computer hobbyists whom he met and befriended at the meetings. Like that of the participants in the Freedom Summer (see chapter 6), Wozniak's social network was becoming dominated by like-minded others. The Homebrew Computer Club was a venue for Wozniak to make ties with others who were as fascinated by computers as he was. Sharing ideas and information was the cornerstone of the Homebrew group. When Wozniak had designed the very first Apple computer, in fact, he photocopied the diagram and description of his design and handed them out at the Homebrew meetings so that anyone who wanted could build an Apple. This was the densely knit, supportive world where the ideas for the design of personal computers were being worked out in give-and-take among the members.

Steve Jobs, however, was not quite so deeply enmeshed in that same electronics-savvy world. His parents, for one thing, were not part of the industry and he had a variety of other eclectic interests – including Eastern religions, philosophy, typeface design, and primal scream therapy. While Wozniak, the actual designer of the Apple computer, was deeply embedded in a small, supportive world of electronics enthusiasts, Jobs was busy making bridge ties to other worlds, the members of which would also be important in the personal computer revolution. Jobs connected the start-up Apple Computer Company (at first housed in his parents' garage) with the best professionals he could find in fields like marketing, customer service, and – perhaps most importantly – venture capital. Although most start-up personal computer companies at the time handled everything themselves, so that the designer of the computer would also be the person in charge of financing the company and marketing the product (with no expertise or resources in either area at his disposal), Jobs recruited outside experts in those fields to work with the small company. For example, while other companies relied on engineers to do their public relations, Freiberger and Swaine write that Jobs turned to the owner of one of the most successful PR firms in the area, Regis McKenna, to handle the advertising for the new company. Initially rebuffed, Jobs continued to hound McKenna until he finally acquiesced to the barefoot, bearded Jobs. "'I don't deny that Woz designed a good machine,' said McKenna. 'But that machine would be sitting in hobby shops today were it not for Steve Jobs. Woz was fortunate to hook up with an evangelist'" (2000: 275).

It was in 1977 at the first West Coast Computer Faire in San Francisco that the Apple II, the computer that would make Apple the most successful personal computer company in the world at that time, was unveiled. The computer fairs brought together companies from all over for several days of interaction. People saw the products and designs of others, met and exchanged ideas, and built ties that had not existed before. These types of institutions functioned like short-term third places where conversation and interaction were non-stop and where the types of shortcut ties that decrease average chain length within the system were made. Computer fairs brought together enthusiasts from all over the country (or even the world) to one place at one time and the weak ties formed there made bridges that facilitated the exchange of ideas outside the immediate Silicon Valley area. At the first West Coast Computer Faire, Steve Jobs secured Apple a prime spot right inside the main doors.

Ties to other companies were critical to Apple's initial success. Beyond the world of hobbyists, who wanted to own computers just because they liked them, potential customers for personal computers needed something useful for computers to *do* before they could be convinced to buy one. Although it is hard to imagine now, in the early days of the personal computer revolution, no one was sure what the average consumer would do with one if he or she got it. The solution for Apple came from another company, Software Arts, headquartered in Cambridge, Massachusetts. Software Arts's product, VisiCalc, was the first financial spreadsheet program developed for a personal computer. At a time when no one was sure that any kind of personal software would find demand from consumers, Freiberger and Swaine write,

> [n]ot only did VisiCalc sell, but the popularity of the program also helped to sell Apple computers. During its first year, VisiCalc was available only for the Apple, and it provided a compelling reason to buy an Apple. In fact, the Apple II and VisiCalc had an impressive symbiotic relationship, and it's difficult to say which contributed more to the other. Together they did much to legitimize both the hardware and the software industries. (2000: 291)

Apple Computer was for a time the only company that spanned the structural hole between the hardware and software worlds.

These connections to people and companies outside of itself gave Apple a position of high betweenness centrality in the system. One of the most important connections that Jobs made for Apple was to the developers and engineers at the Palo Alto Research Center (PARC) run by the Xerox Corporation. The researchers at PARC had developed cutting-edge computer ideas – like the graphical user interface, linked computers for communication, and the mouse – but no one at Xerox seemed at all interested in developing the ideas for the commercial market. Jobs convinced the Xerox executives to let a team from Apple into PARC to see the research there. The developers at PARC were appalled that they were being told to give demonstrations of their research ideas and breakthroughs to a rival company, but they were overruled by executives who probably didn't understand the value of what they had at PARC. In any case, the Apple team was given the demonstrations of the PARC research and then used those ideas in the development of the wildly successful MacIntosh. The ideas that were developed in the small world of Xerox PARC were brought to the outside world through the connection to Apple.

In their study of the networks in Silicon Valley, Castilla et al. (2000) also highlight the importance of movement by employees of the various firms.

> One of the most important aspects of Silicon Valley is the way its labor market works. Extensive labor mobility creates rapidly shifting and permeable firm and institutional boundaries and dense personal networks across the technical and professional population. . . . High mobility reinforces the dense networks, strengthening their role as channels through which technical and market information, as well as other intangibles – organizational culture and trust, for example – are diffused and shared among firms. Engineers not only hop around firms in the same industry; they also move from one industry and/or institutional sector to another – from technical firms to venture capital firms or to university research centers – creating cross-institutional ties and loosely integrating different institutional nodes in Silicon Valley. (Castilla et al. 2000: 220–1)

Castilla et al. point out that not only does technical expertise and information get passed through these broad-ranging networks, but also a culture specific to the area was carried by the workers from place to place so that it diffused across the entire industry. Robert Noyce, the co-founder of Fairchild Semiconductor – a key company whose former employees (known as the Fairchildren) went on to found many of the first important players in the personal computer revolution – and later of Intel, explicitly rejected the hierarchical corporate culture which he felt inhibited the development of good ideas.

> For example, there was no reserved parking at Fairchild, which was conceived of as a democratic community rather than a hierarchical workplace. And this new approach diffused as employees from Fairchild spun off to start their own companies. Everywhere the Fairchild émigrés went, they took the "Noyce approach" with them. It was not enough to start up a company; you had to start up a company in which there were no social distinctions. (Castilla et al. 2000: 225)

The start-up culture of Silicon Valley, with its emphasis on sharing ideas, flexible work schedules, eschewing tradition, and egalitarianism, spread throughout the industry by means of the workers who moved from company to company, maintaining weak ties with former workmates. This culture, which played such an important part in the success of the personal computer revolution, was a combination of attitudes, norms, and values brought together by an integrated network of individuals. Bringing people together also brings ideas together. In the "Closer Look" section below, we will see how we can map the combinations of ideas onto a two-dimensional space.

In line with John Stuart Mill's opinion that communication between dissimilar people is "one of the primary sources of progress," Silicon Valley is a modern example of the success of the small world structure. Small, supportive clusters of like-minded enthusiasts gathered together and shared information and ideas. Those small groups were connected to each other by shortcuts in the network which were often institutionally facilitated. Castilla et al. argue that it was the flows of people across the boundaries of institutional sectors that made Silicon Valley unique. The connections that bridged the structural holes between small worlds of firms and markets, made by the highly mobile members of the workforce, were extremely advantageous to the development of innovative ideas. Moreover, along with information, a "Silicon Valley Culture" was also developed and transmitted through these network ties.

Most of the authors discussed in this chapter have argued that the physical place matters in these networks. Jacobs, for example, claims that the physical layout of the city – such as having short blocks – is critical for facilitating lively interaction among the residents. Oldenburg argues for the importance of the third place – an actual, physical place where people can come together to interact with a diverse set of others. Florida and Clark both find that some cities offer the types of amenities – like restaurants and art galleries – that draw young and talented people to them. But is it possible that new types of communities, which are not necessarily rooted in a physical place, could also serve this function? Can virtual communities provide for the needs of their "residents" as well as "real" places can? Can they do it better? The authors discussed in this chapter all argue that *physical place* matters. But does it? We will turn to this issue in the next chapter.

A closer look: correspondence analysis

In *Distinction* (1984), Pierre Bourdieu performed a correspondence analysis on information about individual tastes and cultural consumption patterns. Plotting the correspondences among the respondents' answers to his questionnaires, Bourdieu found, for example, that people who liked paintings by Picasso and Dali also liked original and exotic cooking, pot-luck dinners, interior decoration that was warm, and friends who were dynamic. On the other hand, people who agreed with the statement "paintings don't interest me" also preferred furniture purchased in department stores, interiors that were clean and tidy and that were easy to maintain, and food that was plentiful and good (Bourdieu 1984: 340). Bourdieu found, that is, that there is a correspondence among tastes.

Correspondence analysis produces a map of a two-dimensional space on which those tastes, attitudes, preferences, dispositions, etc., which often occur together in the same types of respondents, appear close together in space while those tastes, etc., which seldom appear together are far apart. Looking at the correspondence analysis of his data about cultural tastes among the French respondents to the questionnaire, Bourdieu found groups of attributes that regularly appeared together – such as a fondness for Picasso and pot-luck dinners. By adding secondary factors about the respondents, such as their incomes and their fathers' occupations, Bourdieu argued that tastes were a function of the respondents' position in the social structure with regard to economic and cultural capital. People who liked Picasso and pot-luck dinners, for example, were part of that segment of society with high cultural capital and low economic capital. They

Table 7.1 American Time Use Survey data in average hours per day (Bureau of Labor Statistics 2010)

	<HS	HS	SomeColl	Coll&>
TV	3.96	3.81	3.29	2.76
Sports	2.30	2.41	2.93	2.69
Yoga	0.00	0.00	0.00	0.99
Car	1.76	1.68	0.00	1.07
PerfArts	0.00	0.00	2.29	2.59
Classes	2.41	0.00	2.21	1.92
Museum	0.00	0.00	0.00	0.67
Socialize	1.78	1.90	1.73	0.50
Work	7.25	7.65	7.34	7.32

tended to be young (under 30) and have fathers who were junior executives.

To understand correspondence analysis, we will use a matrix of data from the Bureau of Labor Statistics American Time Use Survey (Bureau of Labor Statistics 2010). In this example, instead of looking at individuals' tastes and consumption habits, as Bourdieu did, we will look at groups of people categorized by educational attainment and how they spend their time. We will use four educational groups – less than high school, high school diploma, some college or associates degree, bachelor's degree or higher – and we will look at the average amount of time per day that they spend watching television, attending sporting events, doing yoga, working on car maintenance, attending performing arts, taking classes for personal interest, going to museums, socializing, and working at a primary job. This data is in the matrix shown in table 7.1.

Correspondence analysis treats each row and each column in this matrix as a vector. The vector is an array of values which gives the coordinates of a point in an n-dimensional space, where the "n" is the number of categories (rows or columns) used. Because these high-dimensional spaces are impossible to visualize, we must project the relationships among the points onto a lower-dimensional (two- or three-dimensional) space so as to preserve as best we can the original relationships in the n-dimensional space. Points which were far apart in the n-dimensional space should still be far apart in the lower-dimensional space and those that were close together should still be close together. You can see, for example, in table 7.1 that the vectors for doing yoga and for attending museums are very similar,

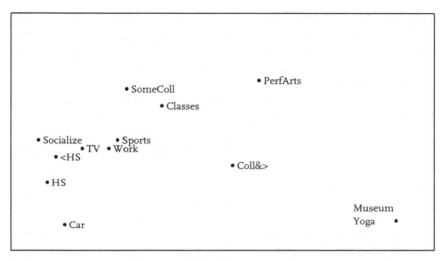

Figure 7.2 Correspondence analysis of American Time Use Survey data

and those two points should therefore appear very close together in the final mapping.

In addition, the correspondence analysis should orient the axes of the plane onto which the points are projected so as to maximize the variation among the points. The x-coordinate in the projected coordinate system picks out the axis along which the most variation among the points occurs and the y-axis picks out the second largest amount of variation. The axes have no a priori sociological interpretation; by analyzing the types of points and their relationships to each other, we must figure out the underlying variables driving the distribution of the points. Bourdieu found a distinction among the points in his dataset based on the economic and cultural capital of his respondents. Other correspondence analyses will, of course, measure other social phenomena.

For example, the matrix in table 7.1 produces the correspondence analysis map in figure 7.2.

Notice that, as predicted from table 7.1, going to museums and doing yoga are in the same space in the map. They are both very far away from doing car maintenance and socializing. They are closer to attending performing arts events than they are to any other activity and closer to the college graduate group than to any other educational level. Work, by contrast, is fairly centrally located to all educational levels.

But how should we label the axes? What are the underlying factors that might be responsible for this distribution of points? One possibility is that the x-axis is measuring cultural capital, with high cultural capital to the right and lower cultural capital to the left. Another way to think about this is in terms of "mass vs. class," with common activities like socializing and watching TV toward the left on the x-axis and more elite activities like going to museums on the right. The y-axis is more difficult to judge. Possibly it is distinguishing between those activities that we tend to engage in with others (attending performances, going to classes, socializing) with those that we do alone (car maintenance, yoga, going to museums).

Correspondence analysis is about the relationships among the attributes that are shared (or not) between groups of actors. We can think about creative places through the lens of correspondence analysis. "Strong-tie advocates" like Putnam argue that our communities are dying from the lack of civic participation in things like bowling leagues. "Weak-tie advocates" like Florida argue that some communities are thriving owing to an abundance of amenities like art galleries. In their history of the personal computer revolution, Freiberger and Swaine argue that the ethos of intellectual generosity was a key ingredient for the success of Silicon Valley. Burt makes a case for diversity and the bridges across structural holes. We could conceivably gather data on different types of cities – those that are dying, those that are thriving, those that are generating innovation, and those that are not. And we could gather data as Bourdieu did for individuals to measure the dispositions, resources, social network structures, diversity, cultural climate, and so on of the communities. The correspondence analysis of that data would then show us a map of the various cultures and subcultures which are made out of the grouping together of attributes, dispositions, and so on. We could then answer questions about the relations between various attributes of communities and the success or failure of those communities and of those cultures with regard to financial well-being, population growth or decline, or production of innovative and creative ideas.

There are several excellent resources for the mathematics of correspondence analysis – especially Clausen (1998) and Greenacre (1984, 1993). It is also covered in Wasserman and Faust (1994) and in Knoke and Yang (2008).

Doing correspondence analysis in UCINET6

Enter the data into a matrix (as was done in table 7.1). Click on "Tools" at the top of the page and choose "scaling/decomposition" from the dropdown menu. Then click on "Correspondence." Enter the name of your matrix into the Input Dataset window and click "OK." You will first be given the values of the factors and the column and row scores. Because correspondence analysis is projecting points in an n-dimensional space onto a lower-dimensional space, it is important that as little as possible of the variance among the original points is lost. The Cum% column in the UCINET output tell you how much of the variance among the original points is captured by the factors to that point. If the cumulative percentage of the first two factors is not sufficiently large, then a two-dimensional map cannot possibly capture all of the important features of the data. If, however, the Cum% of the first one or two factors is large, then we know that the variation along those axes is truly explanatory of the underlying processes. By looking at the Percent column, we can see what percent of the variation among the points is accounted for by each axis.

Behind the values and scores is the correspondence map itself. Note that, of course, the axes are not labeled, as figuring out those labels is the job of the analyst. Note also that although UCINET gives as its default the most important factor with regard to variation in the distribution of points as the x-axis and the second most important as the y-axis, you can choose to look at other axes and to display the map flipped around the horizontal and vertical axes. Areas in the map where attributes cluster together can be read as cultures and subcultures, such as the areas where people with less than high school degrees and with high school degrees are near the activities of attending sporting events, watching TV, working, and socializing. There is another less tight cluster of people with some college education near the activities of attending performing arts events and taking classes for personal interest. There is a very tight cluster of doing yoga and going to museums.

8 How do new communities differ from traditional communities?

Like the Industrial Revolution, which went hand in hand with the rise of urbanization, the personal computer revolution was more than just a technological change – it was also a social revolution affecting the way we organize our lives and our communities. One of the principal components of the computer revolution has been the emergence of computer-mediated communication (CMC) – beginning with bulletin board systems and multi-user domains and expanding to email, texting, and social networking sites. CMC has been extolled by its proponents (e.g., Rheingold 1993) as the wellspring of a new technological utopia which will bring humans together in communities free from the boundaries imposed by physical space and by social distinctions. Critics (e.g., Putnam 2000), on the other hand, have seen the rise of CMC as endangering communities by destroying intimate face-to-face communication with neighbors and other community members and diverting individuals from interest and investment in their own physical communities.

Rethinking the concept of community

Fears about the destruction of communities have existed at least since Tönnies warned about the transformation from Gemeinschaft to Gesellschaft (see chapter 2). Hampton and Wellman note that "pundits have feared that some combination of technological change, industrialization, urbanization, and bureaucratization will destroy community. Isolated individuals would face the state and large organizations in a mass society without intermediate-level communities to give them companionship, support, information, a sense of belonging, and a means of aggregating and articulating their hopes and grievances" (2003: 278). Critics of technological change have feared not only the loss of personal ties, but also the disintegration of the larger community which is built from those ties (Hampton and Wellman 2003: 278). But CMC is only the latest technological change to incite these fears – similar worries arose in response to previous technological changes, including the inventions of the telegraph, the railroad, the telephone, the automobile, the interstate highway system, and the airplane (Hampton and Wellman 2003: 284). Each of these was feared because it had the potential to lure the individual away from home and concentrate his or her interest in more alluring places far away while the local community withered and died from lack of care by its residents. We can see this, for example, in Jacobs's (1961) insistence that city blocks should be short and walkable, with a variety of reasons for people to be out on them, and in Oldenburg's (1989) worries that third places where people can meet up with others to socialize are becoming more scarce (see chapter 7). Sociologists have been worrying about how technological, economic, and political changes would affect communities for as long as sociology has been a discipline. In many ways, in fact, these questions were the impetus for the development of sociology in the first place.

But as we have seen in previous chapters, merely existing in the same local space does not guarantee that individuals will form a cohesive community. Moreover, a lack of efficient means of communication among residents of a community can certainly harm it. For example, we have seen that the urban villagers of Boston's West End lived in densely populated neighborhoods of strong ties and physical proximity, but were unable to communicate effectively with others and come together as a community to save their homes from destruction (chapter 4). Hampton and Wellman point out that in traditional suburban communities – much as in the urban village of Boston's West End – local ties can be *very* local, rarely reaching more than a few houses away and seldom crossing streets or going around corners. This can limit the residents' attachments to the larger community. This is precisely what we have seen in some of the fractured communities we studied in chapter 5.

In reality, communities may never have been the strongly tied, supportive, and cohesive collective that we imagine they once were. Although (as we saw with Wellman and Wortley's analysis of social support in chapter 3) community members such as neighbors and friends provide us with a variety of aid, resources, and different types of support, communities can also turn on some of their members (as some residents of Salem did against the rising mercantile class and as some residents of East Boston did against the Indochinese refugees). Moreover, as we saw in Northeim after the rise of the Nazis, our neighbors are not always available to us – no matter how physically close they may be. Even in less extreme circumstances, Hampton and Wellman argue that many neighborhoods lack the institutional settings and opportunities – like third places and neighborhood-based activities – that give the residents a reason to build ties with each other. The white residents of Princeton Street in East Boston, for example, had no neighborhood meeting places or institutions that could draw the residents together to plan or coordinate activities – fortunately for the Indochinese living there, as it turned out, given that those activities might have been arson.

Instead of thinking of neighborhoods or other geographically bounded spaces as communities which are made up of individuals, it might make more sense to flip the equation in the manner of Simmel (1971) and of Breiger (1974) and instead think of individuals who are made of communities. That is, we can see individuals as members of a variety of communities which may not overlap with each other in any significant way and may not be geographically anchored. Hampton and Wellman argue that communities are, in reality, broad-ranging networks of strong and weak ties with people from a variety of settings – home, school, work, clubs, neighborhoods, kin, friends, and so on. Most individuals in North America have a small, tight core of close ties surrounded by a much less dense web of others to whom they are connected with only weak ties (Hampton & Wellman 2003: 278–9). These types of communities may not match an image of Gemeinschaft-like fellowship and unity, but in terms of social support for individuals, they may be more functional than tightly knit communities are. And in terms of support for *individuality*, they might have distinct advantages.

Cyber utopians vs. cyber dystopians

If traditional communities were never the havens we imagined them to be, how does technological innovation – especially CMC – affect modern communities? What changes – if any – should we expect in our day-to-day lives as more and more of our time is spent in the virtual world of cyberspace? CMC has the ability to forge connections among us, but as Steven Jones points out, "connection does not inherently make for community, nor does it lead to any necessary exchanges of information, meaning, and sense making at all" (1995: 12). In fact, the overwhelming amount of information and the overwhelming number of contacts that are available to us online mean that we teeter toward complete information overload and chaos unless we impose some social order on the virtual world. But what sort of order does it need to be?

The new communities we make online are Simmelian in the way that we pick and choose from among a vast array of groups (and small worlds) in order to put together an individualized community for ourselves. That is, we construct a community for ourselves out of the many choices available to us. But Jones asks of these virtual communities: "What is the nature of individual members' commitments to them? In the physical world, community members must live together. When community membership is in no small way a simple matter of subscribing or unsubscribing to a bulletin board or electronic newsgroup, is the nature of interaction different simply because one may disengage with little or no consequence?" (1995: 11).

This is one of the aspects of the debate between the cyber utopians, who see in the virtual world almost limitless possibilities for better, more egalitarian, more useful, and more engaged communities, and the cyber dystopians, who see instead the virtual world as a place where deep connections and real human interactions go to die. Hampton and Wellman (2003) ask: will the internet weaken community as face-to-face interactions decrease? Will it transform community into a virtual community that is conducted online? Or will it enhance community, adding just another form of communication to those that already exist?

Many of the cyber-dystopian arguments hinge on the private nature of internet use. As is the case with time in front of the television screen, these researchers find that time spent in front of the computer screen is time taken away from in-person interaction with one's neighbors and other community members. Nie et al. (2002), for example, found internet use decreased face-to-face contact with friends, family, and co-workers. The rise of CMC, dystopians argue, is hastening the already rapidly declining investment that Americans feel in their own local communities.

This fear is not unreasonable. Putnam (2000), for example, found a marked decline in civic participation among Americans in the last few decades of the twentieth century as compared with previous decades, with memberships in clubs, organizations, and civic groups all suffering massive declines. Putnam found that "across all these organizations, membership rates began to plateau in 1957, peaked in the early 1960s, and began the period of sustained decline by 1969" (2000: 55). Further, Putnam documents "significant declines in memberships in unions; church groups; fraternal and veterans organizations; civic groups, such as PTAs; youth groups; charities; and a catch-all 'other' category" (2000: 58–9). Even socializing with friends happens significantly less frequently now than it did in previous decades.

In summary, Putnam writes that

> for the first two-thirds of the twentieth century Americans' involvement in civic associations of all sorts rose steadily . . . In the last third of the century, by contrast, . . . active involvement in face-to-face organizations has plummeted . . . [T]he broad picture is one of declining membership in community organizations. During the last third of the twentieth century formal membership in organizations in general has edged downward by perhaps 10–20 percent. More important, active involvement in clubs and other voluntary associations has collapsed at an astonishing rate, more than halving most indexes of participation within barely a few decades. (2000: 63)

More important than just the declining numbers in terms of social and civic participation, though, is the decline in the *diversity* of others to whom we are tied and with whom we interact.

> Local heterogeneity may give way to more focused virtual homogeneity as communities coalesce across space. Internet technology allows and encourages infrared astronomers, oenophiles, Trekkies, and white supremacists to narrow their circle to like-minded intimates. New "filtering" technologies that automate the screening of "irrelevant" messages make the problem worse. Serendipitous connections become less likely as increased communication narrows our tastes and interests – knowing and caring more and more about less and less. (Putnam 2000: 178)

Putnam argues that this will decrease social cohesion. There are, in effect, fewer and fewer weak ties to dissimilar others to hold the society together. Remember that connections to dissimilar others is the basis for Durkheim's idea of organic solidarity, discussed in chapter 2.

Remember also that diversity and eclecticism are the markers of creative communities. Bridge ties to other groups are vital, whether the individual was seeking access to an abortionist (Lee 1969), information about job openings (Granovetter 1974), membership in a social movement (Gould 1995), or technological breakthroughs and innovative thinking (Burt 2004). The heterogeneity of the other people with whom we are in contact is on the decline, Putnam argues – and that is troubling.

What has caused this decline? Putnam certainly does not lay all the blame on CMC, given that the decline began before the rise of the internet. But our ability to form online communities with *only* like-minded others no doubt plays a part. Putnam estimates that

> pressures of time and money, including the special pressures on two-career families, contributed measurably to the diminution of our social and community involvement during these years. My best guess is that no more than 10 percent of the total decline is attributable to that set of factors. Second, suburbanization, commuting, and sprawl also played a supporting role. Again, a reasonable estimate is that these factors together might account for an additional 10 percent of that problem. Third, the effect of electronic entertainment – above all, television – in privatizing our leisure time has been substantial. My rough estimate is that this factor might account for perhaps 25 percent of the decline. Fourth and most important, generational change – the slow, steady, and ineluctable replacement of the long civic generation by their less involved children and grandchildren – has been a very powerful factor. . . . [T]his factor might account for perhaps half the overall decline. (2000: 283)

Instead of seeing the virtual world as part of the problem, other researchers see in the internet and in CMC the possible cure for social disengagement in our communities. Hampton and Wellman (2003) studied community contacts, tie building, and civic engagement in a "wired" suburb of Toronto that they called "Netville." They contend that the internet does not replace social ties of other types, but is merely another tool that people use to connect with each other – much like the telephone.

Hampton and Wellman point out some of the advantages of CMC. The most important of these is that CMC can be asynchronous. That is, unlike the telephone or face-to-face communication, internet communication can happen without both parties being connected simultaneously. "Not only does this afford communication across the continent in different time zones, it affords communication across the street despite different schedules" (Hampton & Wellman 2003: 286). As modern lives become increasingly hectic and schedules become more full, CMC allows people nevertheless to maintain contact with each other. Whereas club meetings or third places that may once have been the institutions that facilitated the maintenance of ties are vanishing, CMC may not be the cause of their decline but instead an adaptive response to it.

A second feature of CMC is the capability it provides for not only one-to-one but also one-to-many communication. "Like a habitually frequented hangout, people show up at their email in-boxes [or Facebook pages] and listen in on the happenings of their communities, interjecting when appropriate, but often just observing. Moreover, email messages are transitive. They can be forwarded to others, including these others in the loop and fostering gossip networks" (Hampton & Wellman 2003: 286). This type of contact, these authors argue, can form the basis of social ties that take place offline in real physical neighborhoods. People can learn much about each other online that will facilitate face-to-face interactions and network building.

This, at any rate, is what happened in Netville. The residents of Netville had high-speed internet connections and a local email discussion list, NET-L. Hampton and Wellman found that, compared to a control group of residents who did not have internet access, on average the residents of Netville who were connected to the local computer network were much more integrated into the community, recognizing three times as many of their neighbors, talking to twice as many of their neighbors, and visiting half again as many of their neighbors as did those residents who were not on the net (2003: 292–3). That is, the use of CMC did not replace face-to-face interaction, but instead seemed to enhance it, giving the wired Netville residents a basis for building ties with each other.

Interestingly, though, the strongest predictor of people actually visiting each other (which was the strongest type of tie that Hampton and Wellman studied) was the length of time that people had lived in the town. The types of strong ties where people actually spent time together in each other's homes were built up slowly over time, not quickly generated online. The types of ties generated through the use of NET-L, in contrast, were more likely to be weak ties. On the one hand, this fits with the cyber dystopians' fears that the types of interaction people find online are shallow and not meaningful, especially compared to the depth and strength of face-to-face interactions. On the other hand, we have seen the strength of weak ties in many situations, including building communal solidarity. It was the lack of weak ties that doomed the West End, after all. As is consistent with what we know about weak ties, Hampton and Wellman found that those residents who used NET-L were connected to people who lived all over the neighborhood, not just those who were especially close by.

And, in fact, CMC did play a role in communal actions in Netville. Not only did residents use NET-L as an efficient and low-cost way to organize neighborhood activities (including a bowling league), they also used it to organize against the housing developer of Netville itself. In contrast to the urban villagers in Boston who were unable to come together to fight the redevelopment of the West End, the wired residents that Hampton and Wellman studied, frustrated with broken promises from the developer, used NET-L to discuss the problems they were having and strategies for addressing those problems, as well as to organize in-person meetings (2003: 303). The residents organized against the developer so quickly and efficiently, in fact, bombarding him with emails about their grievances, that "Based on their experience in Netville, the developer and one of the firm's owners each told us that they would never build another wired neighborhood" (Hampton & Wellman 2003: 303). (This in itself is an interesting point about the vulnerability of technology. The developer can shut down – or refuse to install – the infrastructure for wired communication in a neighborhood. Nazis aside, it would be much more difficult to shut down offline communication among the neighbors. We will return to this point later when we discuss Barabási's research on the structure of the world wide web.)

A different kind of space

Hampton and Wellman found that in Netville the wired residents had larger neighborhood networks and more communication with their neighbors – both online and offline (including making four to five times as many telephone calls). Their social ties were more broad-ranging across the physical space of the neighborhood. There are some interesting implications of this. Hampton and Wellman hypothesize that (2003: 297) the use of CMC, with the concomitant increase in the frequency of communications and the numbers of others with whom we communicate, will decrease the importance of proximity in neighborhoods. This is a different way of thinking about space. Space here is not only geographical but also social. The distance between two actors may be measured by social ties rather than geographic proximity. In the "Closer Look" section of this chapter, we will look at multidimensional scaling, which will give us a method for measuring and mapping out the type of social space to which Hampton and Wellman are alluding. Intriguingly, with regard to the efficient access that the internet provides for users, Wellman and Gulia hypothesize that "[i]t is as if most North Americans lived in the heart of densely populated, heterogeneous, physically safe, big cities rather than in peripheral, low-density, homogeneous suburbs" (1999: 336).

The social space of the web may include more weak ties than traditional communities do, but it is not entirely lacking some of the same kinds of social controls that operate offline. For example, Wellman and Gulia observed that

> those who contribute actively to the [online] BMW car network get their requests for advice answered more quickly and more widely. That is probably why people reply to the entire group when answering an individual's question. ... Moreover, it can be easy to provide assistance to others when the group is large. The accumulation of small, individual acts of assistance can sustain a large community because each act is seen by the entire group and helps to perpetuate an image of generalized reciprocity and mutual aid. People know that they may not receive help from the person they helped last week, but from another network member. (1999: 344)

This has a strong resemblance to the obligations of the gift in Polynesian culture discussed in chapter 3. Norms of reciprocity mean that on the net, as on the scattered islands of the Pacific, the obligations to give, to receive, and to repay may be in force. These norms may be easier to escape than they would be on a small island in Polynesia, but they exist nonetheless.

In this way, the net is quite similar to "real life." Both on- and offline, people have a variety of ties with others, most of which are weak. Wellman and Gulia note that researchers estimate that on average North Americans maintain about a thousand ties, but only a handful of those are truly intimate and fewer than 50 of them are even strong (1999: 350). Nevertheless, these authors point out that the other 950 ties are useful sources of information, support, and the other social goods that we get through weak ties.

But in other ways, the social space of the net is different from the space of "real life." Wellman and Gulia argue that the way in which the internet operates may be changing our own individual communities (1999: 354). The ease of communication – especially the one-to-many broadcast capability of online communication – encourages people to maintain large numbers of connections, while the asynchronous nature of online contact erases the difficulties of communicating over the distance of many time zones. In this way, the internet collapses geographic space that had formerly been a barrier to contact. Wellman and Gulia contend that "[t]his allows latent ties to stay in more active contact until participants have an opportunity to meet in person. By supporting such online contact, the Net may even foster more frequent in-person meetings between people who might otherwise forget each other" (1999: 354).

The shift to a new type of space – measured by social rather than geographic distance – may be the most profound effect that the internet has on our communities. Barabási notes that this is a relatively new phenomenon:

> The ancestors of most Americans lost contact with those they left behind in the old country. From the cattle herds on the prairies or the gold mines of the Rocky Mountains it was impossible to reach loved ones separated by oceans and continents. No postcards, no phone calls. In the subtle social network of those days, it was rather difficult to activate the links that had been broken when people moved. That changed in this century as the mail system, the telephone, and then air travel demolished barriers and shrank physical distances. Today, immigrants to America can choose to maintain their links to the people they leave behind. We can and do keep in touch. . . . The world has collapsed irreversibly in the twentieth century. And it is undergoing yet another implosion right now, as the Internet reaches to every corner of the world. Though we are nineteen clicks away from everybody on the Web, we are only one click away from our friends. They might have hopped three cities and five jobs since we last met in person. But no matter where they are, we can usually find them on the Internet if and when we wish to do so. The world is shrinking because social links that would have died out a hundred years ago are kept alive and can easily be activated. (2003: 39)

Although Milgram found six degrees of separation, Barabási estimates that, owing to the internet, we are now probably much closer to three.

The world, of course, is not *physically* shrinking. But thanks to the internet, it might be *socially* shrinking – at least for some people.

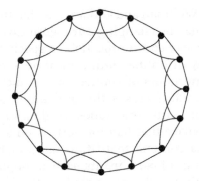

Figure 8.1 Regular network with local clustering and long chain lengths (adapted from Watts 2004: 245, used by permission)

The structure of the web

The social world is shrinking because the internet facilitates the formation of the *small world structure* (Watts 1999a, 1999b, 2003, 2004, Watts & Strogatz 1998). Remember from chapter 7 that the small world structure has both local clustering and short average chain lengths between the members of the system. Figure 8.1 shows a system with local clustering, but long average chain lengths between the members. This is a more formalized version of the network structure that we saw in chapter 3 among slaves when there was no literacy. But as Watts and Strogatz have found, adding even a few ties outside of the local clusters can dramatically shorten the average chain length between nodes in the network, as we can see in figure 8.2. Again, this is a more formalized representation of the slave network when a

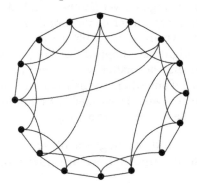

Figure 8.2 Small world network with local clustering and short chain lengths (adapted from Watts 2004: 245, used by permission)

few literate slaves were able to communicate efficiently across large spaces by writing.

The Watts–Strogatz model shows us that a very small number of bridge ties can dramatically shorten the average chain length for everyone in the network. And not everyone in each small world needs to have these bridge ties – just a few people having them will do the trick. This is what the world wide web does. In his research on the structure of the web, Barabási found that

> [j]ust as in society a few connectors know an unusually large number of people, we found that the architecture of the World Wide Web is dominated by a few highly connected nodes, or *hubs*. . . . In the network behind the Web many unpopular or seldom noticed nodes with only a small number of links are held together by these few highly connected websites. (2003: 58)

Like the sociometric stars that Milgram found in the original small world studies – those individuals through whom a large number of letters passed on their way to the final destination – the hubs on the internet are linking pins for the whole system. On the one hand, they mean that we can efficiently connect with the larger network and enjoy all the resources offered there. On the other hand, Barabási argues that the small world structure is vulnerable. "The removal of the most connected nodes rapidly disintegrates these networks, breaking them into tiny noncommunicating islands. . . . We do not need to remove a large number of nodes to reach the critical point. Disable a few of the hubs and a scale-free network will fall to pieces in no time" (Barabási 2003: 117–18). Remember the Netville developer who vowed never to build another wired neighborhood. He also could – and eventually did – shut down the net that existed.

Barabási also found that many webpages – nodes in the internet network – are not connected to the larger system: "[I]n reality not all pages can be connected to each other. Starting from any page, we can reach only about 24 percent of all documents. The rest are invisible to us, unreachable by surfing" (2003: 165).

Moreover, the ties on the web are directional – just because one node links to another does not mean that the second node links back. Recall from our discussion of closeness centrality in chapter 5 that the directionality of ties affects the ease with which two nodes can be connected. A short chain in one direction may be a very long chain in the other. Barabási writes in fact that there are many nodes in the net which cannot be reached at all by surfing. One either already knows that they exist and goes right to them or never sees them at all. Search engines will not find them. Parts of the virtual world are more isolated than any Polynesian island ever was. The space separating those isolated cyber islands from the rest of the net community is, for all practical purposes, infinite.

A closer look: multidimensional scaling

This is a different way of looking at space. Multidimensional scaling (MDS) takes social relationships expressed as degrees of similarity or dissimilarity and maps them onto a two- or three-dimensional space. In this way, it has some similarities with correspondence analysis (see chapter 7). Nodes that have stronger (or closer) relations with each other are closer on the map and those that have weaker (or more distant) relations with each other are farther apart on the map. Berkowitz notes that the

> principal strengths of these methods lies in their use of behaviorally determined measures of the relative "closeness" of elements to one another, rather than some arbitrary a priori scaling of distances. This, once again, is consistent with the radical instrumentalist notion that the properties of systems should be measured using techniques which do not rest on "received" categories, but, as much as possible, derive from observation of the processes through which social systems create or structure themselves over time. (1982: 6)

While in correspondence analysis, the rows and columns of the matrix are vectors for points in space, in MDS, the cell values of the matrix are measures of the relation between the nodes.

One way to think about this is with the distance tables that we often find on road maps. The tables are matrices that give point-to-point driving distances between the various pairs of towns on the map. Table 8.1 is a distance matrix for several cities in the United States – Boston, Chicago, Denver, Los Angeles, New York, and Seattle – as well as two small towns – Chapel Hill, North Carolina, and Lebanon, Kansas, which is the town closest to the geographic center of the continental USA. We produce this matrix by looking at a map and measuring the pairwise distances between the points and then noting them down.

MDS flips this procedure. Instead of starting with a map and making a matrix, we start with the matrix and make a map. What we

Table 8.1 Driving distances in the USA in miles

	Boston	Ch. Hill	Chicago	Denver	Lebanon	LA	NYC	Seattle
Boston		717	984	1971	1658	2985	213	3032
Chapel Hill	717		839	1647	1304	2518	505	2892
Chicago	984	839		1003	691	2017	791	2050
Denver	1971	1647	1003		384	1018	1780	1332
Lebanon	1658	1304	691	384		1401	1466	1644
LA	2985	2518	2017	1018	1401		2793	1137
NYC	213	505	791	1780	1466	2793		2839
Seattle	3032	2892	2050	1332	1644	1137	2839	

are doing is taking the ties between nodes and noting the weight of each, and then positioning the nodes in a Euclidean space so that the weights of the ties correspond to the distances between the points, as much as possible. If we use the matrix in table 8.1 as the basis for MDS, we produce the map in figure 8.3.

Figure 8.3 MDS map of US driving distances

Table 8.2 Facebook friends between cities in the USA in thousands

	Boston	Ch.Hill	Chicago	Denver	Lebanon	LA	NYC	Seattle
Boston		394	6423	3249	21	5411	8493	5432
Chapel Hill	394		208	201	1103	102	346	12
Chicago	6423	208		8991	47	8632	7642	6823
Denver	3249	201	8991		101	5567	4032	5591
Lebanon	21	1103	47	101		58	12	33
LA	5411	102	8632	5567	58		9999	7876
NYC	8493	346	7642	4032	12	9999		3954
Seattle	5432	12	6823	5591	33	7876	3954	

This is not an *exact* match with a map of the USA because driving distances depend on the layout of highways rather than going as the crow flies. But it is pretty close. Note that Lebanon, Kansas, is in the middle of the map and that New York City and Los Angeles are very far apart.

Suppose instead of driving distances, though, we use some measure of social distance? In this case, imagine a matrix made from the number of Facebook friends between all the pairs of cities. Table 8.2 represents this information. (The actual data from Facebook is extraordinarily well guarded, so these numbers are entirely fictitious.) In this case, the higher the number, the more socially close the two cities or towns are.

Figure 8.4 shows the MDS map of the social relations among these nodes. Note that on this map, New York City is closer to Los Angeles than it is to Chicago or Denver. And instead of being centrally located, Lebanon, Kansas, is relegated to the very fringes of the social world. This is a map of social space, where Los Angeles and New York are very close to each other, while small towns like Chapel Hill and Lebanon are sidelined.

Doing multidimensional scaling in UCINET6

After you have entered your matrix and saved it, click on "Tools" at the top of the page and choose "Scaling/Decomposition" from the drop-down menu. Choose "Metric MDS." Enter the name of your matrix in the Input dataset window. UCINET defaults to a two-dimensional display, but you may choose higher dimensions if you like. It is important to decide whether you want the program to treat the cell

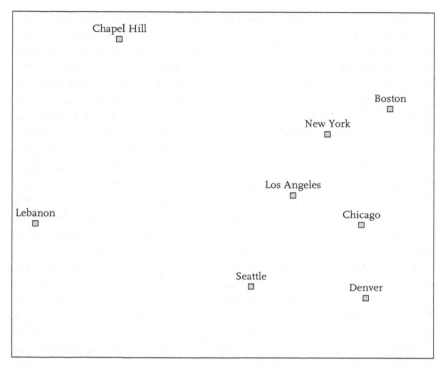

Figure 8.4 MDS map of Facebook friendships

values in your matrix as measures of similarity or of dissimilarity. In the example of driving distances, the cell values are measures of dissimilarity – the higher the value, the farther apart the nodes are. However, in the example of Facebook friends, the cell values are measures of similarity – the higher the value, the closer the nodes are. (Using similarity is simply the inverse of using dissimilarity.)

Click "OK." You will get a page with the coordinates of the points in Euclidean space. Note also that you are given a value for "Final Stress." Remember that the mapping of the nodes into Euclidean space is done to preserve the values of the ties as much as possible, but the social distances may not match spatial distances very well in low-dimensional spaces. The stress is a measure of the fit of the nodes in Euclidean space. In the example of the driving distances, the map produced by MDS has a Final Stress of 0.018, which is quite low – not surprisingly, since the values in the cells of the matrix were taken from a two-dimensional Euclidean space in the first place. If we had measured actual linear distances rather than driving distances, which are constrained by the layout of the highway system, the Final Stress would be 0.00. In the example of Facebook closeness, though, the Final Stress is 0.183. That is, there is more stress – a poorer fit – between the values in the cells of the matrix and the coordinates in Euclidean space in this example. The social world does not, after all, lie on a Euclidean plane. As a rule of thumb, Knoke and Yang say that "stress values below 0.1 are considered an excellent fit, values between 0.1 and 0.2 are an adequate fit, and values above 0.2 are a poor fit" (2008: 82). In general, if the Final Stress values are too high, they may be reduced by going to a higher number of dimensions (from two to three, for example) or perhaps by removing some points.

The next page in the UCINET output is the map itself. Note that you can flip the map along the axes in a variety of directions. This map shows the nodes as they are arranged in social space.

This social space may have more "reality" to it than geographic space, and the communities which inhabit it can affect our lives as much as – or more than –the communities outside our front doors. This space, too, is where we live our lives, and the questions we ask about communities – what do they give us? how do they constrain us? how are they functional or dysfunctional? – are as relevant here as they are in the physical world.

Glossary of network terms

actor: Node in a network. An actor may be an individual or a group and does not necessarily have to "act" in the conventional sense. Two cousins are actors in a family network, two corporate boards that share members are actors in a network of interlocking directorates, and so on.

asymmetric matrix: Matrix where the values of the row, column cells are not necessarily the same as the values of the column, row cells. Examples would be a friendship matrix where some people choose others and are not chosen back or a person-by-group matrix where one dimension of the matrix represents people and the other represents groups to which they might belong. The matrix may or may not be square.

balance: Relations are structured so as to avoid emotional or cognitive dissonance. A balanced triad is a group of three actors whose relations with each other leave no actor in a position of conflicting loyalties. For example, three friends who all like each other would form a balanced triad. So would two friends who dislike – and are disliked by – a third person.

betweenness centrality: Measure of the number of geodesics (shortest paths between pairs of nodes) that pass through a particular node.

cell: Intersection of a row and a column in a matrix.

closeness centrality: Measure of the average length of the chain of ties between one node in a network and all the other nodes in that network.

column: Vertical slice of a matrix.

degree centrality: Measure of the number of direct ties that each node has to other nodes in the network.

density: Proportion of actual ties realized in a network to the possible ties that could have been realized.

dyad: Two connected nodes.

geodesic: Shortest path between two nodes in a network.

image matrix: Matrix using 1s and 0s to show the relations among the blocks of structurally equivalent actors.

index of connectivity: Average length of the network chain between the target and starter group in small world studies.

in-group density: Density of ties among members of a group with other members of the group.

in-group tie: Tie between one member of a group and another member of the group.

interpersonal balance: Triads among actors in personal networks are structured so as to avoid emotional or cognitive dissonance.

matrix: Grid of numbers in rows and columns which represents the actors in a network and the ties among them.

multiplex tie: Relation that has many dimensions between nodes in a network. For example, two people who are friends, relatives, and also workmates have a multiplex tie.

network: Collection of nodes (actors, etc.) and the linkages (ties, etc.) among them.

node: Member of a network.

out-group tie: Ties between members of a group and others who are not members of the group.

relation: Tie between actors in a network. It may have characteristics such as strength and direction.

row: Horizontal slice of a matrix.

small world structure: Networks of tightly clustered nodes which nevertheless have the ability to reach across enormous social spaces relatively efficiently because of a small number of random, far-reaching ties.

sociogram: Picture of a network of relations, where the members of the network are represented by points and the relations between them are represented by lines connecting the points.

strength: Measure of the intensity of the tie between two nodes.

structural balance: An entire network is structured, often into cliques, so that all relations in it avoid emotional or cognitive dissonance.

structural equivalence: When two nodes have the same types of ties to the same others in a network, they are structurally equivalent to each other.

structural holes: Gaps in a network structure where possible ties are absent.

symmetric matrix: Matrix where the row, column values are the same as the column, row values.

tie: Relation between two nodes in a network.

transpose: A matrix is transposed when we flip the original matrix across the main diagonal so that the rows become columns and the columns become rows.

triad: Group of three nodes with relations among them.

uniplex tie: Relation between nodes that has only one dimension.

value: Cell entry indicating the presence, absence, or strength of a tie between the two actors.

References

Allen, W. S. (1984) *The Nazi Seizure of Power: The Experience of a Single German Town 1922–1945*, revised edition. Franklin Watts, New York.

Anderson, B. (1983) *Imagined Communities: Reflections on the Origin and Spread of Nationalism*. Verso, New York.

Arendt, H. (1973) *The Origins of Totalitarianism*, new edition. Harcourt, Brace, Jovanovich, New York.

Aron, R. (1970) *Main Currents in Sociological Thought. II. Durkheim, Pareto, Weber* (trans. Richard Howard and Helen Weaver). Doubleday, New York.

Azarian, G. R. (2005) *The General Sociology of Harrison C. White: Chaos and Order in Networks*. Palgrave Macmillan, New York.

Bailyn, B. (1955) *The New England Merchants in the Seventeenth Century*. Harper and Row, New York.

Barabási, A. (2003) *Linked*. Plume, New York.

Berkowitz, S. D. (1982) *An Introduction to Structural Analysis: The Network Approach to Social Research*. Butterworths, Toronto.

Borgatti, S., Everett, M., & Freeman, L. (2002) *Ucinet for Windows: Software for Social Network Analysis*. Analytic Technologies, Harvard, MA.

Boswell, J. (1791 [2008]) *The Life of Samuel Johnson*. Penguin, New York.

Bott, E. (1956) Urban families: conjugal roles and social networks. *Human Relations* 8, 345–84.

Bott, E. (1957) *Family and Social Networks: Roles, Norms, and External Relationships in Ordinary Urban Families*. Tavistock, London.

Bourdieu, P. (1984) *Distinction: A Social Critique of the Judgment of Taste* (trans. Richard Nice). Harvard University Press, Cambridge, MA.

Boyer, P. & Nissenbaum, S. (1974) *Salem Possessed: The Social Origins of Witchcraft*. MJF Books, New York.

Breiger, R. L. (1974) The duality of persons and groups. *Social Forces* 53, 181–90.

Buck, P. H. (1938) *Vikings of the Sunrise*. J.B. Lippincott, New York.

Bureau of Labor Statistics. (2010) American Time Use Survey. www.bls.gov/tus/#tables.

Burt, R. S. (1992) *Structural Holes: The Social Structure of Competition.* Harvard University Press, Cambridge, MA.

Burt, R. S. (2004) Structural holes and good ideas. *American Journal of Sociology* 110, 349–99.

Calhoun, C. (1998) Community without propinquity revisited: communications technology and the transformation of the urban public sphere. *Sociological Inquiry* 68, 373–97.

Caporael, L. R. (1976) Ergotism: the Satan loosed in Salem? *Science* 192, 21–6.

Cartwright, D. & Harary, F. (1956) Structural balance: a generalization of Heider's theory. *Psychological Review* 63, 277–93.

Castilla, E. J., Hwang, H., Granovetter, E., & Granovetter, M. (2000) Social networks in Silicon Valley. In: Lee, C., Miller, W. F., Hancock, M. G., & Rowen, H. S. (eds.) *The Silicon Valley Edge.* Stanford University Press, Stanford, CA, pp. 218–47.

Centeno, M. A. (2002) *Blood and Debt: War and the Nation-State in Latin America.* Penn State University Press, University Park, PA.

Clark, T. N. (2004) Local amenities are catalysts for stronger development paradigms, or museums and juice bars drive development. Paper presented at the American Sociological Association Annual Meeting, San Francisco, CA.

Clausen, S. E. (1998) *Applied Correspondence Analysis: An Introduction.* Sage, Thousand Oaks, CA.

Collins, R. (1988) *Theoretical Sociology.* Harcourt, New York.

Cross, J. E., Dickmann, E., Newman-Gonchar, R., & Fagan, J. M. 2009. Using mixed-method design and network analysis to measure development of interagency collaboration. *American Journal of Evaluation* 30, 310–29.

Csikzentmihaly, M. (1996) *Creativity: Flow and the Psychology of Discovery and Invention.* HarperCollins, New York.

Davis, A., Gardner, B. B., & Gardner, M. R. (1941) *Deep South.* University of Chicago Press, Chicago.

Durkheim, E. (1933 [1893]) *The Division of Labor in Society* (trans. George Simpson). Free Press, New York.

Erikson, K. T. (1966) *Wayward Puritans: A Study in the Sociology of Deviance.* John Wiley and Sons, New York.

Farrell, M. (2001) *Collaborative Circles: Friendship Dynamics and Creative Work.* University of Chicago Press, Chicago.

Faulkner, R. R. (1987) *Music on Demand: Composers and Careers in the Hollywood Film Industry.* Transaction, New Brunswick, NJ.

Feinberg, M. E. (1985) The social structure of racism in an urban community. Unpublished thesis. Harvard University, Cambridge, MA.

Fischer, C. S. (1984) *The Urban Experience,* second edition. Harcourt Brace Jovanovich, New York.

Florida, R. (2002) *The Rise of the Creative Class*. Basic Books, New York.

Freeman, L. C. (2004) *The Development of Social Network Analysis: A Study in the Sociology of Science*. Booksurge, Vancouver.

Freiberger, P. & Swaine, M. (2000) *Fire in the Valley: The Making of the Personal Computer*, second edition. McGraw-Hill, New York.

Gans, H. J. (1962) *The Urban Villagers: Group and Class in the Life of Italian-Americans*, updated and expanded edition. Free Press, New York.

Genovese, E. D. (1974) *Roll, Jordan, Roll: The World the Slaves Made*. Vintage Books, New York.

Giuffre, K. (1999) Sandpiles of opportunity: success in the art world. *Social Forces* 77, 815–32.

Giuffre, K. (2009) *Collective Creativity: Art and Society in the South Pacific*. Ashgate, Farnham.

Gould, R. V. (1991) Multiple networks and mobilization in the Paris Commune, 1871. *American Sociological Review* 56, 716–29.

Gould, R. V. (1995) *Insurgent Identities: Class, Conformity and Protest in Paris from 1848 to the Commune*. University of Chicago Press, Chicago.

Gould, S. J. (1996) *The Mismeasure of Man*. W.W. Norton, New York.

Granovetter, M. S. (1973) The strength of weak ties. *American Journal of Sociology* 78, 1360–80.

Granovetter, M. S. (1974) *Getting a Job: A Study of Contacts and Careers*. Harvard University Press, Cambridge, MA.

Greenacre, M. J. (1984) *Theory and Applications of Correspondence Analysis*. Academic Press, New York.

Greenacre, M. J. (1993) *Correspondence Analysis in Practice*. Academic Press, London.

Hampton, K. & Wellman, B. (2003) Neighboring in Netville: how the internet supports community and social capital in a wired suburb. *City and Community* 2, 277–311.

Hannerz, U. (1969) *Soulside: Inquiries into Ghetto Culture and Community*. Columbia University Press, New York.

Hannerz, U. (1980) *Exploring the City: Inquiries Toward an Urban Anthropology*. Columbia University Press, New York.

Heider, F. (1946) Attitudes and cognitive organization. *Journal of Psychology* 21, 107–12.

Heider, F. (1958) *The Psychology of Interpersonal Relations*. John Wiley and Sons, New York.

Jacobs, J. (1961) *The Death and Life of Great American Cities*. Modern Library, New York.

Jones, S. G. (1995) *Cybersociety: Computer-mediated Communication and Community*. Sage, Thousand Oaks, CA.

Kapferer, B. (1972) *Strategy and Transaction in an African Factory: African*

Workers and Indian Management in a Zambian Town. Manchester University Press, Manchester.

Knoke, D. & Yang, S. (2008) *Social Network Analysis,* second edition. Sage, Thousand Oaks, CA.

Korte, C. & Milgram, S. (1970) Acquaintance networks between racial groups: application of the small world method. *Journal of Personality and Social Psychology* 15, 101–8.

Kurlansky, M. (1997) *Cod.* Penguin, New York.

Lee, N. H. (1969) *The Search for an Abortionist.* University of Chicago Press, Chicago.

Liep, J. (ed.) (2001) *Locating Cultural Creativity.* Pluto Press, London.

Lorrain, F. & White, H. C. (1971) Structural equivalence of individuals in social networks. *Journal of Mathematical Sociology* 1, 49–80.

Lune, H. (2007) *Urban Action Networks: HIV/AIDS and Community Organizing in New York City.* Rowman and Littlefield, New York.

Marx, K. (1978 [1845]). Theses on Feuerbach. In: Tucker, R. C. (ed.) *The Marx–Engels Reader,* second edition. W.W. Norton, New York, pp. 143–5.

Massey, D. S., Durand, J., & Malone, N. J. (2002) *Beyond Smoke and Mirrors: Mexican Immigration in an Era of Economic Integration.* Russell Sage Foundation, New York.

Mauss, M. (1967 [1925]) *The Gift: Forms and Functions of Exchange in Archaic Societies* (trans. Ian Cunnison). W.W. Norton, New York.

Mayer, A. C. (1966) The significance of quasi-groups in the study of complex societies. In: Banton, M. (ed.) *The Social Anthropology of Complex Societies.* Tavistock, London, pp. 97–122.

McAdam, D. (1988) *Freedom Summer.* Oxford University Press, New York.

McLeod, P. L., Lobel, S. A., & Cox, W. H. Jr. (1996) Ethnic diversity and creativity in small groups. *Small Groups Research* 27, 248–64.

Milgram, S. (1967) The small-world problem. *Psychology Today* 1, 62–7.

Mill, J. S. (1987 [1848]) *Principles of Political Economy.* Augustus M. Kelly, Fairchild, NJ.

Miller, P. (1964) *Errand into the Wilderness.* Harvard University Press, Cambridge, MA.

Moreno, J. (1934) *Who Shall Survive?* Beacon Press, New York.

Newcomb, T. M. (1961) *The Acquaintance Process.* Holt, Rinehart, and Winston, New York.

Newcomb, T. M. (1981) Heiderian balance as a group phenomenon. *Journal of Personality and Social Psychology* 40, 862–7.

Nie, N., Hillygus, S., & Erbring, L. (2002) Internet use, interpersonal relations, and sociability: a time diary study. In: Wellman, B. & Haythornthwaite C. (eds.) *The Internet in Everyday Life.* Blackwell, Oxford, pp. 244–62.

Oldenburg, R. (1989) *The Great Good Place.* Paragon House, New York.

Padgett, J. F. & Ansell, C. K. (1993) Robust action and the rise of the Medici, 1400–1434. *American Journal of Sociology* 98, 1259–1319.

Putnam, R. D. (2000) *Bowling Alone: The Collapse and Revival of American Community*. Simon and Schuster, New York.

Rheingold, H. (1993) *The Virtual Community: Homesteading on the Electric Frontier*. MIT Press, Cambridge, MA.

Rytina, S. & Morgan, D. L. (1982) The arithmetic of social relations: the interplay of category and network. *American Journal of Sociology* 88, 88–113.

Sampson, S. F. (1969) Crisis in a cloister. Unpublished doctoral dissertation. Cornell University, Ithaca, NY.

Scott, J. C. (1985) *Weapons of the Weak: Everyday Forms of Peasant Resistance*. Yale University Press, New Haven, CT.

Scott, J. (2000) *Social Network Analysis: A Handbook*, second edition. Sage, Thousand Oaks, CA.

Shilts, R. (1987) *And the Band Played On: Politics, People, and the AIDS Epidemic*. St. Martin's Press, New York.

Simmel, G. (1971) *On Individuality and Social Forms* (ed. Donald N. Levine). University of Chicago Press, Chicago.

Spanos, N. P. & Gottlieb, J. (1976) Ergotism and the Salem Village witch trials. *Science* 194, 1390–4.

Starkey, M. L. (1949) *The Devil in Massachusetts: A Modern Enquiry into the Salem Witch Trials*. Anchor Books, New York.

Tönnies, F. (1957 [1887]) *Community and Society – Gemeinschaft und Gesellschaft* (trans. and ed. Charles P. Loomis). Michigan State University Press, East Lansing, MI.

Travers, J. & Milgram, S. (1969) An experimental study of the small world problem. *Sociometry* 32, 425–43.

Useem, M. (1978) The inner group of the American capitalist class. *Social Problems* 25, 225–40.

Uzzi, B. & Spiro, J. (2004) Small world networks and imagination: the case of Broadway musicals. Paper presented at the American Sociological Association 2004 Annual Meeting. San Francisco, CA.

Wasserman, S. & Faust, K. (1994) *Social Network Analysis: Methods and Applications*. Cambridge University Press, Cambridge.

Watts, D. J. (1999a) *Small Worlds: The Dynamics of Networks Between Order and Randomness*. Princeton University Press, Princeton, NJ.

Watts, D. J. (1999b) Networks, dynamics, and the small-world phenomenon. *American Journal of Sociology* 105, 493–527.

Watts, D. J. (2003) *Six Degrees: The Science of a Connected Age*. W.W. Norton, New York.

Watts, D. J. (2004) The "new" science of networks. *Annual Review of Sociology* 30, 243–70.

Watts, D. J. & Strogatz, S. H. (1998) Collective dynamics of "small world" networks. *Nature* 393, 440–2.

Webber, M. M. (1963) Order in diversity: community without propinquity. In: Wirigo, L. (ed.) *Cities and Space*. Johns Hopkins University Press, Baltimore, MD, pp. 23–54.

Wellman, B. & Gulia, M. (1999) Net-surfers don't ride alone: virtual communities as communities. In: Wellman, B. (ed.) *Networks in the Global Village: Life in Contemporary Communities*. Westview Press, Boulder, CO, pp. 331–66.

Wellman, B. & Wortley, S. (1990) Different strokes from different folks: community ties and social support. *American Journal of Sociology* 96, 558–88.

White, H. C., Boorman, S. A., & Breiger, R. L. (1976) Social structure from multiple networks. I. Blockmodels of roles and positions. *American Journal of Sociology* 81, 730–80.

Wirth, L. (1928) *The Ghetto*. University of Chicago Press, Chicago.

Wolfe, T. (1970) *Radical Chic and Mau-mauing the Flak Catchers*. Farrar, Strauss and Giroux, New York.

Index